DISCIPLINING STATISTICS

DEMOGRAPHY AND VITAL STATISTICS

IN FRANCE AND ENGLAND, 1830–1885

Libby Schweber

Duke University Press   *Durham & London*   2006

© 2006 Duke University Press
All rights reserved.
Printed in the United States of America on acid-free paper ∞
Typeset in Carter & Cone Galliard by Keystone Typesetting, Inc.
Library of Congress Cataloging-in-Publication Data appear on the
last printed page of this book.

DISCIPLINING STATISTICS

POLITICS, HISTORY, AND CULTURE

*A series from the International Institute
at the University of Michigan*

SERIES EDITORS

George Steinmetz and Julia Adams

SERIES EDITORIAL ADVISORY BOARD

Fernando Coronil	David Laitin
Mamadou Diouf	Lydia Liu
Michael Dutton	Julie Skurski
Geoff Eley	Margaret Somers
Fatma Müge Göcek	Ann Laura Stoler
Nancy Rose Hunt	Katherine Verdery
Andreas Kalyvas	Elizabeth Wingrove
Webb Keane	

Sponsored by the International Institute at the
University of Michigan and published by Duke
University Press, this series is centered around
cultural and historical studies of power, politics,
and the state — a field that cuts across the disciplines
of history, sociology, anthropology, political science,
and cultural studies. The focus on the relationship
between state and culture refers both to a methodological approach — the study of politics and the state
using culturalist methods — and a substantive one that
treats signifying practices as an essential dimension
of politics. The dialectic of politics, culture, and
history figures prominently in all the books selected
for the series.

To my Mother and Father

CONTENTS

ACKNOWLEDGMENTS

The journey from questions to data to new questions to analysis and narrative has been long and many people have helped along the way, both through their faith in the project and their comments on different versions. My special thanks to Eric Brian, Manali Desai, Marion Fourcade-Gourinchas, Steve Fuller, Sarah Gronim, Nathan Keyfitz, Virag Molnar, Paul André Rosental, Silvan Schweber, Simon Szreter, Chris Winship, Robert Wuthnow, Viviana Zelizer, and the reviewers at Duke University Press. While I did not always adopt their many suggestions, their careful reading and thoughtful comments infinitely improved the manuscript, and I am grateful.

INTRODUCTION

The living beings in a population do not constitute a succession in which each one finds its raison d'être in its contemporary antecedents. Each age group is, in fact, the very complex product of those particular events that weighed on each of the ages through which it has already passed, events that could very well have no influence on the groups that preceded it or followed it in the series of ages. . . . This is why the age groups in a population, who make up the population as a whole, have no necessary relation to one another. They are nearly strangers that the hazards of time have brought together, and whose (collective) force is the product of the different adventures that each one has endured.[1]

As we enter the twenty-first century, the notion of a statistical population is part of our everyday vocabulary. Not only do we accept the reality of statistical aggregates, we intuitively understand them to be probabilistic entities. In the mid-nineteenth century, however, neither assumption could be taken for granted. Or rather, neither assumption could be taken for granted if you lived in France. This book begins from an observed contrast between two liberal states, both of which legitimated government action in the name of individual rights and interests. In England, political liberalism went along with an individualist, probabilist understanding of population rates. In France, by contrast, politicians, administrators, and legislators struggled with that understanding.[2] When statisticians reported to them on the mortality of the nation, they responded by asking who or what those figures referred to and whether one could reasonably combine radically different individuals to make up a statistical population. This contrast reflects differences not only in basic styles of statistical reasoning but in the political and scientific institutions in which social statistics and social policy developed.

The comparison of two disciplines, demography in France and vital statistics in England, serves to explore these relations. Both disciplines were "invented" in the nineteenth century, and both supported a new way of thinking about statistical populations, one which involved far greater abstraction and statistical manipulation than was current at the time. In both cases "success" depended on transforming both science and the administration. In the scientific realm it involved a reworking of statistics and of its relation to other sciences. In the administrative realm the adoption of demography and vital statistics was linked to new forms of state intervention, most notably in the area of public health.

The organization of the social sciences into distinct disciplines is generally associated with their incorporation into the university system in the late nineteenth century. This development was preceded, however, by over fifty years of disciplinary activity. During the middle decades of the century, new disciplinary categories and projects were introduced, contested, and elaborated. Some were institutionalized in university-based disciplines, others incorporated into other political or disciplinary projects, and still others abandoned altogether. Proponents of demography and vital statistics were central players in this drama. Their disciplinary activity explicitly challenged the principles by which statistics and the social sciences more generally were ordered. As such it contributed to a transformation in the nature and organization of social knowledge.

The literature on the social sciences is often framed in terms of a central tension between science on the one hand and either policy work or social reform on the other. As the oft-cited title of Mary Furner's book *Advocacy and Objectivity* suggests, the social sciences are generally seen as oscillating between two poles.[3] A comparison of demography and vital statistics highlights a time when these were not the primary axes of differentiation and legitimation.[4] Instead, demography and vital statistics developed around a different set of tensions. In France, these tensions arose over the extent of statistical manipulation, the relation of the individual and the collective, and the balance of speculation and certainty. In England, the scientific status of statistics was discussed in terms of the tradeoff between problem-oriented and comprehensive studies, and a tension between science and opinion (as distinct from advocacy).

While these tensions were political as well as epistemological, the two logics did not overlap, at least not perfectly. Instead epistemological objections to particular projects provided symbolic resources that were evoked in a variety of political contexts. Whereas many studies of science and politics examine how science was used to promote specific interests,[5] this book focuses on the opportunities and constraints which scientific and political institutions posed for the development of scientific knowledge. More specifically, it focuses on the impact of rules governing scientific, administrative, and political practice on styles of statistical reasoning. The book thus combines an analysis of meso-level structures with accounts of agency and historical contingency. Institutionalized rules set the parameters of what could and could not be said and done in both science and administration. Specific attempts to promote new disciplines and new scientific objects drew on these rules and occasionally challenged them. The "fit" between administrative, scientific, and epistemological forms was the result of neither pure interest nor deep homologies, but rather the historical outcome of struggles shaped by and directed at transforming the rules by which resources and recognition were distributed.

Statistics as Social Science

The comparison of demography and vital statistics rests on similarities in their general intellectual programs and differences in the particularities of those programs and in their institutional locations. Both demography and vital statistics constituted themselves around the analysis of official population statistics. As such, they distinguished themselves from survey work, the other widespread "scientific" way to study society at the time.[6] Both traced their intellectual and institutional origins to the "era of statistical enthusiasm" in the 1820s.[7] In both France and England the 1820s were marked by a groundswell of public interest in numbers about society. Newspapers reported the numbers of criminals, insane, sick, and dying. The practice intensified with the first major cholera epidemic in 1831. For the first time newspapers published weekly counts of those afflicted with the disease.[8]

This popular interest supported and was fueled by governmental and scientific initiatives. Statistics were an important tool of representation and management of the nineteenth-century liberal state. One of Napoleon's first administrative acts was to establish official statistical bureaus. While political changes led to the closure and reopening of these offices, the principle that liberal governments needed statistical knowledge to know society and to further "progress" persisted.[9] The contribution of the moral and political sciences was to demonstrate that society was governed by its own natural laws, which existed independent of government action. Only those policies that conformed to natural law could be expected to succeed.[10]

On the statistical front, the "avalanche of numbers" was accompanied by struggles between alternative styles of reasoning. The century opened with a sharp opposition between two distinct forms: political arithmetic and descriptive statistics. Political arithmetic involved using partial data and mathematical formulae to estimate and predict the total size of a population. Descriptive statistics called for comprehensive surveys and head counts to produce reliable data. In the late 1820s public hygienists in France such as Louis René Villermé and the Belgian astronomer Adolphe Quetelet developed a third, explicitly "scientific" form of statistical reasoning. Their approach differed from existing ones in its call for using numbers to identify laws and causes and to develop social policy. On a practical level, it involved the analysis of statistical regularities and manipulation of simple ratios to identify what its proponents referred to as "natural laws."

Both demography and vital statistics laid claim to this third alternative. Both presented themselves as positivist social sciences deserving of scientific recognition, and both called for the use of numbers to identify laws and causes and to develop social policy. They differed, however, in the substantive content that they gave to this program, in the use that they made of it, and in their position vis-à-vis élite science and the administration. A key finding of this book is that there were differences in the styles of statistical reasoning associated with this "scientific" form of statistics.

National Styles

The contrast which I develop between mid-nineteenth-century statistical styles of reasoning in France and England rests on the cases of second-tier statisticians and administrators and their analyses of national population statistics. The concept of a population as a homogeneous entity has been identified as one of the cognitive preconditions for a statistical science of society.[11] One of the curious findings of this book is that English social statisticians and administrators accepted this interpretation with ease while French statisticians and administrators initially rejected it.

For most of the nineteenth century French administrative statisticians (in contrast with mathematicians) struggled with the concept of a national statistical population. A central issue was the conceptual difficulties posed by the act of aggregation. Did it make sense to combine rich and poor in the same category? Were single and married folk really subject to the same hardships and stresses? Or, as the epigraph from Bertillon suggests, was the French population a group of "virtual strangers" with radically different life experiences? By contrast, in England administrative statisticians were singularly indifferent to the problem. They constructed national and local measures of health and well-being without worrying about the "reality" of the underlying population. Eventually French administrators and scholars resolved their problem by positing a radical difference between collective, statistical entities and the individuals who made them up, while their English counterparts interpreted the same statistical representations in atomistic terms.

As readers familiar with neo-institutionalist theory will recognize, this difference corresponds to two distinct models of political sovereignty. Jepperson, in his classification of types of polity, distinguishes between two types of liberal societies: an anti-statist form, in which political authority is seen to lie in civil society, and a statist form, in which the state is seen to embody the interests of "the people," over and above the conflicting interests of individual citizens.[12] In making this distinction, Jepperson is careful to note that strong and weak statism do not necessarily correspond to strong and weak states. Instead, the contrast refers to the nature of political discourse, the boundaries between the state and civil society, and the location of expertise. England, in this analysis, exemplifies the anti-statist form, France the statist form. Both, it should be noted, are depicted as "liberal" anti-corporate polities in the sense that individuals, rather than corporate groups, are the locus of political agency.

These distinctions help to illuminate the contrast between French and English nineteenth-century statistical traditions developed in this book. Whereas most historians of statistics group France and England together as exemplars of the special relation between liberal nation-states and statistics, the comparison of demography and vital statistics highlights a sharp difference in how those numbers were interpreted. The difference lay in both the nature of national statistics as an object and the type of explanation with which statistics were associated. At the level of political discourse, French discomfort with assumptions of homogeneity fit well with a basically conflictual model of civil society. In a parallel fashion, individualist, probabilist constructions in England corresponded with anti-statist political discourse that located sovereignty in the aggregate of individual citizens.

This book focuses on the extensive cultural work involved in introducing abstract statistical concepts of national population among second-tier statisticians and administrators. Among the questions that I ask: Why were English statisticians relatively untroubled by this new abstract concept of population? Why did French statisticians have such a hard time accepting it? And how can one account for the observed contrast between English individualist, probabilist understandings of national mortality statistics and French holist, determinist understandings? The answers, I argue, concern differences in the political function of national mortality statistics and the broader symbolic and organizational conditions supporting them.

The Political Function of Statistics

Far from being a purely technical problem, the interpretation of statistical rates was worked out in a space that encompassed a wide range of knowledge activities. These included anthropology, political economy, public health, administrative statistics, and social statistics. As many authors have pointed out, the social sciences, and social statistics in particular, developed in tandem with the consolidation of the liberal nation-state.[13] Just as the modern state depended on statistics to represent and order social relations and legitimate political authority, so too did statisticians depend on the modern state to produce the official data necessary to fulfill their promise to explain "society" and further "progress." The concept of a national population was central to this ongoing process of articulation and mutual development, and official statistics were an important cultural resource in constructing and diffusing this new collective representation.[14] The resonance of statistical representations and contrasting modes of political legitimation has already been mentioned. The general contrast between a British consensual and French conflictual representation of society paralleled differences in the type of social problem around which new collective representations of the nation were developed, in the boundaries between civil society and the state, and in the political function of statistical representation.

In England national population statistics were produced and analyzed in the context of concerns over poverty ("the condition of England") and public health. As discussed below, vital statistics were one of several forms of knowledge that developed in a politically influential world of social science cum social reform. The project was incorporated into the medical branch of the public health movement and adopted by the movements to reform medicine and reform civil registration. It was institutionalized relatively early in the century in national statistical bureaus and the Statistical Society of London,[15] and in select government bureaus such as the General Registrar's Office and the Medical Branch of the Privy Council. Equally important, the public health movement in England was a model for the new interventionist state. Of all the areas of government action, public health was one of the most intensive.

In this context, the political use of statistics was largely instrumental.[16] Official statistics were published almost immediately and used to determine and justify government intervention in the living conditions of individuals and local communities. The boundaries between science and administration were relatively fluid. Technical developments were introduced in administrative settings. The articulation of epistemological and political concerns was extremely tight, such that debates over particular statistical measures were often (also) debates over policy alternatives.

In France, the new scientific approach to population statistics originated from a similar set of concerns. However, it developed in a different political and administrative climate, in a very different relation to the political and scientific center. A number of factors contributed to the primarily representative function of population statistics in France. First, state intervention was less well developed than in England, leaving far fewer opportunities for the instrumental use of numbers. Second, social statisticians had less access to the policy process than their counterparts in England. Whereas vital statistics developed in a world of strong informal ties between intellectual, social, and political élites, proponents of demography were doubly excluded from power. On the one hand, bureaucratic expertise in France passed through the *grandes écoles*, élite professional schools affiliated with ministries and branches of the civil service.[17] Demographers lacked these credentials and the connections and status that accompanied them. In addition, demographers, like most positivist social scientists, were fervent Republicans. Under the Second Empire, their politics also limited their access to the policy process.

One consequence of this situation was that for much of the Second Empire, French social scientists used epistemic arguments to make political points.[18] These discussions did not, however, contribute to technical developments as they did in England. Instead, the technical development of statistics remained largely divorced from explicit political discourse and policy action. The result was the continuation of a primarily representative form of knowledge initially associated with Napoleon and directed at the political representation of France.

The "Meaning" of Disciplinary Activity

One of the basic premises of this book is that in the nineteenth century, disciplinary activity helped to articulate styles of reasoning with political function. In the course of the century, proponents of both demography and vital statistics explicitly called for recognition of their intellectual projects as separate sciences. In both countries, their disciplinary claims were linked to the introduction of a new, "scientific" approach to statistics at national statistical bureaus. And in both cases, the novelty lay in a new way of using numbers, one which involved greater abstraction and statistical manipulation than administrators usually countenanced. As scholars familiar with the history of population statistics will immediately recognize, none of these intellectual claims were new. To the contrary, political arithmeticians and mathematicians had been manipulating statistical entities since the seventeenth century. Why then did certain individuals go to such lengths to insist that theirs was a "new science," deserving of scientific recognition? What was distinctive about demography and vital statistics? What were statisticians asking for when they insisted that demography or vital statistics be seen as a separate science, rather than a method or an auxiliary form?

These questions situate transformations in population statistics in the context of changes in the organization of knowledge in the second half of the nineteenth century. In the twentieth century discipline formation was generally associated with professionalization and specialization. In the nineteenth century this was not necessarily the case.[19] Proponents of demography and vital statistics did not target the university as an important source of recognition or locus of institutionalization. A comparative study of disciplinary activity surrounding demography and vital statistics thus provides an opportunity to explore a historical question — Why establish a discipline in the nineteenth century — and a theoretical one — How to theorize disciplines, so as to take into account the range of forms that disciplines have historically taken.

The first of these questions is of interest in that it draws attention to changing criteria of what counted as "science" and to how broader institutional conditions, most notably the relation between science and the state, shaped the development of statistical reasoning. As such it offers a comparative institutional approach to the relatively new field of historical epistemology.[20] The more theoretical question is of interest because it opens the way to think about the breakdown and transformation of contemporary disciplinary forms.

Scholars of twenty-first-century social science underline the degree to which knowledge production is increasingly situated at the interstices of "science" and "society" (by which they generally refer to some combination of industry, government, and social movements) in interdisciplinary, multi-disciplinary, and trans-disciplinary forms.[21] As in the nineteenth century, knowledge categories are not stable, yet disciplinary activity remains a central feature of knowledge production.[22] New projects such as bioethics, cognitive science, and even science studies involve explicit attempts to gain specifically disciplinary recognition.[23] Similarly, industry-based research accepts academic criteria of recognition, as evidenced in the demand that industry-based researchers publish in peer-reviewed scientific journals.[24] Rather than abandon "disciplines" as an analytic category, we need to re-think the term, disassociating it from its current identity with exclusive university-based disciplines, self-regulation, and professional associations. The cases of demography and vital statistics require a theoretical approach that promises to help make sense of these latter developments as well.

For a Meso-approach to Comparative Historical Analysis

This book is organized in a four-part historical narrative, tracing the introduction and promotion of demography and vital statistics between 1835 and 1885. It adopts a very specific approach to comparative historical analysis. Whereas most comparative studies involve macro-level categorical comparisons, the approach adopted here is more exploratory and the focus is more meso-historical. In the course of the narrative I follow the development of an ostensibly similar intellectual form in two institutional contexts. However, because both the scientific forms and the institutional contexts changed over the course of eighty years, I also document shifts in the content and location of each. As indicated above, the book is a study in the interaction of agency and structure, where "agency" refers to the competition between carriers of different styles of (administrative) statistical reasoning, and "structure" refers to the set of social and epistemological rules governing the practice of statistics (including rules concerning the division between mathematics and statistics, the division between administration and science, and the proper type of scientific representation). The rules were institutionalized in a variety of scientific and political organizations, ranging from scientific academies and private scientific societies to administrative bureaus and organized social movements. They held for over fifty years, but not for centuries.

One of the methodological challenges in a book of this type is how to identify and follow an object which is itself ill-defined and changing, in a context that is also changing. The solution adopted here has been to begin with very minimalist definitions of demography and vital statistics, and to use them to identify and explore the shifting institutional configurations in which these two disciplines took form. The approach builds on the type of event analysis proposed by Sewell, Griffith, and others.[25] The minimalist definition involves two components: first the historic use of terms and labels to delineate a type of knowledge (or rather, knowledge activity), and second, the professional trajectories of key figures identified with those labels. In France the label is "demography" and the figures are Achille Guillard, who first "invented" the term, and his son-in-law Louis Adolphe Bertillon, who was more successful at promoting the new project. In England the label is "vital statistics" and the key figure is William Farr. The comparison is not, strictly speaking, between two essential categories — demography and vital statistics — but rather between two historically specific instances of those categories — namely, demography in France between 1850 and 1885 and vital statistics in England between 1837 and 1885.

By following these men in their attempts to define and promote demography and vital statistics, I identify key moments and events in the ongoing definition, recognition, and institutionalization of their respective disciplines. In analyzing these events, I ask: What was demography or vital statistics at that moment? What kinds of claims were being made for it? Who was involved in the event? Who were their allies? Against whom did they act? And what were the institutional structures that shaped the dynamics and outcome of the event? An analysis of the shifting content, configurations, and broader social and epistemological logics governing the dynamics within these moments serves to specify the changing contours of demography and vital statistics as objects of inquiry. The comparison between the two cases provides a basis to generalize about the impact of specific institutional arrangements on disciplinary activity more generally.

Before proceeding, it may be helpful to distinguish this approach from two superficially similar ones. For readers familiar with science studies, this approach might seem to correspond to Latour's call to "follow the scientists" as a way of identifying the heterogeneous set of entities and alliances involved in the establishment of a scientific "fact" or theory.[26] But whereas Latour uses individual trajectories to document the negotiated, contingent character of scientific claims, I propose to use them to explore the institutional contexts in which scientists promoted their projects and sought recognition.[27] Similarly, the focus on individuals could be taken as support for a heroic story of great, or at least effectual, individuals. While that story could indeed be told, and in the case of William Farr has been,[28] that is not my intent. Instead, I wish to use the professional trajectories of Guillard, Bertillon, and Farr as heuristic devices to sketch out the contours of the world in which they worked. Stated differently, I want to use them to identify the social and epistemological logics informing the French and British practice of national population statistics.

Far from a comprehensive account of these men's lives, the material that follows uses their trajectories to identify those institutional conditions that account for contrasting styles of reasoning. It begins with the explicit attempts by Farr, Guillard, and Bertillon to found a new science. In Britain, Farr began his campaign for scientific recognition in the late 1830s. In France, Guillard made his first bids for demography in the early 1850s. Both projects referred to a clearly distinguishable form of population statistics, organized around the search for laws and causes and directed at improving administrative statistics in the service of a new social science. Both differed from other forms of administrative statistics in the abstractness of their object (population), the experimental character of their method (involving the use of hypotheses and extensive statistical manipulation), and their intent to develop a distinct social science. Nineteenth-century contemporaries recognized their projects as distinct "scientific" forms of statistics. They also acknowledged the intellectual affinity between them.[29]

Demography versus Vital Statistics

The remainder of this introduction situates the comparison of demography and vital statistics in the context of two literatures: one on disciplines and disciplinarity and the other on the history of nineteenth-century statistics. The first of these two discussions traces the shifting place of disciplines in the history and sociology of science. While "disciplines" have always had a place in these literatures, they have not always figured as an object of inquiry in their own right. The discussion here highlights those approaches which problematize and theorize "disciplines" and discipline formation. As indicated above, I take from institutionalist approaches a focus on the importance of mechanisms of recognition for producing and authorizing scientific knowledge, and from constructivists an appreciation of the fluid, negotiated character of disciplines and scientific criteria. The theoretical contribution of this book lies in the integration of these points into a comparative institutional framework and in the abandonment of a priori distinctions between science on the one hand and politics, administration, and the state on the other.

The final section of this introduction situates my comparison of demography and vital statistics in the literature on nineteenth-century statistics. The literature is vast and has been summarized and dissected numerous times. My discussion is limited to those aspects directly relevant to the historical processes examined in this book. These include the conceptual difficulties surrounding assumptions of homogeneity and causation in social statistics, and the competition between alternative forms of administrative statistics. The discussion serves two purposes. First, it identifies the contribution of this book to the current historiography. Second, it makes a case for a processual, institutional, comparative approach to the history of statistics and science.

The narrative of demography and vital statistics begins around 1835 and ends in 1885. The periodization of this book corresponds to two distinct institutional logics. In parts I and II of the book, I examine the introduction and initial promotion of demography and vital statistics in the context of a relatively stable mid-nineteenth-century institutional structure. The term "structure" refers to the set of rules associated with dominant scientific organizations, administrative organizations, the policy process, the circulation of élites (social, political, economic, and intellectual), and the according of scientific recognition. The story begins with the creation of national statistical bureaus. In 1834 the British government created the General Registrar's Office (GRO). Two years later the French government established the Statistique Générale de la France (SGF). For the period under consideration, these institutions were responsible for publishing national population statistics. They were also one of the primary target audiences for both demography and vital statistics. In the course of the century, advocates of both projects struggled with other contenders to impose their vision of statistics on these bureaus. The specificity of both demography and vital statistics lay in the demand that official statistics be redesigned to meet the needs of "science" as well as administration.

The period is also marked by distinct forms of politics and relations between science and the state. In France the relatively authoritarian regime of Louis Napoléon relied upon and reenforced the authority of élite scientific structures, most notably the scientific academies. Recruitment to the high civil service was dominated by the Napoleonic system of grandes écoles. In England, by contrast, the period was marked by an unusual configuration of relatively weak political parties and ministerial bureaus, coupled with "experts" and an educated public that played an active role in politics and the policy process. Social science experts had direct access to the policy process through organizations such as the Statistical Society of London and the Social Science Association and their appointments to key administrative positions.[30]

Parts III and IV focus on the years 1878 to 1885. In both France and England this short period was marked by new, specifically scientific challenges to the authority of demography and vital statistics and a transformation in the scientific and administrative arrangements that had supported them. In England, a revival of partisan politics and reassertion of Treasury control over administrative bureaus effectively excluded amateur social scientists from the policy process and altered the relation of science and the state. In France, Republican success in the Parliamentary elections of 1877 cleared the way for the incorporation of positivist scientists into government. While this situation removed obstacles to the institutionalization of demography as a separate science, it eventually led to the demise of demography itself. In the course of the 1880s the demographers' program for population statistics was taken over by traditional intellectual élites and quasi-official scientific organizations. In contrast to England, where reform of the civil service altered channels of access to the policy process, in France bureaucratic experts continued to be recruited internally. The result was that while components of demography were adopted by competing, better-established groups of statisticians and administrators, the discipline itself did not survive. The period ends with the dissolution of specialized demographic institutions in France, the transformation of vital statistics into a form of professional knowledge in England, and the dissolution of the International Congress of Statistics, an institutional resource for both disciplines in their attempt to reform administrative statistics.

In researching this book, I have focused almost exclusively on published records — including transactions of conferences and scientific and administrative meetings, articles, editorials, reports, and institutional records — for it is these records that document the state of the public debate and reactions to different statistical and disciplinary claims. As Alain Desrosières has pointed out, one of the challenges that comparativists face is how to negotiate imbalances in the historiography.[31] The recent outpouring of historical studies of statistics and the relative absence of systematic comparative work has produced a somewhat skewed picture of nineteenth-century statistics. We know a lot about certain aspects of statistics in some countries and less about those same aspects in other countries, either because they have yet to be documented or because they were irrelevant to the broader questions used to frame earlier studies. Early-nineteenth-century French statistics and mid-nineteenth-century English vital statistics have been extensively documented, while French demography and social statistics in the third quarter of the century remain relatively unexplored. This book fills that gap.

By tracing the history of disciplinary claims concerning vital statistics and demography over a seventy-year period and across two countries, this book provides an account of the diffusion and ongoing reformulation of this new style of statistical reasoning among practitioners rather than innovators, and the emergence of distinct national traditions. It also provides historical material to reconsider sociological understandings of disciplines, disciplinary activity, and scientific production more generally.

Disciplines and Styles of Reasoning

Scholars of disciplines and disciplinary activity tend to adopt one of two approaches: an institutionalist approach and a science studies approach. These correspond to two distinct phases in the sociology of science. The discussion that follows reviews the contribution of each to the study of disciplinary activity and underlines the analytic concepts that inform this book.

The Sociology of Science

The first explicit attempts to theorize disciplines can be traced to the sociology of science as it developed in the late 1930s and in the decades following the Second World War. The "institutionalist" approach began from the assumption that scientific development was guided by internal epistemological criteria. Disciplines, in this view, were social communities that shared a set of scientific norms and practices. Disciplinary gatekeepers ensured conformity to these rules by linking them to mechanisms of scientific recognition, including prizes, publications, grants, and jobs. Thus whereas economic activity was governed by profit, scientific activity was governed by the distribution of recognition. Modern research universities were identified as the historical guarantors of disciplinary autonomy, which was presented as a condition of "success."[32] My book builds on institutionalist work that emphasizes the role of scientific recognition in constituting disciplines and producing scientific knowledge. It differs from that work, however, in the disassociation of recognition from any a priori assumptions concerning the content of scientific norms and the role of universities in protecting them. Instead, I begin with empirical questions: who grants recognition, under what conditions, and according to what criteria?

In the 1970s a number of groups challenged the institutionalist approach to science. Criticisms focused on the failure of sociologists to study the content of scientific knowledge. Whereas the institutionalists built on a view of science as the product of creativity, scientific procedures, and epistemological criteria of assessment, proponents of the Sociology of Scientific Knowledge (SSK) treated science as a social and discursive practice.[33] Instead of formal organizations and formalized rules, sociologists of science turned to the study of informal groups, micro-level social interaction, practical manipulations, instruments, recording devices, and rhetorical styles. Whereas institutionalists explained scientific growth by means of formal organizational structures and norms, proponents of SSK sought to account for the authority of specific claims by the contingent events, alliances, and heterogeneous associations through which the claims were constructed. While these developments were extremely fruitful for the history and sociology of science, they tended to sideline the study of disciplines.[34]

Throughout the 1970s and 1980s, historians of science continued to talk about disciplines. However, they paid little attention to what the term might mean or to the assumptions implicit in their use of the concept.[35] In the absence of more systematic reflection, they often adopted a narrow, American-based model of disciplines as relatively autonomous scientific communities. Disciplines were studied as carriers of strong professional identities with little or no necessary relation to the content of scientific knowledge. This organizational bias was reversed in the 1980s under the dual influence of Michel Foucault and ecological approaches to the sociology of science. Both developments introduced spatial metaphors into the study of knowledge. My focus on the relations of demography and vital statistics to anthropology, political economy, public health, administrative statistics, and social statistics builds directly on these developments.

Ecological studies of science generally take either a political economy or a cultural approach. In the 1970s Charles Rosenberg called for an ecology of science which analyzed science in terms of processes of competition and entrepreneurship. The approach was exemplified by Kohler's oft-cited monograph on biochemistry.[36] Fifteen years later, under the influence of Foucault and others, Gieryn called attention to the extensive symbolic work involved in delineating science from non-science. The problematic was quickly picked up and applied to the study of disciplinary boundaries.[37] Both approaches drew attention to the processes involved in demarcating disciplines one from the other.

When pushed to their logical conclusion, cultural approaches underlined how boundary work constituted the very entities whose status and authority the boundaries were designed to affirm. Abbott went so far as to suggest that we think about entities such as disciplines and professions as the result of a process whereby heterogeneous elements (including types of people, types of work, and types of organizations) are yoked together to constitute new things.[38] Case studies, in turn, documented a range of mechanisms or processes used to constitute disciplinary entities. These include the writing of canonical histories,[39] the use of demarcation criteria to include or exclude particular projects, and the use of metaphors to create conceptual spaces.[40]

For the purposes of this book, one of the primary theoretical contributions of the ecological approach has been to shift the focus of theorizing from disciplines as (stable) entities — be they knowledge categories or professional communities — to disciplinary activity.[41] A second important point is the fundamental instability of disciplinary categories. One of the difficulties in telling the stories of nineteenth-century demography and, to a lesser extent, vital statistics is that these disciplines, by twentieth-century criteria, failed. Stated more radically, they never existed, at least not qua disciplines.[42] As such, their stories are more about the assertion of disciplinary claims than the institutionalization of stable entities.

Julie Klein and her colleagues have recently coined the term "disciplinarity" to underline the fluid, ever-changing character of disciplinary entities.[43] As the cases of demography and vital statistics indicate, disciplinarity began well before the institutionalization of disciplinary categories into professional, university-based communities and persisted well after the first set of departments and disciplines was established. From a theoretical perspective, the emphasis on the fluid nature of disciplinary categories is useful in that it decouples the study of disciplines from the study of twentieth-century university-based forms and opens the way for a more general inquiry into the social and epistemological logics associated with disciplinary activity.[44] Instead of assuming that we know what disciplinary activity is about, scholars need to interrogate the substance of disciplinary claims and the consequences of explicit disciplinary activity. They also need to ask about the conditions supporting different types of disciplinary forms.

For an Institutional Study of Disciplinarity

This book offers a meso-level, comparative institutional analysis of disciplines. It takes from the early institutionalists an acknowledgment that criteria of recognition are important, as is the relation of science, civil society, and the state. Instead of treating discipline formation as a proxy for scientific development and asking about the conditions of success and failure, the book uses disciplinary activity to explore the articulation of social and epistemic logics in a variety of settings. In comparing demography and vital statistics, I take from studies of disciplinarity their emphasis on the negotiated, contested, fluid character of knowledge categories. But whereas much of this work explains particular outcomes in terms of a chain of contingent events, I begin from the premise that nineteenth-century statisticians worked in worlds that were highly structured, in which some arrangements were easier to negotiate than others and institutionalized rules favored certain outcomes over others. The advantage of a systematic comparative analysis is that it allows one to identify those rules and the variety of ways in which they impinged on knowledge forms.

This general statement leaves me with a number of questions. The first is: What kind of institutions shape disciplinarity? The answer, I suggest, lies in the rules and mechanisms governing the distribution of recognition.[45] To focus on these rules and mechanisms is to combine the institutionalist insistence on recognition as an important mechanism of social control in science with the insights of historical epistemology concerning variations in the criteria for defining science (or, in this case, statistics).[46] Stated more generally, historical epistemology is the study of "competing forms of facticity." Whereas most scholars in the historical epistemology tradition focus on the discursive conditions of possibility, this book offers an institutional version of the same research agenda.

A second question raised by my formulation concerns the nature of disciplinarity or disciplinary activity. If disciplinary activity does not necessarily result in the creation of stable, institutionalized disciplinary entities, how can one recognize it? What is it about? And why does it matter? The usual approach to these questions is to define disciplinarity as the struggle to establish a discipline. The cases of nineteenth-century statistics are instructive in that they challenge this assumption. They suggest that scientists may appeal for scientific recognition not because they want to found an autonomous community or entity, but rather to transform the criteria by which they are being evaluated and thereby gain entry into an already existing knowledge arena — be it a specific science such as political economy or a professional activity of some sort. They also imply that stabilization is a rarity and that therefore stabilization, and not its absence, must be explained.

According to this approach, disciplinary activity is an explicit call for scientific recognition as a distinct knowledge category. The question of just what the category is — whether it involves the creation of specialized professional identities or incorporation into the university system — is an empirical problem. The basic premise of this book is that the substance of disciplinary claims will vary with the criteria for scientific recognition and the broader institutional context in which those claims are made and rewarded.

What distinguishes them from more specific knowledge claims or bids for material resources is the specific rhetorical form that they take. In contrast to other types of claim, disciplinary claims make an explicit appeal to epistemic criteria.[47] As such, they are necessarily designed both to gain recognition for the speaker and his or her intellectual project and to either affirm or transform broader rules of what counts as knowledge.

The Specificity of Statistics

Before moving on to the contributions of this book to the history of statistics and population statistics more specifically, it is perhaps helpful to address the objection that statistics are a special case. As the analysis that follows indicates, one of the nineteenth-century issues in the meta-discussions surrounding statistics concerned its status. As the opening speaker asked at the meeting of the International Congress of Statistics in 1869, is statistics a science, an auxiliary science, or a method?[48] And from my perspective, does statistics provide a useful case for the study of disciplinarity? The question, it seems to me, needs to be considered from two perspectives. The first is empirical, the second theoretical. On empirical grounds the issue is the specificity of statistics. Was statistics a special type of knowledge, diffused throughout a myriad of social institutions and practices, different in kind from other categories of scientific knowledge in circulation at the time? Or, was it "merely" an extreme instance of a more general phenomenon, namely the consolidation of disciplinary categories outside the academy and élite scientific institutions in a heterogeneous variety of social spaces?

Certainly statistics was not unique in its extra-scientific location. Political economy for most of its history was part of a broad public discourse. Leading "scientific" articles appeared in popular, nonspecialized journals, and important ideas were shaped by practices in agriculture, industry, commerce, government, and the press.[49] Similarly, anthropology developed in the context of the travels of independent scholars abroad and the implementation of colonial policy, as well as through the conversations of "scientists" at home. And ethology was as much a method as a "science." It is thus difficult, at least on empirical grounds, to dismiss attempts to establish statistics as a science by arguing that it occupied a different social location or that some people did or do not consider it to be one.

This observation connects to the theoretical point. If the literature on disciplinarity has one lesson to teach us, it is that we should not presume that we know what an object is before it is — and even then, it might change.

The argument that statistics was not a science would seem, at some level, to be doing just that. More generally, these observations raise the question of the role of theory in constructing my own object of inquiry and the intuitive difficulty of getting our heads around an approach that focuses on processes rather than objects. This book begins from the observation that at certain moments in time, certain people made explicit bids for recognizing a particular approach to population statistics as a separate science. It is the fact of making those bids, of doing that cultural work, that I am taking as an index of disciplinarity. Moreover, by labeling it "disciplinary work" I am clearly suggesting that these instances, once examined, may contribute to a more general understanding of the phenomenon of disciplinarity.

The specificity of disciplinarity as a theoretical problem is that it promises to shed light on the relations between social and epistemic considerations and logics. Far from being a self-contained argument, the debate over whether statistics was or was not a science was linked to debates over what counted as a science more generally and what type of knowledge statistics was (or was to be). At different moments, in different places, participants in the debate put forward different definitions of science and used those definitions to authorize their embrace or rejection of specific forms of statistics. Science was variously defined as hypothetical knowledge, certain knowledge, deductive knowledge, and inductive knowledge; alternative, competing styles of statistical reasoning were accepted or dismissed. Moreover, the adoption of one position or another was tied up, in complicated ways, with views on the causes of poverty and depopulation, on the proper relation between science, the administration, and politics, and on the scope of political action.

Thinking about Nineteenth-Century Statistics

Scholarly work on nineteenth-century statistics can be divided into two general literatures: a history of mathematical statistics and a history of administrative statistics. The division reflects both a historical division between the two types of activity for most of the nineteenth century and differences in the historiography. In both cases, the literature has moved from internalist histories, focused on specific instruments and techniques, to cultural and political studies of the construction of statistics and their social consequences. This book builds on the questions and findings of the cultural and political approach. It differs from other studies in this genre in its comparative design and in its focus on the scientific and epistemological consequences of different institutional arrangements.

Mathematical Statistics

The history of mathematical statistics was transformed in the 1980s by the publication of the two-volume edited set *The Probabilistic Revolution*, and a series of monographs that followed.[50] Together, this body of work shifted the focus of scholarship from the study of ideas and techniques to the study of styles of reasoning and practices. As Hacking has defined it, a "style of reasoning" is a cluster of types of objects, types of explanations, types of statements, and types of institutions that establish what counts as knowledge.[51] Like "disciplines," "styles" yoke together heterogeneous items, which once brought together serve to map out and organize a variety of social phenomena. Like the concept of "disciplines," the concept of "styles" draws attention to the articulation of social and epistemological logics.

THE GAP BETWEEN EULER AND GALTON For the most part, histories of statistics have been organized around an almost teleological interest in mathematical statistics. Historians of nineteenth-century statistics have been particularly preoccupied with the movement from probability theory in the late eighteenth century to the invention of mathematical statistics in the late nineteenth.[52] The question that lurks behind many of these histories is how to explain the long gap between these crucial developments. Why did it take over eighty years for mathematicians to move from Euler's "invention" of the method of least squares to Galton's and Pearson's use of the "error curve" to model social and biological phenomena? If most of the techniques of probability theory were developed in the late eighteenth century, why did it take until the early twentieth century for mathematical statistics to be established as a distinct discipline, as evidenced by the creation of the biometric school?[53] And why was it only after the Second World War that working statisticians began to routinely use probability theory and mathematics more generally?[54]

One of the contributions of the new history of statistics has been to shift the focus of inquiry from the "invention" of mathematical techniques to the objects, explanations, and claims that accompanied their development. As Stigler points out, the biometricians' accomplishment was not simply to have found a technical solution to the problem of how to combine probability theory and the empirical study of societies. Rather, the techniques of correlation and regression analysis introduced a new style of reasoning organized around the independent effect of probabilist statistical laws on the distribution of physiological and social characteristics in relatively homogeneous populations.[55] The introduction of this new style depended not only on the "invention" of new techniques but also on new types of data, new concepts, new statements, and new institutions.

Pursuing this logic, the "lag" between the invention of probability theory and the invention of mathematical statistics can be explained by the absence of these extratechnical elements. In this account, the history of nineteenth-century statistics becomes a story of the introduction and eventual linkage of the heterogeneous elements constituting the probabilist style of statistical reasoning. Crucial developments include the introduction of official statistical bureaus, new political uses of statistics, and new concepts amenable to statistical formulation.[56]

Historians of nineteenth-century statistics often single out Quetelet's work as a milestone in the path from Euler to Galton. His contribution is seen to lie in his use of error theory, and more specifically the binomial distribution, to establish homogeneity. Addressing French concerns about the meaning of aggregate statistical measures and distributions, Quetelet interpreted the seeming symmetrical distribution of social, moral, and physiological characteristics around a mean in terms of a fictional "average man," corresponding to an underlying anthropological type. The assumption in much of the literature is that Quetelet's work refocused statistical work on the study of averages. It was only in the late nineteenth century, or so the story goes, with the linkage of eugenics and mathematical statistics, that social statisticians shifted their attention to the study of variations, distribution, and differences. This impression is faulty, however, at least as concerns population statistics. Both French and English statisticians rejected Quetelet's use of the "average man,"[57] and many called for the analysis of parallel series rather than averages. A comparison of demography and vital statistics provides an opportunity to explore the ambivalent reception of Quetelet's specifically scientific form of social statistics and the nonlinear movement from eighteenth-century political arithmetic to twentieth-century biometrics.

A second contribution of the new history of statistics has been to draw attention to the day-to-day work of practicing mathematicians and statisticians. This focus has served both to expand the settings relevant to the history of statistics and to complicate the story. In place of a linear history of progressive discovery, nineteenth-century statistics emerges from this narrative as the product of fits and starts, played out at the interstices of science, politics, administration, and a variety of different publics. Curiously, this recognition has not led to systematic studies of the organizational or institutional logics governing statistical practice. Instead, historians tend to treat nineteenth-century social statisticians as a relatively homogeneous, unstructured group of individuals, engaged in a variety of practices, who at different moments introduced different elements of what would later become mathematical statistics. While specific actors and "inventions" are often located in specific institutions, those institutions generally serve as place holders. The nature of those institutions or their situation at a particular moment in time is not used to explain why a particular event happened or why it happened the way that it did. Nor are the processes connecting different moments ever explored. Nineteenth-century administrative and social statistics are presented as the repository of concepts that subsequently contributed to the solution of mathematical problems. The result is a sort of "thick description" in which a myriad of illuminating moments attest to the extensive cultural work that filled the gap between eighteenth-century mathematical theory and early-twentieth-century biometrics.

TOWARD A COMPARATIVE INSTITUTIONAL ANALYSIS OF STATISTICS This absence of institutional analysis is particularly striking when it comes to discussions of nineteenth-century critiques of statistical reasoning. Many historians note nineteenth-century objections to assumptions of homogeneity and to statistical forms of explanation more generally. The Royal Academy of Medicine ruled in 1837 that statistics should not be used in clinical medicine, on the grounds that they were irrelevant to the diagnosis of individual cases. Auguste Comte criticized the use of mathematics to study morals. Hacking similarly identifies a "silly season of determinism," in which social statisticians, physicians, and administrators criticized the concept of statistical law for its negation of free will.[58] While historians note these concerns, they do not systematically analyze the social and institutional position of the critics and the effect that these criticisms had on the development of statistics or the social sciences. Instead, they cite them as evidence of the general confusion surrounding the interpretation and use of statistics for most of the century.

One exception to this absence of systematic institutional analysis can be found in the comparison that both Porter and Hacking make between Prussian statistics on the one hand and French and British statistics on the other.[59] The association of France and Britain makes sense for a number of reasons. The term "statistics" was initially introduced by the cameralist school in the German-speaking parts of Europe in connection with inquiries into the wealth of the ruler. The term referred to the systematic, qualitative description of the state's resources, including its population, territory, and agricultural and commercial production. It was only in the early nineteenth century that observers appropriated the term "statistics" to refer to the numerical description of society. This shift happened first in France and Britain. The new form of statistics combined political arithmetic, which used mathematics to estimate population, and the cameralist description of the sovereign's state. Statistics, in its nineteenth-century version, was a numerical form of social science that explored the size, health, wealth, and moral state of the population.

Both Hacking and Porter contrast the French and British embrace of an atomistic, probabilist style of statistical reasoning, in which official statistical data was analyzed for evidence of laws and causes, with Prussian objections to the very existence of statistical laws. They explain this contrast by means of the "fit" between statistical and political objects. In France and England the nineteenth century was marked by the adoption of a liberal political philosophy according to which the political legitimacy of the government rested on its ability to foster the well-being of individual citizens. This vision assumed a radical distinction between "society" and the state, and called on the state to respect the natural laws governing the development of society.[60] Statistics promised to identify those laws. In Prussia, by contrast, politicians worked with a model of society as the product of the state. The role of government was to further the interests of the state and cultivate national culture. While statistics might describe the current resources of the state, it promised little in the way of political legitimation or direction. Prussian statisticians explicitly rejected the very concept of statistical laws, denying them any predictive or explanatory force.

Hacking's comparison of (French and English) liberal and Prussian statistics points to the primary form of "institutional" explanation currently found in the history of statistics. Whereas political and social historians and historical sociologists seek explanations in the interaction of structure and agency, calling on concepts such as resources, conflict, mobilization, and institutions to explain specific outcomes, historians of statistics tend to focus on the "fit" of statistical and other cultural representations. This latter approach is extremely helpful in analyzing the consequences of particular statistical forms for representing and reproducing power relations, be they class, gender, or colonial forms. However, it does little to explain why statistical representations assumed one form rather than another or developed in one direction rather than another. Moreover, as the comparison between French demography and English vital statistics illustrates, the focus on thick description and representations often obscures the social and epistemological logics that structure the production and diffusion of different styles of reasoning. Viewed as free-floating collections of heterogeneous forms, French and English statistics appear quite similar. The same general set of ideas and practices circulated in both countries. Viewed from the perspective of the social logics governing the circulation of those ideas, however, they emerge as quite different. One of the substantive historical contributions of this book lies in the identification of some of those differences and an exploration of the institutional conditions that supported them.

Considering the eventual development of mathematical statistics, these differences between the French and English cases may not be important. In both countries they applied to a world of social reformers, social statisticians, and administrators whose activities had little or no direct effect on the development of probability theory or on the work of English biometricians and their contribution to mathematical statistics. At the same time, they are not completely irrelevant. One of the underlying premises of this book is that the same institutional differences that account for differences in administrative styles of statistical reasoning, and in the diffusion of a "scientific" version of statistics among reformers and social scientists, also explain why the center of mathematical statistics shifted from France in the beginning of the nineteenth century to England at the end of the century, and why the French initially rejected marginal economics while the English embraced it.[61] In addition, these contrasts shed light on national styles of reasoning. More specifically, they help to illuminate the well-known contrast between French realist, collectivist forms of social thought and English nominalist, atomistic forms.[62]

Finally, the analysis that follows helps to make sense of the objections to social statistics and their consequences for the subsequent development of the field. It points to the counterintuitive nature of statistical concepts and styles of reasoning and to the enormous amount of cultural work that went into transforming them into common-sense assumptions and ways of thinking. This cultural "work" involved the "yoking" of statistical objects such as population with specific social and political problems, such as poverty, public health, and depopulation. Differences in how those political problems were handled and in the political function of statistics directly affected the interpretation and use that states and scientists made of ostensibly similar numbers.

Administrative Statistics

ADMINISTRATIVE STATISTICS AS REPRESENTATION The history of administrative statistics has followed a path parallel to that of mathematical statistics, albeit a somewhat separate one. The literature can be divided into three categories: technical studies, cultural studies, and social histories of official statistics. This book builds on the third category, which examines the social, political, and organizational logics governing administrative practice. As with the literature on mathematical statistics, it differs from those studies in its use of comparisons to explore the effect of political and social institutions on knowledge production and in its focus on the effect of those institutions on differences in national styles of reasoning, rather than on the reproduction of social inequalities or state authority.

With a few notable exceptions, histories of official statistics before the 1980s were designed to help current users negotiate historical data. Their aim was to inventory existing statistics and comment on their accuracy and reliability.[63] More recently, historians have extended this line of inquiry from the data to their production. There are now a number of excellent histories of official statistics, documenting changes in the organization, production, and output of the census.[64] Many remain driven, however, by a concern with the accuracy and consistency of the data and with the eventual mathematization of administrative statistics.

In the 1980s the cultural and linguistic turns in history and sociology transformed the study of official statistics.[65] Cultural theories of the state placed the work of political representation at the center of historical inquiry and drew attention to the role of the census in the imaginary of social relations and the constitution of the political nation.[66] Similarly, Foucault's identification of "population" as one of the primary objects of modern political power gave a new currency to population statistics in particular and administrative statistics more generally.[67]

Both the cultural study of state formation and Foucauldian studies of the knowledge-power nexus treat statistics as a form of representation. They thus encourage studies which explore the relation between statistical and political representations. Work in this vein highlights the role of statistics in political legitimation, in representing and therefore constituting the nation-state, and in introducing and reproducing new social hierarchies.[68] My study of the relation between statistical representations of population and modes of political legitimation builds on these insights. It differs from many cultural studies of statistics in its focus on knowledge as a practice, rather than a representation.

A second contribution of this literature has been to highlight the use of statistics and other political technologies in state control of the population. Administrators use these technologies to enumerate and classify individuals according to common sets of criteria and inscribe them in standardized forms. The rise of the nation-state and colonial government both depended on breaking existing collective identities and introducing new ones. They also depended on standardizing and classifying individuals, so as to better manage them. Official statistics were a central tool in both processes.

These two problematics underline two distinct political functions of official statistics: representation and instrumental control. Following Hacking, historians tend to link the two, such that representation is treated as a condition of both scientific and political action, which in turn transforms representations.[69] The comparison between the political function of population statistics in France and England suggests, however, that these two functions may fruitfully be thought of as separate.

Representation as a political function refers to the ideological use of statistics to document, and thereby constitute, the nation as an entity with external boundaries and internal hierarchies. While the symbolic boundaries that it establishes and re-enforces may inform state intervention, statistics do not themselves enter into its everyday exercise. An instrumental use of statistics, by contrast, points to the adoption of statistical indices as tools of state intervention. In France, population statistics were developed and deployed in the service of representation, whereas in England they served a largely instrumental role. These differences between representative and instrumental uses, I will argue, had significant implications, not only for the interpretation and use of official numbers, but also for the epistemological criteria by which forms of knowledge were authorized and rewarded.

ADMINISTRATIVE STATISTICS AS PRACTICE An important recent development in the history of administrative statistics has been the shift from analyzing representations to studying concrete processes by which such representations become the object of political and scientific action. Moving beyond representations, scholars such as Thévenot and Desrosières have drawn attention to what they describe as the "investment in form."[70] "Form" refers to statistical representations, the symbolic form and associated style of reasoning. "Investment" refers to the material, social, and symbolic conditions that must be put in place for the representation to hold. It thus extends beyond financial investment to include the procedures, social relations, and meanings that stabilize particular practices. For official statistics, these range from elaborating statistical categories and adopting specific techniques to collecting, recording, collating, manipulating, and publishing data to maintaining the network of private citizens, data collectors, inspectors, administrators, officials, and users involved in these processes. The advantage of the concept of "investment in form" is that it draws attention not only to the technical tools used to stabilize statistical objects but to the importance of social, political, and commercial arrangements as well.

At the same time that Thévenot and Desrosières have theorized the problem of investment, a number of social historians have examined the production of official statistics. Studies such as those by Bruce Curtis, Silvana Patriarca, Alain Desrosières, and Simon Szreter treat official statistics not as self-contained documents but as products of broader social, political, and administrative processes. Far from a simple innovation, the introduction of and investment in specific statistical forms were the product of extensive political struggle.[71] The stakes included not only who would run statistical bureaus and what kind of statistics they would collect, but basic political ontologies. Central issues included which groups were to be empowered, which would be excluded, on what basis resources would be distributed, what counted as a social problem, and who had the authority to define the nation. Moreover, the struggles were almost always both epistemological and political. Whereas most historians focus on the political and ideological consequences of different outcomes, this book examines the scientific and epistemological consequences of those same administrative struggles.

Histories of Population Statistics

Various parts of the historical narrative developed here have been analyzed by other authors, albeit with different questions in mind and from different theoretical perspectives. A brief review of the relation of this book to these literatures serves to underline its contribution. Stated very generally, most histories of population statistics, demography, and administrative statistics adopt a Whiggish perspective when defining their topic. They focus on those nineteenth-century moments that directly contributed to twentieth-century developments. Viewed from this perspective, vital statistics is generally mentioned in passing, while nineteenth-century demography is completely ignored. Similarly, nineteenth-century histories of public health and social statistics pay a great deal of attention to France in the first half of the century and England throughout the century, but largely ignore French developments between roughly 1851 and 1885, in large part because those developments did not contribute to twentieth-century developments.

This imbalance in the historiography reflects the negative effect of the Second Empire and the early decades of the Third Republic on both public hygiene and social science. But it also obscures the cognitive and institutional logics shaping statistical activity at the time. In addition it contributes to a tendency to misread French developments by assuming that what was true for public hygiene and social statistics in the first half of the century continued to be true in the second. The result is an image of France and Britain as more similar than they actually were, at least as regards social statistics.

This chronological gap in the historiography is clearly evidenced in the genre of social history cum biography. A number of excellent biographies of key figures in the English public health movement and French public hygiene movement explicitly address their statistical work. The two best-known of these works are Coleman's biography of Villermé and Eyler's of William Farr. Both authors use their subjects to explore the world of public health research, and both underline the importance of their subjects' liberal political commitments and social reform concerns for their scientific work. Coleman's book documents the state of statistics and public health in the first half of the century; Eyler's book covers the middle quarters of the century. Organizational histories of these movements cover similar periods.[72] In all these cases the story of France in the second half of the century is missing, in large part because there were no "great men" who straddled science and politics, at least not in the areas of public hygiene and social statistics. Louis Adolphe Bertillon is probably as close as one comes, and his influence was relatively minor, at least with respect to the twentieth-century development of statistics, public health, and even demography. Why were there no heroic figures in these fields? One answer, I suggest, is that the institutional conditions did not allow for them.

One of the themes of this book is the relation of demography and vital statistics to the public health movement. In England vital statistics linked its fortunes to the medical branch of the public health movement; in France demography distanced itself from the public hygiene movement. This contrast is related both to the intellectual substance of the programs in each country and to broader institutional factors, including the nature of the two public health movements, channels of access to the policy process, and relations in England and France between orthodox medicine, public health, élite science, and social statistics. These differences influenced the content and institutional distribution of alternative styles of statistical reasoning. While a number of scholars point to these differences in passing — noting the absence of medical statistics in the work of the French national statistical bureaus and the professionalization of the English public health movement relative to the French — they do not relate them to variations in scientific developments and epistemological rules.[73]

A similar set of observations can be made concerning histories of population statistics proper. A number of accounts mention demography and vital statistics. However, they do so in the light of of later historical developments. Viewed from the perspective of mathematical statistics, vital statistics plays a small, relatively insignificant role in that history, and French nineteenth-century demography is totally absent. Similarly, viewed from the perspective of the contemporary discipline of demography, eighteenth-century French political arithmetic and nineteenth-century vital statistics figure as intellectual precursors, while nineteenth-century French demography is, once again, irrelevant (except for its contribution of the name).[74]

Turning to work on nineteenth-century statistical movements, the English "movement" is far better documented, in part because it was far more active. There is a large literature on the private statistical movement and different organizations that composed it.[75] None of these studies, however, explore the relations between different organizations and their consequences for the content of statistical knowledge. My comparison of demography and vital statistics thus complements this work by examining the institutional logics that account for differences in the axes of differentiation between statistical projects in the two countries. In France the key issues would seem to have been the degree of abstraction of statistical entities; in England the defining issue was the relation between opinion and science.

While most histories of administrative statistics and social science focus on either a single country or very general trends, a few adopt a comparative approach, similar to the one developed here. The first, most striking example of this genre is Westergaard's history of nineteenth-century statistics (1932), which provides a systematic, albeit noncritical, description of administrative practices in different countries.[76] More recently, Stuart Woolf and Alain Desrosières have both engaged in comparative research. Both signal macro-level differences in the nature of the state. Focusing exclusively on France and Britain, Woolf contrasts the role of educated élites in England with the role of the state in France in promoting statistics.[77] In a similar vein, Desrosières underlines the contrast between centralized statistical production in France and decentralized administrative statistics in England.[78]

While both sets of observations identify important overall differences, they cannot be directly applied to vital statistics and demography. In England, decentralization was accompanied by indirect centralization. Official statistics were the product of a relatively efficient, well-coordinated administrative infrastructure linking local and central offices. This decentralized, yet coordinated system was a crucial condition of possibility for the success of vital statistics. In France, by contrast, tensions between local and national government and between ministries significantly limited the statistical apparatus, rendering centralization largely ineffectual and depriving demography of the administrative resources essential to its program. These comments underscore the need for more meso-level institutional analyses of how specific arrangements directly impinged on the development of specific research practices.

Finally, this book touches on material that has recently been analyzed from a Foucauldian viewpoint. Scholars such as Mary Poovey and Joshua Cole have examined nineteenth-century debates surrounding population statistics from the perspective of the constitution of "mass culture" and the introduction of new divisions and domains within that "social body."[79] Poovey argues that the emergence in Britain of an image of a national, mass culture in the 1860s depended on the prior elaboration and institutionalization of statistical practices directed at representing the national population as a single entity. Moreover, she shows how the representations were elaborated in conjunction with specific social problems and concerns for social reform. Similarly, Cole's analysis of debates surrounding population statistics in France underlines how statistical discourse contributed both to representing the population as an entity and affirming social hierarchies, most notably those related to the family and women. Both Poovey and Cole examine some of the same debates that are analyzed in this book. Cole's work in particular highlights the immense difficulty that statisticians, administrators, and the public had with using statistics to establish causation. At the same time, his focus, like Poovey's, is on the social consequences of statistical "investments in form."

My own analysis complements this work by examining the scientific consequences of these debates. One of Foucault's many contributions was to highlight the extent to which the domain of the social was simultaneously political and epistemological. New modes of political action were intimately linked to new ways of knowing and new types of object. However, the novelty or specificity of these more epistemological dynamics is not always immediately evident. It is only by comparing French discussions with those conducted elsewhere that the specificity of each case comes through. In France, debates over population statistics circled around the representative function of the knowledge. Epistemological objections concerned the reality of statistical abstractions, and technical discussions were relatively rare. In England, by contrast, comparable debates took a very different form. Few if any of the participants even commented on the homogeneity or reality of statistical representations. They actively debated the choice of variables and selection of statistical indices, and technical debates were often a proxy for political debates (and vice versa).

These contrasts point to differences in the articulation of political, epistemological, and technical issues in policy debates. Moreover, they point to differences in the dominant styles of statistical reasoning. Thus, while both French and English reformers, politicians, and administrators used statistics to constitute and address social problems, they did so in different ways. One of the contributions of this book is to document those differences and to situate them in differences in the political function of statistics and in the rules of scientific, and more specifically statistical, recognition.

STATISTICAL INTERNATIONALISM Before turning to the historical narrative it is important to say a few words about statistical internationalism and its role in promoting a specifically scientific form of administrative statistics. According to some historians, Quetelet's most significant contribution to the development of nineteenth-century statistics lay not in his proposal to apply probability theory to statistical regularities, but rather in his untiring work to promote the standardization and improvement of official statistics. Already in the 1830s Quetelet was involved in establishing the Statistical Society of London and in designing the British census of 1841. That same year he was appointed head of the Belgian Central Statistical Commission. In 1842 he conducted a municipal census of Brussels, and in 1846 he organized the Belgian national censuses. Quetelet explicitly designed these different censuses to serve the needs of scientists. The experience involved him in producing official data and launched him on a second career devoted to persuading statisticians and administrators across Europe to adopt the same, "scientific" standards for official data.

Quetelet's crowning achievement in this respect was the creation in 1853 of the International Congress of Statistics.[80] The congress was one of the first international scientific congresses in Europe and was quickly imitated by other sciences. It met nine times between 1853 and its dissolution in 1878. The congress brought together heads of national statistical bureaus from across Europe as well as independent statisticians and scholars. As such, it marked a significant innovation or change in the conventions of scientific communication. Whereas eighteenth-century political arithmetic had developed through the correspondence of scholars, the nineteenth century was marked by the introduction of public scientific congresses as a vehicle of communication and standardization.

In the 1850s and 1860s the International Congress of Statistics was primarily devoted to introducing uniform administrative procedures. For example, one of the early resolutions called for decennial censuses, directed at the actual population (*population du fait*) rather than the legal population (*population de droit*). In later years, participants also took on questions of statistical theory and methodology. In 1867 the congress resolved to create a section to deal with statistical questions connected to the theory of probabilities, and in 1868 it called on administrators to analyze deviations from the mean as well as the means themselves. As noted in the following discussion, the congress provided an important forum for developing and promoting a specifically scientific version of administrative statistics and producing internationally comparable data. It also provided a valuable resource for advocates of this approach in their home country. This was especially so in France, where demography was initially excluded from élite scientific and political institutions.

PART I

The Struggle for

Disciplinary Recognition:

Why "Invent" a Discipline

in Nineteenth-Century France?

CHAPTER ONE

The "Invention" of Demography, 1853–1855

The question "Why establish a discipline in the nineteenth century?" serves to shift the researcher's attention from familiar features of contemporary disciplines, be they intellectual or institutional, to the act of discipline assertion itself. In the realm of demography the question leads to France, to the self-taught botanist and Republican political speaker Achille Guillard and his son-in-law Louis Adolphe Bertillon. The year is 1853, in the early years of the Second Empire, a period of political repression in which citizens, including scientists, need official permission to assemble in a group of more than three. Many outspoken Republicans have fled Paris for fear of imprisonment, leading academics have resigned their posts rather than swear allegiance to the new regime, and practicing social scientists are obliged to temper their words so as to avoid censorship. The occasion is the publication of a book entitled *Élements de la statistique humaine, ou démographie comparée*, in which Guillard announced the birth of a new science, demography.

Very little has been written about Achille Guillard and his role in the founding of demography as a discipline. Those accounts which exist repeat the version presented by his grandchildren in a memorial volume for their father.[1] According to their account, demography was conceived in prison in the early 1850s by Guillard and his future son-in-law. Incarcerated for their support of the Republican cause, the two men supposedly developed demography as a response to the failure of the Revolution of 1848. Curiously, none of the accounts that repeat this founding myth ask about the content of the original project. None attempt to explain what about this first version of demography rendered it a response to the collapse of the Second Republic, and all take for granted the association between intellectual project and disciplinary activity.

This first chapter uses Guillard's attempt to assert the existence of demography as a distinct science to explore three parallel sets of questions.

First, what was demography in this initial version? Second, what do Guillard's efforts to establish demography as a discipline and their reception tell us about the institutional structures shaping social statistics at that moment? Third, what was the institutional significance, in this particular case, of explicit disciplinary activity? In other words, what was Guillard asking for when he linked his intellectual program to the recognition of a new discipline? What changes would discipline formation have introduced?

Guillard's Initial Project: Reforming Political Economy

The Intellectual Project

The content of Guillard's original project for statistics can be discerned in two short texts, which he submitted to the *Journal des économistes* in 1853. The first was a letter to the editor, Joseph Garnier, entitled "On the need to record the age of death."[2] In his letter, Guillard used the occasion of the creation of cantonal statistical offices to define what he referred to as *la statistique humaine* (soon to become demography). According to Guillard, statistics was the only science that established with certainty, thanks to its reliance on numbers, the "state of the nation." The aims of *la statistique humaine* were (1) to identify variations in the state of the population according to sex, age, location, and race; (2) to inquire into the causes of that condition; and (3) to make that information available to legislators and economists in their pursuit of progress.

In some respects, demography was yet another version of the Enlightenment project to use social science, and more specifically statistics, to hold legislators accountable to the "natural" laws governing society. Its audience was the liberal economists who dominated élite social science at the time. More specifically, demography challenged the use of Malthusian arguments to reject state support for the poor. Curiously, responses to Guillard's proposal focused not on the political stakes but on technical issues concerning data, statistical entities, and the limits to statistical manipulation.

Guillard's original project encompassed a campaign to improve official statistics so as to meet the needs of science, extensive discussions of how to use existing data by correcting for known omissions and verifying the data by comparing different sources, and discussions of the choice and use of different statistical measures. Beginning with the state of existing knowledge, Guillard decried the absence of precise knowledge about local population movements (births and deaths) and their cause. In particular, Guillard called attention to the failure of the decennial summaries of civil registries to specify ages of death. These data were essential for establishing the age structure of the population, which in turn influenced mortality rates.[3] Far from being unusual, this focus on administrative practice was characteristic of French nineteenth-century statistics. Mathematicians measured their work by the logic and skill with which they manipulated numbers, but statisticians based their authority on the quality of the raw data and their administrative value. The novelty of Guillard's approach lay in his extension of population statistics from the art of data collection to the selection and manipulation of alternative statistical indices. As suggested below, this emphasis challenged existing boundaries between mathematics and statistics and between "scientific" and "administrative" forms of social statistics.

While statistics were an important component of Guillard's original intellectual project, they were not its raison d'être. A second article, published in August 1853, outlined what for Guillard constituted the substantive contribution of demography to social knowledge.[4] Like the first letter, the text was published in the *Journal des économistes*. The occasion was a discussion at the Académie des Sciences Morales et Politiques on the subject of Joseph Garnier's article "Population," which had appeared in his *Dictionnaire d'économie politique* in 1852. All three publications were associated with political economy, and Garnier was a leading spokesman for the discipline.

Guillard entitled his article "On Birth Statistics in Relation with the General Question of Population." His analysis consisted of a series of statistical demonstrations of what he claimed to be the true law of population and was presented as a refutation of Malthus's theory that population growth outruns subsistence. According to Guillard, the laws of nature are such that the population automatically proportions itself to the existing level of subsistence. As evidence, Guillard cited official statistics for France and Belgium. In each country an increase in economic prosperity had been accompanied by a decline in both mortality and natality and an increase in longevity. According to Guillard, nature automatically adjusts the number of births to the food supply, thus ensuring the maintenance of a natural equilibrium.

In developing this argument, Guillard directly challenged Garnier's position that overpopulation was the cause of poverty and that the only way to avoid suffering was for individuals to take responsibility for their situation by limiting their reproduction.[5] While the message was clearly political, Guillard saved his passion for statistics. The thrust of his argument was that economists needed to turn to statistics to resolve their theoretical differences. Without such tools futile debates, such as that over population, would never be resolved and political economy would never become a real science.

The Initial Response

In 1853 neither of Guillard's two articles mentioned the term demography; in 1854 all of his articles did. The main event which would seem to have intervened between these two dates was the unequivocal rejection of Guillard's manuscript by the Académie des Sciences Morales et Politiques. Unfortunately, the archives of the academy contain no record of the reasons for this rejection. The only traces are the editorial comments that Joseph Garnier published in response to Guillard's two articles of 1853. Rather than discuss either Guillard's refutation of Malthus or his program for political economy, Garnier took on Guillard on his own ground, namely the use of statistics. Garnier opened by countering Guillard's call for improving administrative statistics, dismissing them as a scientific source. He criticized Guillard's statistical demonstration of Malthus's principle of population by questioning the ability of statistical observation to reveal laws.

According to Garnier, the successful limitation of population growth by a fall in the birth rate in France and Belgium did not of itself establish the universality of this mechanism. First, two cases were not enough to establish a law, and second, the use of national averages obscured the considerable variation or disequilibria displayed at the local level by both France and Belgium: "Now, if the result evoked by Mr. Guillard was not only a national average, but the expression of what *really* happened in the bosom of all the families (elements of this average in France, in Belgium and everywhere) . . . if it (his measure) was the expression of facts which were constant and universal for the present and the past; if everywhere and always the fathers of families and their progenitor shared in the law of the equation of subsistence, oh! then we would believe that nature on its own takes responsibility to regulate births. Until now, and as we have seen in millions of special cases, it is death, proceeded by the suffering of *misère*, which has contained and contains populations within the limits of subsistence (emphasis and parenthesis added)."[6]

The issue for Garnier was thus not a question of theory, but rather the relation of statistical averages to reality and the possibility of establishing a law based on statistical observations.

Criteria of Recognition: The Boundary between
Theory and Observation

Political Economy under the Second Empire

Garnier's criticisms of Guillard's project for statistics can be interpreted in two ways. Either he used the statistical aspect of Guillard's work to raise political objections which in the climate of the authoritarian empire he preferred not to debate publicly, or he was genuinely troubled by Guillard's use of numbers. Nor are the two explanations mutually exclusive. Each is supported by the evidence. The epistemological argument highlights a basic feature of French liberal economic thought, while the political argument calls attention to the institutional strategy which economists adopted in the first decade of the Second Empire. A brief review of the history of French political economy serves to clarify Garnier's position.

In choosing the liberal economists as his main target, Guillard aimed at the élite social science of the time. Intellectually, the French political economists were first and foremost committed to the principles of the free market and individual liberty. The introduction of the social question during the 1840s divided them between ultraliberals, who insisted on individual responsibility and viewed the question of poverty in moral terms, and moderate liberals, who felt that the state should regulate certain excesses introduced by industrialization.[7] In contrast to their English counterparts, French liberal economists were largely excluded from politics and policy making. It was only in the 1860s that their discourse gained political authority. The significance of this exclusion for the history of statistics is that while in England political economists' policies were tested by practical legislative experiments, in France the discourse developed as a largely intellectual construct.

With the establishment of the Second Empire, the possibility that liberals might obtain legislative backing for their policy of free trade became more realistic. In 1853 political economy was in a dominant, albeit precarious position. The collapse of the July Monarchy in 1848 had put an end to its period of institutional security. Under the provisional government, the chairs of political economy at the Collège de France and the École des Ponts et Chaussées were temporarily closed. With the creation of the Second Empire in 1851, the economists' position was marginally secured. According to Le Van Lemesle, the liberal economists retained their institutional position during the 1850s by adopting a defensive strategy in which scientific goals were suspended. In the first decade of the Empire, economists emphasized the vocational dimension of their knowledge and its contribution to maintaining public order and conciliation between classes.[8] At the same time, they based their scientific credentials on the specifically deductive character of their knowledge. While both these factors are more than sufficient to explain why Guillard's project was rejected by the economists, they do not explain the substance of Garnier's criticisms.

Political Economy and Descriptive Statistics

As noted above, Garnier criticized Guillard's projects on two grounds: he rejected the adequacy of administrative statistics, and he challenged the ability of statistical observations to identify underlying laws. Both positions expressed a basic set of epistemological assumptions concerning the identification of natural laws and the relations between observation and theory. They were among the defining premises of political economy as a science. They were also an important axis of social differentiations, dividing between liberal political economy and other human sciences.

The founding father of French liberal political economy was Jean-Baptiste Say, and it was his writings on methodology and the relation between political economy and statistics that set the terms of the debate.[9] Say's position can be described in terms of his distinction between two types of science (descriptive science and experimental science) and two types of statistics (descriptive statistics and political arithmetic). According to Say, experimental sciences were those sciences such as physics, chemistry, and political economy which aimed at identifying general laws and causal relations. Descriptive sciences such as botany, natural history, and statistics, by contrast, were classificatory endeavors. Whereas experimental sciences explained natural phenomena, descriptive sciences proceeded by naming and classifying observations. These differences corresponded to the types of knowledge that the two types of science produced. Political economy identified general, universal laws of nature that surpassed the particularities of time and place. By contrast, statistics, unable to take into account either history or general causes, produced a punctual, static image of society. In addition, the problems of data collection and multiple possibilities for error rendered most official data unusable for scientific purposes. Say's model for political economy thus provided for a clear division of labor or disciplinary map, whereby economists used *deductive* methods to identify natural laws which statisticians illustrated or validated. Although political economists under the July Monarchy consistently included statistical work in their journal, under the Second Empire they reverted to this strict hierarchy.[10]

In 1853 Joseph Garnier was the permanent secretary of the Society of Political Economy, editor in chief of the *Journal des économistes*, professor of political economy at the École des Ponts et Chaussées, and the author of one of the definitive treatises of political economy at the time. He had also recently coedited the widely read *Dictionnaire d'économie politique*. Garnier used these forums to transmit what he himself described as "the most generally acknowledged doctrines" or "normal opinion" of the liberal school, rather than introduce any new ideas.[11] Both institutionally and intellectually, Garnier's position was that of gatekeeper. His self-appointed role was to protect Say's intellectual legacy.

Among the liberal economists, Garnier was notable for his relative openness toward statistics and mathematics. For example, it was on his initiative that the mathematical works of Léon Walras were published in the *Journal des économistes*. While Garnier gave voice to a wide range of intellectual positions in the *Journal des économistes*, he did not present them as equally authoritative. Instead, he used his editorial powers to instruct readers on how they should evaluate the different articles that he published. As gatekeeper of the discipline, Garnier affirmed Say's position: descriptive statistics, yes; formalization of any kind, no; and a clear division of labor between theory and statistics. This position explains both Garnier's willingness to publish Guillard's letters and the content of his editorial comments. As self-appointed gatekeeper, Garnier may have welcomed the opportunity to expound on the limits of statistical analysis.

This reading suggests yet another reason for economists' initial reaction to demography. Not only did it challenge their reading of Malthus and upset their defensive institutional strategy, it also directly violated the epistemological boundary between observation and theory at the heart of the liberal economic project. In calling attention to these transgressions, Garnier effectively used the editorial column of the *Journal des économistes* to reenforce the disciplinary map that served to legitimate political economy. He also clearly indicated to Guillard that liberal economists were not interested in Guillard's attempt to improve their science.

The View from Republican Science, I

While liberal economists were Guillard's primary audience, they were not his only one. The term "demography" was first used in 1854 in the newly created *Revue du XIXᶜ siècle*. Founded during the early years of the Second Empire as the *Revue Babel*, the journal was one of many short-lived attempts to give voice to Republican intellectuals. Six months after its founding, the editors changed the name of the journal and invited a number of new authors to join its ranks, including both Achille Guillard and Louis Adolphe Bertillon. The latter's inclusion among the contributors situates them in a broader circle of Republican intellectuals and in opposition to liberal political economists who worked in state-recognized institutions and were identified with the monarchy.

The introduction to the first issue locates the journal in a positivist Republican ideology of science. The opening editorial affirmed the journal's commitment to the unity of science and bewailed the detrimental effects of disciplinary specialization on the "Progress of Science." The value placed on unity was partly grounded in the belief that society should be governed by the unified study of nature, rather than juridical contracts.[12] It also challenged liberal economists' strict division between experimental and descriptive sciences and their exclusion of statistics from the discovery of laws.

Reworking the Project

Guillard's article for *La revue du XIXᵉ siècle* was entitled "Human Statistics: The Conservation of Children, Frustrated Births." It differed from his contributions to the *Journal des économistes* in two major respects. First, in this positivist version all discussion of Malthus and political economy disappeared. Second, the discussion was framed in terms of explicit disciplinary claims. The text was divided into two sections, on the demography of childhood and the demographic method. The opening sentences contained what was to become Guillard's standard introduction: a definition of the new science and concern for its low status and the consequent neglect of human statistics: "We mean by human statistics the mathematical knowledge of populations, of their general movements, of their physical, intellectual, moral, civil and social state. Its domain is very vast; it embraces the succession of generations, the duration of life, the relations of man with nature, in one word, all the type of facts and studies which are directly related to the species, its needs, its suffering, and its well being. This science can, in its realization, claim the rightful title, taken from the ancient motto: (cited in Greek and in French): I am man, and all that is of man is the object of my concerns. It might perhaps be well defined as the natural and social history of the human species."[13]

As the quote indicates, demography followed in the tradition of Condorcet and Comte. It called for a comprehensive social science based on the scientific, and in this case statistical, study of society. Another innovation in the article was the introduction of a system of specialized signs designed to facilitate the formalization of statistical analysis. A lowercase letter was the number of times an event was recorded in a population (for example, "n," for *naissances*, or number of births), a capital letter was an annual average ("N" for the average annual number of births), and a subscript was the number of people in an age group ($n_{(0-1)}$ for the number of children between the ages of zero and one).

The question which interests me here is not why Guillard chose these particular symbols, but rather why he invented terms and symbols at all. The answer, which Guillard provides in his article on method in botany, is that it is through the introduction of new concepts, which bridge the gap between theory and observation, that science advances.[14] Discipline formation, for Guillard, thus involved the elaboration of new, ever more comprehensive vocabularies, directed at creating a single, general science.

The Path to Disciplinary Activity

The idea of discipline formation as a move toward a comprehensive science was a positivist Republican idea. That said, 1854 was not a year during which many intellectuals engaged in disciplinary work. Guillard was the only one of the contributors to the *Revue du XIXe siècle* to call for the recognition of their project as a separate science. Thus, while Guillard may have taken the form from the positivist cultural arsenal, the timing of his disciplinary claim cannot be explained by this reference group. Instead, I would argue that the explanation lies more with the initial reception of the project among economists.

The publication of *Éléments de la statistique humaine, ou, démographie comparée* in 1855 brought together the two versions of Guillard's project, those of political economy and discipline formation. As noted above, the book can be divided into two parts, the body of the text, which was written before February 1853, and the introduction and annexes, which would seem to have been written for the book version. In terms of the content, nothing in the book version is new. Demography is defined as the statistics of human collectivities — the study of natural divisions. Its aims are to identify the laws of population, defined in the broadest sense as those laws pertaining to the size of the population, and its education, morality, vigor, and well-being. Finally, its scope is limited only by the restriction of demography to the quantitative study of society.

According to Guillard, demography is the mathematical study of population. The important point here is a distinction between mathematics and arithmetic, and the relation of each to statistics. While arithmeticians study absolute numbers, statisticians study averages and regularities. One of Guillard's criticisms of Garnier was precisely that he supported "arithmetic" rather than statistics. The result, Guillard argued, was that economists' statistical findings were limited to punctual descriptions of limited scientific value.

Three elements distinguish the introduction of Guillard's book on demography from his earlier texts. These include the clear distinction which he makes between political economy and demography, his explication of what was formerly an implicit political program, and finally, an attempt to forge an alliance with administrators. All three are part of a clear attempt to alter the epistemic rules governing political economy and to insert demography therein.

Guillard makes the first point in his discussion of the historical development of the social sciences. The aim of the emerging science (demography) is to reorient social science away from the study of a "fantastic ideal" and toward the observation of facts. This development is associated with an expansion in the object of study to include "all the conditions of life in the exclusive interest of the masses." He continues: "From which it results that, just as the *science of wealth* must become, by the progress of knowledge, the science of the common well-being, similarly the science applied to large numbers must be transformed, by a better direction of its studies, into the science of all the numerical means [averages] which interest humanity. Demography is thus the common reservoir into which all the currents of statistics must flow."[15] The quote points to a shift in Guillard's conception of how *la statistique humaine* relates to political economy. Whereas in 1853 he presented demography as a component of political economy, or a corrective to it, by 1855 demography had become a more general, more scientific form of knowledge, destined to replace political economy.

Turning to the administrators, Guillard's introduction repeated the themes of his earlier text, in which he insisted on the value of official statistics and the need to improve them. The specificity of demography lay in its reliance on official data. Demographers depended on the efforts of administrators for the advance of their science. "The large numbers, which are the atomical material, the simple bodies of the statistics, cannot be collected by individuals. It is necessary to wait for the ministerial bureaus, organizations that, by their nature, are repelled by movement, and, for lack of control, depend on routine. All that the adept of the science can do, is to compare the numbers which the [administrators] are willing to furnish, and to call for those which he lacks. This is why the progress of statistics is slow."[16] In linking demography to the development of administrative statistics, Guillard effectively entered into direct competition with liberal economists for the support of the administration.

The final point, which Guillard's book highlights, concerns the political color of demography. In the annex of the book, Guillard reprinted a series of letters that he had exchanged with various economists, notably Garnier. The letters help to explain the relation between demography and the failure of the Revolution of 1848. The link lies in Guillard's Enlightenment belief in Progress as a natural law and in his definition of Progress as an increase in the well-being of the population. As he explained in response to Garnier:

> Does the population of workers increase beyond that which is needed? NO, since our industrial centers maintain themselves through an incessant immigration. But if it were to be demonstrated . . . that workers in our factories increased to the progress of the majority of our co-citizens, then I would say "to work statisticians!" Economists, to the rescue! Research, discover what is the exceptional cause that maintains these laborious families in a state against nature, and indicate the remedy to those who should and can apply it. What is this suffering class lacking? Is it knowledge of the art of living? Provide them with prodigious and large instruction, such as Rossi wanted. Is it the dignity and independence that comes from property holding? In effect, our peasants live better, much better, since they possess the land that they cultivate and are masters of their profession. What can be done such that the factory worker too may become master of his (profession).[17]

This quote clearly situates Guillard's concern with laws of population and demography in the context of an ongoing debate over the causes of poverty and unemployment. French liberal economists used Malthus's theory of population growth to defend their opposition to state intervention in the economy. Concretely, the issues at stake were limits on the length of the working day, the creation of workers' associations, and the redistribution of landed property. Demography constituted an attempt to defend these measures, while appealing to economists' own language of natural laws.

This position explains why Guillard turned to the statistical study of population. Paradoxically, his intention was not to found a new discipline based on the exclusive study of what we today refer to as demographic variables, but rather, as he explained it, to demonstrate once and for all the irrelevance of population to analyzing the causes of poverty and the conditions for economic progress. Guillard thus studied population in order to persuade economists to return their attention to properly economic problems and abandon their moralizing approach to unemployment and poverty. His argument can therefore be seen as an early attempt to dissuade economists from making rhetorical use of supposedly natural laws (or, in the twentieth century, biological laws) to set a priori limits on the possibility of social progress and change.

Why Demography and Why Discipline Formation in 1855?

The initial assertion of demography in 1855 provides a number of insights into both nineteenth-century discipline formation and the institutional structures supporting a scientific approach to administrative statistics. It also provides a first insight into the issues shaping the introduction and reception of national statistical populations as a scientific and political entity. Whereas theories of discipline formation often take the basic disciplinary categories for granted, focusing on whether such claims led to the establishment of a set of formal, continuous organizations, the above discussion asks about the act of making a disciplinary claim. Why did Achille Guillard link his program for political economy to a disciplinary discourse in 1855? The historicization of the question draws attention both to the local conditions shaping the ongoing reformulation of disciplinary maps and the variety of disciplinary forms.

Guillard's turn to disciplinary work in demography can be explained by his position in the "scientific field," and in particular the system of social-science disciplines as specified by the relations of political economy and positivist science. Three factors would seem to have contributed to Guillard's disciplinary endeavors: his initial failure to gain scientific recognition from an established, élite scientific audience (the political economists), the availability of an alternative, newly constituted scientific community that supported his project, and the place of discipline formation in the cultural repertoire of that community. The crucial factors were the explicitly epistemological character of the initial criticisms and the use of disciplinary claims to assert an alternative set of explicitly epistemological criteria.

For Guillard, the call for recognizing demography as a separate science was aimed not at establishing a new, semi-autonomous community of researchers but rather at achieving scientific recognition. Guillard sought recognition first from positivist, Republican scientists and then from the orthodox scientific community. This goal corresponded to the form of the envisaged discipline. Far from a specialized discourse or set of practices, demography followed the positivist model of a comprehensive science, building on and abstracting from lower-level sciences (in this case political economy and descriptive or "arithmetic" forms of statistics) in the name of scientific and social progress. The stakes were not organizational but scientific, or, more specifically, epistemological. They had to do with what counted as statistics.

Between 1853 and 1855 Guillard made a number of attempts to gain recognition from political economists for his particular combination of abstract statistical reasoning and socialism. His writings on statistics were all submitted to mainstream liberal economic journals. The gatekeepers of political economy responded by rejecting the project, not for its political content but on epistemological grounds. In criticizing Guillard's project for its excessive abstraction and use of numbers to identify laws, Joseph Garnier affirmed a clear division of labor between political economy and statistics. Political economy was responsible for theory and explanation; statistics was limited to observation and description. Guillard's proposal that numbers could be used to identify laws of population was rejected on the grounds that it violated this basic rule. The editorial column in the main political economy journal was an important mechanism in enforcing this cognitive boundary.

While political considerations clearly figured in this judgment, Garnier's use of epistemological arguments pushed Guillard to respond in kind. His turn to discipline formation can be explained by the support that he found in the newly created positivist journal *La Philosophie Positive*, and in the epistemological character of the debate. Rather than specialization or professionalization, discipline formation sought a reworking of the cognitive rules in such a way as to make a place for demography, by broadening the use of numbers to include the identification of laws and causes.

At the same time, the case of Guillard provides a first insight into the formal and informal organizations shaping the world of social statisticians at the time. The world of French social science was divided into two distinct spheres: an élite sphere associated with the state-supported Académie des Sciences Morales et Politiques and peopled by liberal political economists, and a second, more marginal Republican sphere, associated with the short-lived *Revue du XIXe siècle* and supported by positivists and scientific materialists. Each sphere was associated with a distinct epistemological model for the practice of science and statistics. The liberal economists called for a purely descriptive form of statistics, in which the authority of numbers rested on a one-to-one correspondence between observations and numbers, while positivist scholars envisioned a more active role for statistics in constructing abstract entities and exploring laws and causes.

Turning to the problem of statistical entities, Guillard's bid for recognition of demography as a separate science demonstrates the counterintuitive nature of abstract statistical populations, while the economists' reactions to Guillard's proposal shed light on the political and scientific issues at stake in the debate. Garnier rejected Guillard's use of national averages on the grounds that it obscured the experiences of individuals. Averages, he argued, said nothing about the actual experience of those individuals to whose lives they applied. More to the point, their lives could not be generalized at all. Thus they were irrelevant to a discussion of scientific laws and to the formulation of social policy. Garnier's responses point to a sharp boundary between scientific and administrative knowledge and the location of statistics on the administrative side of the boundary. But they also point to the explanatory, or rather rhetorical, function of statistics in political economy and public life. Far from being an explanatory tool, statistics were seen as a resource to illustrate already established laws. This position was clearly expressed in the distinction between explanatory deductive sciences and descriptive sciences. But it was also evident in the way administrators, public health officials, political economists, and statisticians used statistics in their discussion of social problems. As we will see, this use contrasted sharply with that in England in approximately the same period.

CHAPTER TWO

The Neglect of Demography, 1855–1867

Guillard's attempts to establish demography as a separate science had little impact on statistics or on the division of social-science knowledge. Political conditions precluded any serious institutional innovation. In the 1860s the emperor relaxed restrictions on public assembly and expression, opening the way for a flurry of disciplinary activity. Numerous new scientific societies were created in 1859 and 1860, including the Société d'Anthropologie and the Société de Statistique de Paris. Republican positivists multiplied disciplinary categories and organizations in an attempt to advance knowledge and society. Demography remained, however, the work of an increasingly marginal, socialist scholar, Guillard.

The term "demography" only appeared twice in scientific publications in the course of the decade: once in 1861, in one of the first volumes of the *Journal de la société de statistique de Paris*, and a second time in 1865, as an entry in a new edition of Nysten's medical dictionary. The first was the work of Guillard. In the second instance it was his son-in-law, Louis Adolphe Bertillon, who took the relay. While neither event contributed to the intellectual history of statistics or the establishment of demography as a discipline, both serve to map out the institutional setting in which those developments would subsequently unfold. Guillard's attempt of 1861 draws attention to the creation of the Société de Statistique de Paris and associated changes in the relations between statistics and the administration, while Bertillon's professional trajectory and initial engagement with demography point to the role of élite academic medical science and anthropology in the development of statistical reasoning in France

Discipline Formation in the 1860s

The Société de Statistique de Paris

Chapter 1 left the story of demography in 1855 with the publication of Guillard's book *Éléments de la statistique humaine, ou démographie comparée*. The book fell on deaf ears. The liberal economists at whom it was aimed treated it as a work of statistics, and thus irrelevant to the theoretical considerations by which they defined themselves. It was only in 1860 that Guillard made a second attempt to assert the relevance of his project for economists. The occasion was the founding of the Société de Statistique de Paris, an organization that united liberal economists and national administrative statisticians. The creation of the society affirmed and nuanced the existing hierarchy between a descriptive approach to statistics, associated with administrative statistics and supported by liberal economists, and the more experimental, abstract approach of medical men and public hygienists. It also provides a second illustration of how intellectual developments were linked to specific social problems, such that the authority and diffusion of the first depended on the political fortunes of the latter.

The immediate context for the creation of the Statistical Society can be found in the desire of liberal economists to consolidate their newly won political influence.[1] On 23 January 1860 Napoléon III signed a free-trade treaty with England. The treaty was the work of Michel Chevalier and constituted a decisive victory for liberal economists. Unfortunately for them, the treaty evoked widespread opposition. Most importantly for my story, much of the criticism was framed in statistical terms. Chevalier created the Société de Statistique de Paris to develop a statistical defense of free trade.[2]

To launch his project, he brought together liberals sympathetic to statistics and administrative statisticians. As noted above, by the 1850s liberal economists had shifted their attention from the "masses" to the economy and the promotion of free trade. This focus distinguished them from liberal Whig reformers in England who remained focused on "the condition of England." The alliance of liberals and administrators involved a readjustment of certain boundaries in economists' disciplinary map and a reenforcement of others. On the one hand, the creation of the society marked a relaxation of economists' previous strictures against the use of official statistics in science; on the other hand, it provided further institutional backing for their descriptive, atheoretical model of statistical knowledge.

The success of the alliance was partly due to the "fit" between economists' view of statistics and that of administrative statisticians at the Statistique Générale de la France (SGF), the French national statistical bureau created in 1832 and first directed by Alexandre Moreau de Jonnès. According to Moreau de Jonnès, the aim of the SGF was to describe the state of the nation, rather than to identify its natural laws of development or to develop policy. The interest of statistical representation was that it provided an index of the well-being of the nation and thus of the legitimacy of the current government. These aims were associated with a descriptive model of statistics that conformed to liberal economists' epistemological model for statistics.

Practically, this aim translated into an insistence that official numbers must correspond as closely as possible to real observations. The ideal statistical publication was a series of tables which laid out the facts, without commentary.[3] Like the liberal economists, Moreau de Jonnès objected strongly to political arithmetic. In the first half of the century, this position led him to exclude public hygiene from the SGF on the grounds that its knowledge was purely speculative. In contrast to the situation in England, the SGF did not collect information on the causes of death.[4]

Moreau de Jonnès resigned from the SGF in 1852 and was replaced by Alfred Legoyt, a professional administrator and advocate of political order.[5] While Legoyt differed from Moreau de Jonnès in his focus on the practical work of data collection as the key to good statistics, rather than on the work of classification and analysis, he shared a descriptive approach to statistics. His book *La France statistique*, published in 1843, is striking for the absence of the word "science." Administrative statistics, according to Legoyt, was the practical, factual side of economic science. Like Moreau de Jonnès, Legoyt argued that statisticians should follow the facts, and refrain from any investigation of causes.

As this brief review indicates, the work of the SGF rested on an epistemological commitment to descriptive statistics, whereby numbers were interpreted as summaries of immediately observable facts. While administrators and economists had different reasons for promoting statistics, they shared a common set of epistemological criteria. The creation of the Société de Statistique de Paris in 1861 thus strengthened the descriptive model. Like all societies under the Second Empire, the Statistical Society was established with an authorization from the prefecture of police. Its first meetings were held in the Hôtel-de-Ville, indicating its quasi-official status. The initial board of the new society was composed of leading liberal economists, including Michel Chevalier as president, and Louis Wolowski, Léonce de Lavergne, Victor Foucher, and the Marquis de Fontette as vice-presidents.

Alfred Legoyt, the head of the SGF, was the permanent secretary and remained in that position throughout the Second Empire. In his opening address Chevalier stressed the sisterly relation between political economy and statistics. Statistics, he argued, deserved to be recognized, despite the disdain of many economists.[6]

Thus the Société de Statistique de Paris represented a conscious effort to shift the cognitive boundaries of political economy so as to make a place for a certain type of descriptive statistics. It also involved extending the liberal model for statistics to administrative statistics and the Société de Statistique de Paris. To national-level administrators, the alliance with the liberal economists was welcome. For most of the nineteenth century, French statistical bureaus were institutionally very weak; the establishment of the Statistical Society offered an important opportunity to strengthen their position within the administration and increase their autonomy.

The Société de Statistique de Paris was not limited to administrators and economists. As the only scientific organization devoted to statistics, it also provided a forum for moral and medical statisticians working on questions of poverty, crime, and public health. Inclusion does not always signal agreement, however. For its first two decades the society was divided between administrators, led by Legoyt, and moral and medical statisticians, led by Bertillon.[7] Once again, social divisions were organized around epistemological criteria. Administrators persisted in their commitment to purely descriptive statistics, while moral and medical statisticians followed in Villermé's footsteps, using statistics to identify laws and causes.

It was in this institutional context that Guillard launched his second attempt to assert the existence of demography as a discipline. In 1861 he published a paper entitled "Démographie (lois de population)," in which he addressed the criticisms that the professor Wappäus at Göttingen had made of his book.[8] Guillard's article opened with a defense of demography as a science and of the scientific potential of official statistics, despite their imperfections. It also summarized the main findings of demography to that point, including the propositions that the population adjusts to the level of subsistence, that its growth is solely due to an increase in work and its products, and that there is no necessary relation between the size of the population and the length of life. As in 1855, the economists and administrators in the society published Guillard's text and expressed their disapproval by ignoring it. No mention is made of the article in the transactions of subsequent meetings, nor do other authors use it as a starting point for their own work. The refusal of the gatekeepers to respond to Guillard's attempt to promote demography within the Société de Statistique de Paris points to the dominance of the liberal economists and their descriptive form of statistics. It also reflects a tacit agreement that statisticians should not be allowed to address the basic principles of political economy.

Demography and Nysten's Medical Encyclopedia

The next attempt to promote demography as a discipline came in 1865, when Louis Adolphe Bertillon wrote an entry for a new edition of the *Dictionnaire de médecine, de chirurgie, de pharmacie et des sciences qui s'y rapportent*.[9] The dictionary was edited by the physiologist Charles Robin and the positivist philosopher Émile Littré, the main carrier of a nonspiritual version of Comtean positivism who had been among the contributors to the *Revue du XIXᶜ siècle* in 1855, together with Guillard and Bertillon. While politically out of favor, both Robin and Littré were nonetheless central in Parisian medical circles and more specifically among proponents of the "new medicine."[10] Both men were leading members of the Faculté de Médecine de Paris and the Royal Academy of Medicine, and both were active members of the Société de Biologie, a positivist, Republican stronghold. In its most general form, their approach to medicine echoed and re-enforced the Republican project for science described above. The keywords of their project were observation and experiment, the unity of knowledge, and a rejection of a priori schools of thought or theories in medicine.[11] During the mid-1860s a number of proponents of this philosophy of science launched encyclopedic projects of one kind or another aimed at imposing a new, more comprehensive scientific model of medical knowledge, which included not only physiology, anatomy, and chemistry but the social sciences as well.

Louis Adolphe Bertillon contributed a number of entries to the new medical dictionary, of which the two of particular demographic interest are those on demography and on population. The article on demography outlines Guillard's disciplinary project, while the article on population spells out Bertillon's own intellectual commitments. It was only in 1873 that Bertillon actively incorporated the promotion of demography into his own professional identity. Bertillon's reticence was directly related to his model of the French population as a society of "virtual strangers," made up of individuals and groups with radically different life experiences, thereby rendering national statistical indices meaningless. As we will see, Bertillon was far from alone in his unease. The "reality" of statistical indices was a recurrent theme in scholarly and political discussions of the national population, be it over the issue of infant mortality, degeneracy, or depopulation.

Bertillon's Initial Project: Reforming Public Hygiene

On the eve of the Revolution of 1848, Louis Adolphe Bertillon was a medical student at the Faculté de Médecine de Paris. The revolution interrupted his studies, but it also introduced him to a circle of Republican thinkers and scientists who were to significantly influence his subsequent career. He was befriended by both the Republican historian Jules Michelet — who is often credited with having inspired the Revolution of 1848 — and the medical researcher and future anthropologist Paul Broca. Bertillon completed his medical studies in 1853. In a clear political statement, he dedicated his thesis to his teacher A. Deville, who had been exiled in 1851 for political activity.[12]

A reading of Bertillon's doctoral thesis, entitled "On the Reaction of a Number of Elements of Hygiene to the Length of Life" [*durée de la vie*], gives an idea of his intellectual project at the time when his future father-in-law was preparing his manuscript on demography. Like Guillard, Bertillon was committed to a particular use of statistics, one that incorporated elements of Quetelet's social physics but did not fully embrace it. In the first sentence, Bertillon states his intention to deal with "the laws which govern the *durée de la vie humaine* in the society of our century."[13] As Bertillon goes on to explain, he is interested in the length of life as a measure of human prosperity.

The basic framework of Bertillon's project was thus similar to that of Guillard. Both men focused on the measure of longevity as an index of prosperity. In the tradition of political economy and public hygiene, prosperity was conceived as the sum of individual well-being. Thus, while both men defined their object as the study of the collective, their aim was to increase the well-being of the greatest number of individuals. This focus led each of them to emphasize the distribution or pattern of experiences summarized by a single measure. Like Guillard, Bertillon insisted that it was not population size or growth that provided a measure of the state of the population, but rather the number of individuals surviving into adulthood.

Bertillon's project differed from Guillard's, however, on a number of points. First, Bertillon developed his approach in the context of public hygiene, rather than political economy. In contrast to Guillard, who directed his attention to evaluating Malthusian laws, Bertillon presented his work as an application of new methods in medical science to the concerns of public hygiene. Second, Bertillon was much more cautious than Guillard in his use of statistics, especially concerning the "reality" of abstract statistical rates and the scientific authority of the new "scientific" administrative style. Borrowing from Quetelet, Bertillon called on statisticians to distinguish between natural, physiological averages and arithmetic averages. The first were taken from a homogeneous or natural population, such that the average value and the probable value were one and the same. Thus, with heights taken from a racially uniform population, the average height will also be the most common or likely height. Arithmetic averages, by contrast, were averages calculated on the basis of a heterogeneous population. An arithmetic average had no actual referent and did not correspond to the probable or most common value. In Bertillon's terms, it was artificial.[14]

Whereas Guillard assumed that measures of mortality and longevity necessarily corresponded to a homogeneous population, Bertillon focused on the heterogeneity of the underlying population. The population, he explained, is not composed of a single group, but of many subgroups (what we would call generations or cohorts), each with its own probability of living and dying. The average length of life is an artificial summary of the experiences of infants, adults, and elderly people. Its value does not correspond to the most common age in the population. An average age of forty-three could easily correspond to a population with high infant mortality and high longevity, in which those who survived infancy had a high probability of living to an old age, or to a population with relatively low infant mortality and fewer very old people. Average age was thus an artificial or arithmetic average and as such a poor indicator of the hygienic conditions or well-being of the population.

For Bertillon, the "artificiality" of what he called arithmetical rates raised a serious challenge to Quetelet's project and, by extension, to that of Guillard. In Bertillon's mind, the French population was not a single entity whose movements could be described in terms of the interacting forces of mortality and natality, or even (economic) production and mortality, but rather a heterogeneous composite of individuals and cohorts, each subject to its own personal history. The point was similar to that voiced by the administrator Moreau de Jonnès when he criticized statistical averages as "fictions." Moreau de Jonnès used this argument to reject the use of abstraction in statistics, thereby affirming the authority of the descriptive style, but Bertillon used it to guide statisticians in the choice between different abstract measures. Vitality, he argued, was best measured by mortality tables, which took into account age-specific mortality rates. In seeking the causes of observed regularities, Bertillon favored the comparison of serial results rather than averages. As an illustration, he cited the work of the hygienist Louis René Villermé, who had compared series of mortality rates with the distribution of rents. In a nonmathematical form of correlation analysis, the tendency of mortality rates to increase in inverse proportion with rent was taken as proof of a causal relation.[15]

Viewed from the perspective of the history of statistics, Bertillon's position in 1853 challenges the conventional view that nineteenth-century statisticians were obsessed by averages and that only with Galton and Pearson in England in the late nineteenth century did they turn their attention to distributions. It also suggests that in France, one of the obstacles to the development of social statistics (and demography) was ontological. Guillard's project, like that of Quetelet and Villermé, rested on the claim that there was a collective reality, distinct from the individuals which composed it, and which was subject to structural forces or laws. In contrast, Bertillon, like most medical men, resisted all attempts to efface individual differences, much more to posit a supra-individual reality. Curiously, in England administrators and statisticians involved in similar statistical operations were singularly unconcerned by these ontological considerations.

Statistics and the "New" Medical Science

The Academy of Medicine and Medical Statistics

The usual image of the founder of a discipline is one of a person with a coherent intellectual project devoted to its intellectual and institutional promotion. The depiction certainly fits with what we know of Claude Bernard and Louis Pasteur, two of Bertillon's better-known contemporaries who founded new disciplines (or rather appropriated and transformed existing ones).[16] It does not, however, fit with Bertillon's story. Instead, his career was shaped by a series of invitations to apply his technical expertise to problems of public and political concern. Both the invitations and Bertillon's commitment reflected a new conception of medicine which emerged in the 1860s and took over the élite medical community based in Paris. This new vision called for establishing medicine on a strictly scientific basis, dealing with *causes prochaines* rather than *causes finales*. As such, it was part of a broader movement toward the development of positivist science.[17]

In the course of the 1850s the editors of various medical journals called on Bertillon as a statistical expert to defend against critics the use of the smallpox vaccine. Later in his career, scientific journalists and public health officials asked him to explore the problem of wet-nursing and infant mortality. This work in turn led him to address growing political and public concern over the threat of depopulation. From an institutional perspective, Bertillon used this work to gain recognition from the élite medical community. Like Guillard, he framed his bid for scientific recognition in terms of a need to widen and thereby transform the criteria of what counted as knowledge. And like Guillard, his turn to explicit disciplinary activity came in response to definitive rejection from élite science on epistemological grounds. While Guillard focused his attention on the gatekeepers of political economy, Bertillon focused on the Academy of Medicine.

Like much of his subsequent work, Bertillon's work on the effect of the vaccine was designed to instruct his readers in the interpretation and use of statistics. The most important general lesson concerned the difference between statistical effects and real changes. His articles highlighted distortions introduced by assuming that the number of births is equal to the number of deaths in a population (a common assumption at the time) and that mortality rates are constant over time, especially in a geographically mobile population. Bertillon associated changes in age-specific mortality rates with the heterogeneous (nonorganic) nature of a population composed of unrelated cohorts. In discussing the effect of population growth on ratios and tables, Bertillon provided his readers with a lesson in how to work with abstract models. He showed how a decline in infant mortality increased the number of children surviving into adulthood, thereby creating the false impression that adult mortality had increased.

Bertillon's work on the vaccine set his intellectual agenda. More specifically, it led him to undertake a much more systematic study of mortality rates by *département* and Parisian district (*arrondissement*). Initially, his aim was to develop a data base that would allow him to apply his serial method. His intention was to compare the ranking of departments by mortality with their ranking by proportion of the population vaccinated. It was this work which led him to identify the disproportionately high rate of infant mortality in the area around Paris and to put the blame on the practice of wet-nursing.[18]

In 1858 Bertillon reported his findings to the Academy of Medicine, but his study was buried by a committee established to look into his claims. It was only a few years later, when the problem became a political issue, that Bertillon's work was revived and he was credited with the "discovery." For the next twenty years much of Bertillon's statistical work focused on developing an increasingly detailed mapping of age-specific mortality by department. In 1866 Quetelet asked him to do the work which the Statistique Générale de la France had failed to do, namely to construct an up-to-date mortality table combining census and registration data. Bertillon's table was the first "modern" mortality table produced for France and served as a point of reference for decades afterward.

Another study, which brought Bertillon to the attention of the Academy of Medicine, involved his analysis of differential mortality within the city. By the 1860s Haussmann's radical architectural restructuring of Paris had fostered a great deal of discontent. To defend the project, Paris administrators published a series of statistical reports documenting improvements in the health of the city. Bertillon responded with a number of articles refuting these claims.[19] Again, a political debate framed in statistical terms led Bertillon to a new topic and provided him an occasion to repeat his lessons on the proper manipulation of numbers. As with the vaccine, Bertillon picked the reports apart, reversing their findings by revealing flaws in the statistical analysis.

The Société de Statistique de Paris and the Division between State and Medical Statistics

Bertillon continued his pedagogic work at the Société de Statistique de Paris. In 1866 he published a paper that he had previously presented at the Academy of Medicine on the statistical measurement of longevity (and mortality).[20] Bertillon identified eleven measures of vitality under four names then in use by statisticians. He reviewed each one, discussing its construction, its significance, and the types of work for which it was and was not appropriate. To illustrate his technical argument Bertillon took six departments, selected "by chance," and demonstrated that their relative rank varied depending on which measure was taken. The paper illustrated the two main components of Bertillon's intellectual agenda — a concerted campaign to educate relevant publics in the use and interpretation of statistics and a cautionary lesson against the creation of (artificial) statistical entities. To appreciate the importance of this work, it is helpful to keep in mind the absence of formal statistical education at the time. In a period when statistics were just beginning to be incorporated into public understandings of society and political arguments, such lessons were revelatory. For historians of statistics, Bertillon's career highlights the processes by which statistical common sense was shaped in the nineteenth century and the state of public reasoning at the time.

The paper on the measurement of mortality was an occasion to insist on the need to take into account the effect of age structure on the different values, and how the observed age structure was in turn affected by births, deaths at different ages, and migration. Again, the lesson for Bertillon was that the population could not be considered a unified whole. "The result is that the living who survive to each age, $p^0 \ldots 1, p^1 \ldots 2 \ldots$ do not constitute a succession. Each term is in fact the very complex product of events which burdened each age which it passed, events which could very easily not have influenced the groups which preceded or succeeded them in the series of ages . . . no theoretical calculation can thus determine these values (vitality at different ages), nor allow for the discovery of the succession of terms which make up the list of the living."[21] For Bertillon, insistence on empirical observation was tied up with an anti-essentialist conception of population. Far from a distinct collective entity, a statistical population for Bertillon was an artificial, heterogeneous construct which could only be evaluated empirically.

The publication in 1866 of the second version of the paper for the *Journal de la société de statistique de Paris* was significant for Bertillon's subsequent career, establishing his reputation as a statistician outside medical circles. Bertillon was one of the founding members of the Société de Statistique de Paris. However, until this point he had remained a somewhat marginal participant. He spoke occasionally at the meetings of the society, largely on issues of medical statistics. More importantly, his criticisms of current uses of statistics and his concern to improve the quality of administrative data, especially in the areas of mortality statistics and the nonexistent data on causes of death, brought him in direct conflict with the head of the SGF and permanent secretary of the Société de Statistique de Paris, Alfred Legoyt.

As mentioned above, the society was divided into two camps, one led by Alfred Legoyt, who supported a descriptive model of statistics consistent with the political economists' vision, and the other by Bertillon, who called for a more "scientific" approach to statistics. Within the society Legoyt was the dominant figure. During the 1860s almost all the topics which we today associate with demography, such as mortality, marriage, and population growth, were monopolized by Legoyt, who as head of the SGF was the only one to have access to official data. The importance of Bertillon's article was such that even Legoyt was obliged to cite it in his technical discussions.

In summary, between 1853 and 1865 Bertillon's intellectual work focused on the promotion of medical statistics. His primary audience was the Academy of Medicine. While historically statistics had been confined to the sphere of public hygiene and rejected as a tool of therapeutics (much as statistics had been confined to pure description among the political economists and rejected as a tool of theorizing), positivist calls for a more scientific approach to medicine in the 1850s and 1860s opened the way for a reconsideration of the relevance of statistics. With hindsight, it is easy to see that the laboratory and the experimental method (in the sense developed by Pasteur and Bernard) were to replace clinical observation. In 1855, however, that victory was far from evident, and Bertillon was welcomed as a colleague by advocates of a more "scientific" medicine. Thus in 1855 and even in 1865, he had every reason to believe that his project for medical statistics would be an integral part of the new scientific medicine that was taking over Paris.

Within the Société de Statistique de Paris, Bertillon confined his contributions to traditional public hygiene topics. The difference between his scientific vision for statistics and the descriptive model, developed by the liberal economists and administrators, brought him into conflict with their main spokesman for statistics, Alfred Legoyt. During the 1860s Legoyt's institutional dominance relegated Bertillon to a somewhat marginal position within the society. At the same time, Bertillon's active campaign to join the Academy of Medicine probably minimized the frustration which that marginalization might otherwise have caused. All the papers that he published in the *Journal de la société de statistique de Paris* were reprints of works written for other organizations or spheres.

The View from Republican Science, II

The Société d'Anthropologie de Paris

Bertillon's pedagogic work at the Academy of Medicine and at the Société de Statistique de Paris was paralleled by a similar investment in the newly founded Société d'Anthropologie de Paris. The history of the Second Empire has traditionally been depicted as having been divided between two periods, a repressive phase extending until 1859 and a more liberal phase. While this chronology has been debated,[22] it holds for the social sciences. Before 1859 almost no scientific societies were established, and those that already existed reduced their activities significantly. Between 1859 and 1860 a large number of societies were created, including the Société d'Anthropologie and the Société de Statistique de Paris, both of which played a major role in the subsequent history of demography and statistics. This growth in new organizations would seem related to a significant relaxation in the restrictions on assembly and free speech, although no formal legislative changes were made. It was at this point that Bertillon left Montmorcy and his medical practice for Paris and the life of a full-time savant.

His decision to return to the capital coincided with the creation of the Société Anthropologique de Paris by Paul Broca. Broca and Bertillon were friends, and Bertillon's return to Paris may have been motivated by Broca's invitation to join him in the endeavor. From the beginning the Société d'Anthropologie had a clear scientific and political orientation. All nineteen of the founding members were medical doctors, all were Republicans, all were anticlerical, and all were positivists. The initial institutional success of the society was in part due to Broca's explicit attempt to keep politics out of the society. While the society was later to become a base for radical Republicans and scientific materialists, before 1866 it was dominated by moderate Republicans.[23]

Broca's professed aim was to put anthropology on a positivist basis, similar to that of medicine. In his early pronouncements he envisioned an encyclopedic or umbrella science devoted to the study of the human race. The relevant sciences included zoology, anatomy, physiology, hygiene, ethnology, history, archeology, linguistics, and paleontology. His goal, like Bertillon's, was to develop a science of man or of the human race (as compared to ethnography, which was a science of the human races in their specificity). As Broca explained: "Once the distinction between the races is admitted, an enormous field suddenly opens up for scholarly investigation. It is no longer a matter of merely completing or rectifying the classifications and descriptions of Blumenbach, but of seeking the origin of the permanent varieties, of the hereditary types, of the simultaneously diverse and graduated characters that constitute the races."[24] In practice, the field that Broca established consisted largely of what we would today term physical anthropology and race.

Anthropology and the New "Scientific" Statistics

The above description suggests a number of reasons why Bertillon might have been attracted to Broca's project. Beyond their friendship,[25] they shared a commitment to introducing the numerical method in clinical medicine. In addition, Broca's disciplinary project was situated in the same positivist scientific culture that Guillard had drawn upon to frame his project for demography. Both anthropology and demography were defined as the science of man and the study of the human race. Like Guillard, Broca situated his project in a theory of the development of knowledge and civilization, whereby sciences such as demography or anthropology were only possible after a certain level of progress had been reached. For both men scientific development depended on a radical turn to the empirical method.

To prepare himself to contribute to Broca's project, Bertillon attended Quatrefages's lectures in anthropology at the Museum of Natural History. He also took part in discussions of a wide range of issues at the society's regular meetings. Of all the topics that he worked on, that of polygenism most directly influenced his work on population statistics. Anthropologists at the time were divided between those who believed that the human species developed from a single race and those who posited multiple origins. Broca and Bertillon were polygenists. To establish their thesis, they measured and classified human skulls. These data provided the one and only time when Bertillon attempted to apply Quetelet's claim that normal statistical distributions can be taken as evidence of an underlying homogeneous population (a claim contained in Quetelet's concept of "the average man").

The question was: How to establish common origin? The usual method was to examine skeletal remains. But how to determine if two skeletons came from the same race or a different one? The problem, Bertillon suggested, could be treated as a special case of the more general issue of how to establish the likelihood that an observed measure actually appeared in an underlying population. The solution, he suggested, was to be found in the study of averages and the distribution of observations around the mean. Bertillon began his exposition by drawing on Quetelet's example of the circumference of the chests of Scottish conscripts, and how they were distributed. As Quetelet had demonstrated, the observed measures were symmetrically distributed about the mean such that (in Bertillon's terms) the arithmetic average corresponded with the physiological mean. Among Scottish military recruits, the average circumference was also the most likely (frequent). Moreover, Bertillon explained, once the underlying distribution was known, it was possible to calculate the likelihood that a single new observation would occur in the population.

Quetelet used this demonstration to establish the existence of an "average man," or underlying human type; Bertillon applied it to the concerns of anthropologists and argued that it provided a tool to distinguish between racially pure and mixed populations. Following his reasoning of 1853, Bertillon argued that the presence of what we would call a normal distribution confirmed that the underlying population corresponded to a distinct race. To demonstrate this method, Bertillon presented a comparison between the heights of conscripts from two regions of France, the Finistère and the

Doubs. Whereas in the Finistère the observed distribution followed a bell-shaped curve, thus indicating the presence of a single race, in the Doubs the distribution of heights traced a double hump, suggesting the presence of a crossed or mixed population, one constituent of which was short and the other tall. In the Doubs, the calculated average was "purely arithmetic," an "artificial compromise" between two true or anthropological averages. The serial method, Bertillon argued, was the only method capable of discovering this otherwise hidden reality.[26]

From the perspective of the history of demography, the crucial feature of this work was that it led Bertillon to acknowledge the possibility of using statistical measures to identify an otherwise invisible, underlying reality. It also serves to underline his ontological concerns and the obstacles that they posed to his embrace of demography. Like the administrative statisticians of the period, Bertillon insisted on a close correspondence between statistical measures and "reality." His application to social data of Quetelet's program for social physics (or Guillard's more general version) thus depended upon his prior acceptance of the existence of collective objects. In 1863 Bertillon accepted that anthropometric data could be used to discern the existence of racial groups; he did not, however, go so far as to accept the idea that French population statistics might also be produced by an underlying collective entity constituted by internal forces of mortality and natality rather than immediate environmental or accidental causes.

Why Not (Yet) Demography and Why Not (Yet) Discipline Formation

Bertillon's intellectual trajectory in the 1860s illustrates the conceptual obstacles that the counterintuitive notion of a national statistical population posed to the diffusion of a new, more abstract style of statistical reasoning, associated with the work of Quetelet and the application of probability theory to social statistics. In the second half of the nineteenth century, versions of this new style were promoted under the heading of a "scientific" approach to administrative statistics. Demography constituted one of the clearest versions of this project. While Bertillon's reluctance to embrace his father-in-law's idiosyncratic new science can be taken as a personal story, the argument developed here is that his position reflects a broader sensibility, one shared by liberal economists, administrative statisticians, and even proponents of more experimental, positivist forms of science.

The case rests on Bertillon's status as one of the most technically proficient, "scientific" statisticians of his generation (keeping in mind that the focus here is on second-tier statisticians who participated in the Société de Statistique de Paris, the Société d'Anthropologie, national and municipal administrative bureaus, and debates on social issues at the various élite academies). The extent of this unease with the "reality of statistical measures can be seen in policy debates over population problems during the Third Republic. In Bertillon's individual case, the possibility of a meaningful statistical construct first arose in the context of his work on polygenism and the measurement of race. However, it was only when this more collectivist concept was married to widespread concern over depopulation that national population statistics ceased to be challenged as fictions, opening the way for a more "scientific" form of administrative statistics.

In 1865 Bertillon juggled two distinct models for how to do statistics and for the type of knowledge that they produced. One, which he associated with medicine and the study of (contemporary) society, was limited to the identification of observable, mechanistic causal relations between immediate causes and individuals. The other, which he developed in association with Broca and the problem of polygenism, used statistics to identify otherwise invisible collective entities governing the character and growth of observable human populations. The tension between the two models points to the extent to which even the most sympathetic of statisticians struggled with the "reality" of statistical populations, at least when it came to their own national population. Thus even as public hygienists were happy to treat the poor, the primitive, and the dispossessed as statistical aggregates driven by underlying collective forces, they balked at extending this logic to their own national population.

The tension between Bertillon's two intellectual projects also underlines the social and epistemological logic shaping the circulation and evaluation of ideas in Second Empire France. Far from being an integrated scientific community, the world of social statistics was organized into a number of distinct spheres, each with its own hierarchy of types of knowledge and its own model for statistics. Focusing exclusively on Bertillon's career, one can identify at least three distinct spheres and associated cognitive maps. The first, which we encountered with Guillard, is the world of liberal economists. Until 1860 statistics had been dismissed as a descriptive form of knowledge with little relevance to policy making or even explanation, but with the founding of the Société de Statistique de Paris and the alliance of administrators and economists around issues of free trade, statistics was elevated to a relevant, albeit secondary form of knowledge. Throughout the

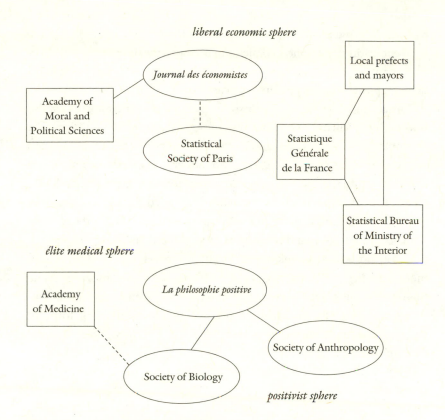

liberal economic sphere

Journal des économistes

Academy of Moral and Political Sciences

Local prefects and mayors

Statistical Society of Paris

Statistique Générale de la France

Statistical Bureau of Ministry of the Interior

élite medical sphere

Academy of Medicine

La philosophie positive

Society of Anthropology

Society of Biology

positivist sphere

Figure 1. The World of Social Statisticians, France, 1853–1865: Social and Epistemological Spheres as Viewed from the Perspective of Bertillon's and Guillard's Professional Trajectories

Second Empire, liberal economists worked with a cognitive map that distinguished between deductive, explanatory knowledge and descriptive, statistical knowledge.

The second sphere, to which Bertillon tried to gain access, was that of orthodox élite medicine. In 1836 a long debate on the numerical method at the Academy of Medicine had led to the dismissal of statistics as irrelevant to clinical medicine and confined statistics to the lesser science of public hygiene. Bertillon's medical publications were part of an attempt to reopen the debate. In the 1860s his efforts were for naught.

Finally, during the Second Empire a version of Quetelet's more abstract, scientific use of numbers to identify laws and causes flourished in specifically Republican, positivist scientific organizations and among moral reformers. Intellectually, it was associated with a general attempt to establish a materialist science. Socially, the effort was supported by municipal administrators, medical men, and Republican social scientists. Figure 1 depicts the different institutional spheres or fields that shaped the development of mortality statistics in the 1850s and 1860s, as revealed by attempts to establish demography as a distinct disciplinary category.

The advantage of this type of institutional analysis is that it draws attention to the articulation between epistemological, institutional (scientific), and political logics. The creation of the Société de Statistique de Paris marked a reworking of the cognitive boundaries of political economy and an inclusion of a specific, descriptive form of statistics into the set of relevant forms of knowledge. This reformulation depended, however, on a strict policing of recognized forms of statistical knowledge. Within the Society, leading administrators and economists monopolized discussions of population statistics and economic topics, limiting medical men and carriers of moral statistics to the study of social problems and public hygiene. While this division might seem reasonable given the social identity of the different participants, it masks an epistemological struggle over acceptable forms of statistical manipulation and a political divide between supporters of the monarchy and Republicans.

CHAPTER THREE

The Reinvention of Demography, 1867–1878

The dates for the birth of a discipline are always difficult to establish. For demography there are three contestants: 1855, when Achille Guillard published his book *La démographie figurée* and the term "demography" was first introduced to the scholarly public; 1873, when Louis Adolphe Bertillon provided his first formulation of the project that was subsequently to be institutionalized as demography; and 1876, when the discipline was established in the form of a course, a journal, and a congress. The preceding chapters examined the first of these markers and laid the background for the latter two. The discussion that follows continues the story of demography by examining Louis Adolphe Bertillon's active engagement in discipline formation in 1873 and in the move from discourse to formal organizations between 1876 and 1878.

As in my analysis of the first attempt to found demography in 1855, the discussion is guided by an interest in the phenomena of nineteenth-century discipline formation. I wish to understand why someone in France, in the third quarter of the nineteenth century, would engage in disciplinary activity and why someone else might not. With demography this problem translates into several questions: Why did Bertillon refrain from disciplinary work before 1873? Why did he adopt a disciplinary discourse in 1873? And why, or rather how, did he succeed in institutionalizing that claim between 1876 and 1878? I also want to use these questions to reconstruct the institutional setting and epistemological rules in which demography was promoted.

The argument I develop is that Bertillon's turn to demography can be explained by the introduction of new conceptual resources and the constraints associated with existing institutionalized cognitive rules. The key conceptual development was the politicizing of the fear of depopulation, and the collectivist concept of the French national population that this problem authorized. Bertillon's association of his statistical work with his father-in-law's new discipline of demography was directly linked to his engagement in the debate over depopulation and the solutions that it provided to his ontological struggles over the referent of statistical rates. The shift from rhetorical pronouncements to institutional activity was preceded by a series of rejections from the gatekeepers of academic science. Between 1873 and 1878 Bertillon was denied recognition by the Academy of Sciences, the Academy of Moral and Political Sciences, and the Academy of Medicine. It was only after this triple defeat that he directed his attention almost exclusively to promoting demography as a separate science.

The Debate over Depopulation

French concern over population, or rather depopulation, increased dramatically in the last years of the Second Empire. The importance of the debate for the history of demography lies both in the introduction of a new, abstract concept of population into liberal political discourse and in the political relevance that the debate gave to statistics and statisticians. More directly, the debate marked a turning point in Bertillon's career, providing him with intellectual and institutional resources, which transformed his work.

Declining Birth Rates and the Liberal Economists

Among intellectuals, the debate over depopulation can be traced to discussions held by liberal economists about the censuses of 1856 and 1866. The 1856 census was the first (in the brief, fifty-year history of the French census) to report a decline in the overall rate of growth. In some departments the death rate exceeded the birth rate. Far from frightening French liberal economists, these figures were initially received with complaisance. Most economists interpreted them as evidence that Malthus's preventive checks against overpopulation were operating. It was natural, in this view, that as civilization progressed and as more citizens became property holders, more of them would act with foresight and moral restraint. Only Léonce de Lavergne, a member of the Academy of Moral and Political Sciences, warned against the dangers of depopulation.

While de Lavergne's fears were not shared, his articles placed population growth on economists' agenda. An initial article in 1857 was followed by a series of papers and discussions on French population growth in the *Journal des économistes* and at the Academy of Moral and Political Sciences.[1] Official statistics provided a catalyst for these discussions. They did not, however, dictate the terms of the debate. Instead, the discussion circled around the consequences of rural migration for agricultural production. "Depopulation," in this context, referred to the depopulation of the countryside, rather than to the absolute size of the French population.[2]

In 1857 Bénédict Augustin Morel published his widely acclaimed treatise *Traité des dégénéréscences physiques, intellectuelles et morales de l'espèce humaine*,[3] which introduced the psychological concept of degeneracy to the French public. According to Morel, environmental and hereditary factors were gradually transforming and perverting what had once been the perfect human type, thus contributing to the degeneration of the species. In terms of population, it is important to note that Morel's book did not introduce a collective notion of degeneracy. The threat to France lay in the growing number of degenerate individuals (cretins, criminals, the insane, etc.), rather than in the transformation of a collective entity.

Thus in the late 1850s two separate intellectual developments placed population statistics at the center of attention among savants. While French liberal economists rejected the alarmism of de Lavergne and Morel, they accepted the intellectual challenge which both sets of arguments posed. Between 1857 and 1866 the liberal economic press published a series of articles on the topics of population growth, depopulation, and degeneracy. One article, which placed statistics at the center of both these debates and which altered the statistical concept of population, was a text by Alfred Legoyt entitled "On the Supposed Degeneracy of the French Population."[4] The article is striking for its combination of a historical and essentialist account of national population growth.

Legoyt opened his article with the standard exceptionalist account of recent population statistics. The period 1854–59, he explained, had been particularly harmful for France. The combined effect of an especially severe cholera epidemic, insufficient harvests, and two major wars temporarily suspended the laws that governed French population growth. Some people, Legoyt noted mistakenly, took these events as evidence of the physical degeneracy of the race. Legoyt wrote his article to dispel this view with the support of facts.

While Legoyt refuted the depopulationist position, he accepted the abstract, holistic concept of population which it supported. This much is evident in his suggestion, cited above, that one can remove exceptional years to arrive at the true laws of population. Until this point Legoyt had introduced mortality statistics as the traces of contingent, historically specific events; in this article, he discussed them as the product of underlying laws, characteristic of the race, and accidental causes.

In 1856 the debate among liberal economists over the census focused largely on the impact of internal migration. Read through this lens, the census of 1866 brought welcome news. According to the official figures, the annual rate of population growth over the last decade had increased (albeit somewhat artificially, given the annexation of Nice and Savoie), and the number of departments subject to a loss of absolute population (because of migration, slowing rates of "natural" growth, or both) had declined.[5] This news should have reassured scholars and politicians worried about the threat of depopulation. But far from welcoming the new figures, French economists renewed their cries of alarm. According to Charbit, this concern can be explained by more general anxiety over France's military strength relative to Germany and the challenge of populating the colonies. While both issues were a longstanding source of concern, it was only in 1866 and thereafter that they were explicitly linked to the overall growth rate.[6] From that point on "depopulation" became a political catchword to express French fears concerning the (assumed) waning of the nation's military, political, and cultural supremacy. This change in the political meaning of population statistics in turn re-enforced the new holistic concept that Legoyt, in his defense of the opposite position, had introduced into the technical discussion a few years earlier.

Infant Mortality, Wet-Nursing, and the Academy of Medicine

These discussions were important chiefly because they fed into a second set of debates at the Academy of Medicine over the causes of infant mortality. In contrast to the debates at the Academy of Moral and Political Sciences, the discussion at the Academy of Medicine was conducted in statistical terms. Speakers framed their arguments in terms of the proper manipulation and interpretation of statistical data. As such, the debate constituted an important forum for linking a new, holistic concept of population with demography, defined as the use of statistics to identify laws and causes. The debate over the "mortality of *nourrissons*" (infants sent to wet-nurse) opened with an impassioned speech by Dr. Boudet. He began by defining the problems as belonging to public hygiene and as appropriate for discussion in the Academy of Medicine. His argument rested largely on the national importance of the issue. "The military, agricultural and industrial strength of a nation," he told the academy, "depends on the number and energy of its citizens. The Empire is surrounded by strong nations whose populations approach her own. Thus, it is incumbent on her, at the risk of decay, to watch over the increase and vigor of future French generations."[7]

In 1867 the minister of public instruction asked the Academy of Medicine to discuss the mortality of infants sent to wet-nurse.[8] The relation between the practice of wet-nursing and unusually high rates of infant mortality was first signaled by Louis Adolphe Bertillon in 1857. However, it was only in 1866, with the publication of a series of alarmist articles by several hygienists, that the ministry was moved to call for a proper inquiry. In discussing the issue, the academy linked infant mortality with the decline in the birth rate, the strength of the nation, and moral degeneracy. In the course of the debate Broca objected strongly to this association. At the end of the session he offered to provide statistical evidence to support his claims.

The president of the academy accepted the offer. A few months later, Broca presented a paper entitled "On the Supposed Degeneracy of the Population." The paper launched a debate which equaled—in length and vigor—that which the academy had just concluded on infant mortality. The debate is of interest for what it reveals about the state of statistical reasoning among medical men at the time.

Depopulation, Degeneracy, and the Academy of Medicine

The year 1867 was one in which the Academy of Medicine heard a great deal about population phenomena. It was also a year when they learned a fair amount about statistics. Broca's main point in the debate over infant mortality had been to convince the academy of the need to establish a special statistical bureau to collect ongoing data on infant mortality. True, he told his colleagues, they already had much information, enough perhaps for their own needs, but not enough for them to know what to do. What they needed were precise, truly scientific documents. His lessons in how to read and use statistics were aimed at demonstrating the value of the method and the need for scientific expertise, which he referred to as "demography."[9]

Broca's criticism was directed at Mr. Brochard, an administrator responsible for the central office in charge of *nourrissons*.[10] Brochard had conducted a study showing that the mortality rate of *nourrissons* passing through his office was considerably less than that of infants assigned to wet-nurses by small, local offices. The issue, ever present in France, was one of centralization. But it was also a question of the value of special institutional-level studies by those with first-hand knowledge of their data versus more comprehensive official studies conducted by administrators. The distinction is relevant in that it echoed a debate between the authority of private local studies and that of national-level official statistics.[11]

Broca's criticism concerned the figures themselves. The author, he explained, had only examined a single neighborhood (*arrondissement*) for a period of two years. Thus the data base was inadequate. Many of the babies who died in 1858 were placed in homes in 1857, and many of the deaths due to conditions in 1859 occurred in 1860. Nor could one assume that these two effects canceled each other out. The problem, Broca explained, was characteristic of statistical work. All statisticians know it, which is why they require data extending over many years consecutively.[12]

A second, more complicated, statistical lesson concerned the interpretation of rates. Having demonstrated that the absolute number of births continued to increase, Broca went on to consider the significance of the declining rate of birth: "There is no doubt that the number of births relative to the population is decreasing. But what does that prove? Only that the second figure is increasing more rapidly than the first. And what conclusions does that suggest? That the growth of population, not being due to an increase in natality, is due to a decrease in the mortality and a lengthening of life."[13] The number of births, he insisted yet again, did not have the near exclusive importance attributed to it. It was a false criterion of the prosperity of a population. The point was one which Bertillon had developed at length before the Société d'Anthropologie in the context of his work on acclimatization.

The failure of Broca's audience to appreciate his point may have been due to an already ingrained natalism. But it was also due to the novelty of a statistical mode of thinking according to which a population could be conceived of in terms of flows and balances rather than as a composite of individuals. Guérin's statistical refutation combined statistical ignorance and perspicacity. Taking on Broca's argument relating population growth to an extension in the length of life, Guérin accused him of double counting: "When after one or many censuses we observe an increase of population superior to that resulting from an excess of births over deaths, the difference can not be attributed to a greater longevity of survivors, since each of them only counts for a single unity which they represent at the point of departure, and which is the number of years attained since, regardless of when the census is done: it is only through double counting that it can be otherwise."[14]

Although this initial objection was unfounded, Guérin's second point was more solid. Having (he thought) disproved Broca's explanation, Guérin returned to the original problem: How to explain a population growth disproportionate with the birth rate? The response, he argued, lay in the effect of migration. In his view Broca unquestioningly accepted Legoyt's (ungrounded) assumption that immigration and emigration canceled each other out. The insight was a good one, and Broca's failure to take it into account highlights another incipient feature of what was to become demography after 1870, namely the construction of a formal model of population growth which excluded the effects of migration.

Guérin's application of his argument, however, left something to be desired. In the absence of data, he made an equally unfounded assumption that the absolute difference between births and deaths provided an index of migration. As Broca explained in his counterattack, population data are notoriously inexact. "While the civil registers in France are well maintained, the data collected at the communal level and centralized in the chefs-lieux can be criticized. The mortality lists include foreigners who died during a trip to France and fail to include Frenchmen who died during a voyage abroad. As for the censuses, they will never be more than approximate. They contained a large number of double counts and many omissions. The 'population flottante' frequently produces double counts, as the same person can be counted at the residence of his family and at his temporary residence. The omissions, even more numerous, are due first of all to the soldiers posted outside of our territory . . . and secondly to a miscounting of infants between 0 and 1."[15]

I have taken the space to spell out these arguments in detail because they illustrate the state of statistical expertise among "shopkeeper statisticians."[16] The confused state of savants' common sense concerning the nature of population as an object is clearly illustrated by the contrast between Guérin's and Boudet's statements. In contrast to Boudet, who conceived of the link between population and national strength in classical eighteenth-century terms—whereby each individual constituted a resource, and the strength of the nation was measured by the aggregate of its resources—Guérin's discussion revolved around an abstract notion of population as constituted by the interaction of different forces—those of natality, mortality, and longevity.

One of the legacies of debates such as these was to render this second, abstract notion of population familiar to its audience. The interest of the debate at the academy is that it reveals in a very nuanced way the symbolic process by which the consolidation of a set of linkages or associations—between infant mortality, the distribution of heights, military aptitude, declining birth rates (along with increases in the absolute number of births), depopulation, and decadence—provided the context for introducing this conceptual shift. It also shows how differences between the individualist and collectivist concepts of population were worked out in the context of technical discussions over the proper use and interpretation of statistics.

Bertillon, Demography, and Depopulation

Demography and the French Association for the Advancement of Sciences

Bertillon's engagement in the active promotion of demography as a discipline was directly linked to his association of demography and depopulation. The military defeat to Germany in 1870 and concomitant fall of the Second Empire and creation of the Third Republic created new opportunities for Republican social scientists. In 1872 the organizers of the Medical Congress of France asked Bertillon to address them on the French population and the dangers of depopulation. Whether the request came from Broca—who had introduced the topic into the medical community—or was based on Bertillon's reputation as a statistician is not clear. What is clear is that Bertillon was taken by surprise. Unable to put together a talk on the topic on such short notice, he declined.

In the following year Bertillon was better prepared. In 1873 the organizers of the second annual meeting of the French Association for the Advancement of Science asked Bertillon to address the congress on the same topic.[17] This time he accepted. Two features distinguish Bertillon's speech from his earlier writings: his use of the threat of depopulation to frame his speech and his explicit bid for the recognition of demography as a science. In what was only a slight rewriting of history, Bertillon presented his own work on differential mortality as having been motivated by a concern with contemporary problems of population. "It was in effect, Messieurs, in order to resolve the problems of the population that it seemed to me to have been absolutely necessary to abandon the method of semi *a priori* conceptions, which was almost exclusively used until now. . . . Messieurs, the French population by its weak rate of growth. . . . is becoming a subject of legitimate concern, because, more than ever, it is the force which decides the destiny of nations."[18] Whereas until 1872 Bertillon had presented his work as an effort to document the vitality of the population and promote public hygiene, in 1873 this goal was replaced by his newfound concern about depopulation and national strength.

This change in frame corresponded to a change in Bertillon's conception of population as an entity and the types of causal relations directing its growth. Until this point Bertillon had adhered to a contingent model of explanation, similar to that developed by the administrator Alfred Legoyt in his analyses for the Statistical Society of Paris. In 1873 Bertillon presented a different model. As he explained to his audience: "Messieurs, my work does not deal with the painful times nor with accidental fatalities which have all of a sudden transformed our weak rate of growth into the visible and cruel decline of which you know. My research aims at the constant, little known, but important causes which, in full monarchical prosperity, have not ceased, from the beginning of the century, to weigh (on us) and which moreover have increased."[19]

This declaration of the existence of long-term causes was followed by a systematic discussion of the nature of population as an object. The statement is important in that it spelled out what was to be the core of Bertillon's project for demography. He explained:

> The population of a nation depends on two factors: on its natality which unendingly furnishes the new layers of the collectivity, and on its mortality, which reaps, clearing up every age!
>
> But, if births and deaths (as assimilation and dis-assimilation for the individual) are the two fundamental acts in the development of the social body, the so to say anatomic composition of this social body, and the climatic and mental environment within which it develops, have the greatest of influences on each of these two movements. It is thus that, on the one hand, relations exist between the force of the different groups of age, of sex, of civil state, of profession, and on the other hand, the intimate qualities of these anatomic elements of the social body resulting from the degree of wealth, of instruction, of moral elevation, of habitation, etc. have a large influence in its intestinal movements — births, marriages and death — by which the nation exists, renews itself and grows or lowers itself. They must thus be reviewed, measured and placed in relation with its movements.[20]

Population, in this new conception, was divided between an anatomical or intestinal component and a climatic or environmental one. The task of demography was to study population movement by tracing the internal dynamic rooted in the interaction of births, marriages, and deaths and to specify the impact of external environmental factors on that movement.

In this new model, population movement was granted a privileged position as the independent variable, conceptualized in terms of how the forces of natality, nuptiality, and mortality interacted. Whereas earlier texts had emphasized these measures as merely indicating when individuals entered and exited from the population, in 1873 they were presented as forces. Similarly, whereas previously the "state" of the population had been the object of interest (the dependent variable), in this new formulation its interest lay in what it told the observer about future population movements. The moral, intellectual, and physical states of the population were important because they influenced the intensity of the forces of mortality and natality. The interest of this depiction, which was to become the conceptual core of demography, is that it presented the population as an abstract, self-contained statistical object amenable to mathematical modeling. As noted in the discussion of depopulation in chapter 2, this notion originated when population growth was introduced as an object of interest in and of itself. What Bertillon did in his speech of 1873 was to provide a systematic elaboration of this general concept.

In summary, the important features of Bertillon's formulation were his acceptance of long-term structural causes, his model of population as a self-contained object, and a focus on births and deaths over migration as factors that accounted for population movements. These three points were intimately related. It was because population was the product of long-term, permanent causes that it could be conceived of as a collectivist entity, distinct from the individuals and individual events which constituted it. Similarly, it was because those forces lay in the forces of mortality and natality, and not in external environmental or political factors, that they could be treated as autonomous and subject to mathematical formalization.

This latter insight allowed Bertillon to resolve his problems concerning the determinism of statistical laws. He concluded his speech with the claims which he had had so much difficulty sustaining in his dictionary definitions of 1865: "Messieurs, this rapid review of the . . . intrigues of mortality has highlighted this capital fact: that the chances of life and of death are, like other phenomena, subject to constant laws, there, as elsewhere in nature, there is no trace of personal governance."[21] In 1865 Bertillon had insisted on the indeterminism of mortality rates; after 1873 he echoed Quetelet's argument that the determinism of statistical laws applied to collective reality, but not to individual behavior.

The last section of Bertillon's talk before the French Association for the Advancement of Science included another innovation, at least in French discussions of population. Whereas until this point the discussion of causes had been largely qualitative, in 1873 Bertillon presented statistics as a tool of causal analysis. It was only the absence of adequate data, Bertillon explained, that prevented the use of statistics to explain long-term declines in the birth rate. Relevant statistics included mortality statistics by profession, month, wealth, department, and cause of death. Unfortunately most of these data were unavailable, either because they had not been collected or because the administration had not published them.

To illustrate the potential value of such information, Bertillon presented an analysis on the basis of what little he had, namely mortality by month on a national scale. In a type of analysis which had been perfected by William Farr in England, Bertillon used the data to measure the difference between "premature" and "naturally determined" mortality. This difference, he argued, represented the margin within which governments could act to redress the menace posed by declining population. According to this model, each population had its natural force of mortality (and natality) — the famous constant causes. Beyond that, each population was subject to an additional modicum of mortality due to poor hygienic conditions, faulty legislation, and poor distribution of resources. This line of reasoning suggested that demography could potentially be a practical tool of administration, rather than a simple mirror or register of the imprint of history on the French people.

For Bertillon, the turn to disciplinary assertion was thus associated with the development of a more focused, tighter intellectual project. Rather than break with his earlier institutional aspirations, Bertillon continued to pursue them, only this time in the name of demography. Between 1873 and 1877 he attempted to gain scientific recognition for his project from the quasi-official world of French academic science. The bid took him outside the sphere of Republican science into what were for him new social and intellectual arenas. It was at this point that the type of cognitive rules and corresponding boundaries which Guillard had encountered twenty years earlier came into play.

The Turn to Discipline Formation

Bertillon's New Project: La démographie figurée

Bertillon's attempt to gain academic recognition proceeded on a number of different fronts. He submitted *La démographie figurée* — his first book-length work — to essay competitions at the Academy of Moral and Political Sciences and the Academy of Sciences, and he renewed his candidacy for a position in the Academy of Medicine.[22] Published in 1874, *La démographie figurée* is a good example of how Bertillon's formulation of demography post-1873 combined his earlier projects for promoting statistics in medicine with his new commitment to discipline formation, his new, holistic concept of population, and his new political concerns for the strength of the French nation.

La démographie figurée consisted of thirty-nine maps and eighteen tables bracketed by a brief introduction and a conclusion. Each map indicated mortality rates by department. Departments were shaded to indicate areas with particularly high or low rates. Finally, the tables broke down the figures by age, sex, civil status, and various measures of mortality. While the use of graphic representations had been introduced into French statistics in the first half of the century, the technique was rarely used. This reluctance can be explained both by the cost of reproduction and by an epistemological objection. As noted above, administrative statisticians such as Moreau de Jonnès preferred tables of numbers on the grounds that they retained a one-to-one correspondence with the individual data from which they had been drawn.[23]

Bertillon himself provided two explanations for his use of maps. The first was that they allowed the reader to process a great deal of information quickly and that they fixed that information in the observer's mind more effectively than a complicated table of numbers would have done. The second was that they revealed an otherwise invisible underlying reality. As Bertillon explained: "This mode of expression has an even more precious advantage: with numerical notation, one only finds the relations which one seeks because one suspected them *a priori*, whereas figurative representation allow one, by the near simultaneity of the reading, to seize distant unexpected relations, which jump at the eyes, and which are new precisely because, not having been suspected, they were never tried."[24] This notion of the power of statistical analysis to identify previously unsuspected relations can be related to Bertillon's newly acquired belief in the existence of constant causes or patterns associated with a particular population and with the political use of demography. While these concerns had not shaped his original research, they did justify the practical value of demography.

The Academy of Moral and Political Sciences

The first test of Bertillon's book came in 1875 with the announcement of an essay competition for the Prix Victor Cousin in the section of Political Economy, Finances, and Statistics at the Academy of Moral and Political Sciences. The topic of the competition was to "study the movements of the population and observe the causes to which they are subject; signal what about these causes might be accidental or normal and regular, and show to what extent and how each of them operates; research the causes for the movement of the population within a single state and indicate the effects."[25] The final data for submissions was 31 December 1874, and Bertillon's book was among them.

The usual procedure for such competitions was that each work was assigned to a reviewer who reported on the manuscript. The committee then met to consider the relative merits of the submissions, and the official reporter issued a written statement declaring the winners and providing a brief discussion of the reasons for the choice of each work. Like the editorial comments in the *Journal des économistes*, these comments allowed gatekeepers of the discipline to specify the criteria of recognition appropriate for a particular type of work and the hierarchical relations between forms of knowledge.

The initial reporter for Bertillon's work was Émile Levasseur, a liberal economist who had made a career by excelling in the quasi-official élite educational system, notably at the École Normale Supérieure, an institution designed to train the state's élite educational corps. By 1874 he was one of the most highly placed economists of the time. Of the four existing chairs in political economy, Levasseur held three, the other being occupied by Joseph Garnier. He was a member of the Academy of Moral and Political Sciences and a professor at the Collège de France.

In terms of demography and statistics, Levasseur was among the liberal economists who supported the use of numbers. A review of discussions at the Academy of Moral and Political Sciences indicates that he consistently defended the value of (descriptive) statistical data in the face of criticism. While economists such as Joseph Garnier and Jules Simon criticized official data for their unreliability, Levasseur insisted that even approximate data provided valuable indications about social reality. Finally, like Bertillon, Levasseur only became interested in the significance of falling birth rates after 1871. Both these factors explain Levasseur's favorable report on *La démographie figurée*. The report presented the book as a contribution to medical science rather than political economy, and Bertillon was awarded second prize.[26]

The book was not, however, spared a more critical reading. In the official report, Garnier criticized Bertillon for his use of statistics. He noted that while Bertillon recognized the need to study population over short periods, he lacked the data to study yearly fluctuations by department or in other countries.[27] Garnier also noted that Bertillon's analysis rested wholly on relations or coefficients (what we would call rates) rather than absolute figures.[28] Garnier attacked this approach, suggesting that in abandoning the statisticians' insistence on a one-to-one correspondence between figures and observed reality, Bertillon introduced an element of speculation which undermined the authority of his figures: "This manner (of working) has a danger, that is to lead statisticians to reason on (the basis of) calculated figures, rather than reasoning on figures obtained by the record of facts, in the manner of what is called political arithmetic of the last century. It is thus that the author went to a great deal of trouble to establish hypothetical figures of the French population, year by year, from 1801 to 1869, with the real population as given by the quiquennial censuses."[29]

Garnier's criticisms echoed those which he had made of Guillard's work twenty years earlier. They reveal both a failure to appreciate the distorting influence of variations in age structure on directly observed numbers and a reasonable concern over the dubious value of census data for the calculation of annual rates. More to the point, his comments point to the dominance among political economists of a descriptive model for statistics. In comparing Bertillon's work to that of political arithmeticians, Garnier sent a clear message to his readers that Bertillon's practices were not to be imitated. As Moreau de Jonnès argued, only observed numbers provide a guarantee of certainty.

The Academy of Medicine

In 1875 Bertillon submitted his candidacy for the newly created position in the section of *associés libres* at the Academy of Medicine. This time, in contrast with his attempts of ten years earlier, his candidacy was based on his credentials as a statistician. The commission appointed to consider his application consisted of Mr. Bergeron, one of the two doctors responsible for reintroducing the issue of infant mortality in 1868; Mr. Roussel, the author of the legislation of 1874 designed to regulate the wet-nursing industry; and Paul Broca, designated the official reporter for the commission. All three sympathized with Bertillon's argument about the contribution of statistics to medical science.

Broca's report presented Bertillon's candidacy as an occasion for the academy to retract its earlier strictures against the use of the numerical method in medicine. He based his claim on the importance of the method for the public health work of the academy and changing circumstances, which rendered earlier injunctions obsolete. According to Broca, the absence of statistics in the academy could be explained by the state of the art in 1820, when the academy was reestablished: at the time statistics was not yet a science and the SGF did not yet exist.[30] Broca concluded his opening remarks with a plea not only to include statisticians in the academy but to recognize the place of "human statistics" in public medicine. He also used the occasion to echo Bertillon's oft-repeated call on the government to improve official statistics by publishing age-specific data on marriages and deaths for those under twenty-five years of age.[31]

Broca then proceeded to review the various statistical papers which Bertillon had presented to the academy, highlighting three features of Bertillon's work. The first was his use of statistics to discover otherwise unseen phenomena. Here Broca noted Bertillon's priority in linking infant mortality with wet-nursing and his identification of unnaturally high mortality among married males between eighteen and twenty, suggesting the need to raise the minimum age of marriage. The second feature was Bertillon's unique combination of medical and statistical knowledge and the specialized skill required to adapt official data to medical purposes. Finally, Broca signaled the accessibility of Bertillon's work to nonspecialists, notably through his use of maps. The key characteristics which Broca stressed were originality and comprehensiveness.[32]

As was customary, Broca's speech was complemented by a pamphlet that Bertillon had compiled with a list of his major publications and activities.[33] The pamphlet opened with a clear statement of his desire to be elected not (only) on his own merits but on those of the new discipline for which he spoke: "To justify the introduction of Demography into the circle of medical sciences, I can do no better than to recall the following words, delivered by Mr. Broca before the Academy."[34] Bertillon then proceeded to reprint a number of paragraphs from Broca's speech calling for the inclusion of statistics among the medical sciences. To buttress the argument, Bertillon noted that both the editorial council of the *Dictionnaire encyclopédique des sciences médicales* and Messrs. Littré and Robin in their revised edition of the Nysten medical encyclopedia included demography in the circle of medical knowledge.

As a strategy, this coupling of Bertillon, demography, and statistics certainly served to fix Bertillon's name with that of demography and to consolidate his professional identity around his new discipline. It did not, however, further his chances in the Academy of Medicine. The vote was a resounding defeat. Bertillon received one vote and the position went to Amédée Dechambre. To what extent the result can be read as a rejection of demography as a medical science and of Bertillon, rather than as a vote for Dechambre, is difficult to establish. Certainly, Bertillon had not followed the accepted route to the Academy of Medicine (in contrast to Broca, who had accumulated most of the competitive honors available in medical research and surgery before his own election).[35] And just as certainly, Dechambre had a stronger record than Bertillon. Regardless of the reasons, the association of Bertillon with demography in the course of the campaign gave the defeat a double significance. In choosing Dechambre over Bertillon, the Academy of Medicine also ruled that statistical credentials on their own were not sufficient to merit entry into their circle.

From the perspective of demography, Bertillon's defeat was decisive in that it led him to abandon medicine as his primary frame of reference. Until 1875 Bertillon consistently presented his work as a contribution to public hygiene and the new medical science; now he situated it in the more general context of social science. Bertillon's defeat also led him to shift his institutional orientation. Whereas until 1873 Bertillon consistently presented his work first to the Academy of Medicine and only then to other societies and journals, after 1875 he abandoned the medical world and that of academic science more generally. While the disappointment at being rejected by the Academy of Medicine was more than enough to explain this reorientation, its effect was exacerbated by a parallel rejection from the even more illustrious Academy of Sciences.

The Academy of Science

In 1876 Bertillon submitted *La démographie figurée* for the Prix Montyon in statistics at the Academy of Science. The Prix Montyon was the most prestigious form of scientific recognition available to statisticians, awarded to all statisticians of note in the course of the nineteenth century.[36] The prize was created in 1817 both to counter the negative political reputation of statistics at the time and to compensate for the closure of the first national statistical bureau, the Bureau de Statistique de la République, in 1811. In contrast to other academic prizes, the Prix Montyon did not set a particular question; instead, it sought to encourage a certain type of statistical work. Moreover, it functioned as a type of professional recognition, in a period when there was no formal training, no accreditation, and no specialized roles for statistical experts.

As at the Academy of Moral and Political Sciences, the published reports that accompanied the award of the prize were the main vehicle by which the academy communicated and imposed its model for how to do statistics. The ideal statistical practice was defined in opposition to both political arithmetic and political economy. In contrast with practitioners of political arithmetic, members of the academy insisted on a clear separation between statistics, which was limited to data collection, and mathematical analysis. This division was associated with their own monopoly over mathematics. Statistics, in this conception, was neither a method nor a science. Instead, the art of statistics lay in the personal observation and registration of data. The main characteristics of a good statistician were those of care, attention, and a moral commitment to assembling true facts. The statement accompanying the Prix Montyon and the judges' reports explicitly condemned economists' use of numbers. Statistics consisted of careful, certain knowledge, but political economy involved speculative generalization. The authority and scientific value of statistics lay in the certainty of the knowledge, which in turn depended on procedures of data collection.

These specifications led the academy to privilege small, local studies at the expense of those at the departmental and national level. The members of the academy believed that it was impossible to collect reliable data on a national scale. Instead, they envisioned a process whereby numerous private scholars would collect hard data locally and send them to the academy to be used by mathematicians. The role of the statistician, in this division of labor, was to oversee and thereby guarantee the certainty of the raw data.

The model which I have just described was introduced in 1817. One of the striking features of the Prix Montyon was the constancy of the criteria by which submissions were judged. This continuity can be attributed to the tenure of the mathematician Jules Bienaymé as official reporter for the committee. Bienaymé was appointed to the position in the early 1840s; he was still there in 1876 when Bertillon submitted his book.

This fundamental difference in the nature and role of statistics can be clearly seen in the contrast between Bienaymé's official report on *La démographie figurée* of 1877 and Bertillon's rejoinder. Bienaymé opened his report with a general statement condemning the use of secondary sources. In using data which they have not personally collected, Bienaymé explained, the authors of these works are unable to attest to the exactitude of their numbers, and thus of their conclusions. Their work is no more than economic conjecture and cannot be used to control the quality of administrative statistics.[37] These and similar points can be found in almost every report of the

Prix Montyon. They are important to the historian of statistics in that they demonstrate the academy's blanket rejection of official data, despite the considerable improvements in the work of the SGF. Turning to Bertillon's text, Bienaymé signaled three faults: Bertillon's publication of rates rather than absolute numbers; his technique for calculating mortality rates, which Bienaymé subjected to a mathematical critique; and Bertillon's use of the term "demography," which Bienaymé judged unacceptable.[38]

Bienaymé's principled objection to the use of official data was, as I have shown, a central theme in all his reports. His criticism of Bertillon's use of rates rather than real numbers would seem to echo the concerns of Moreau de Jonnès in the 1830s and 1840s. Placed in the context of Bienaymé's position as mathematician in the Academy of Science and his model for statistics, however, it can be understood as an expression of his concern that statisticians produce data which could be used for mathematical analysis. To mathematicians Bertillon's statistical summaries were indeed useless. In Bienaymé's words, his work could not be considered "statistics properly speaking."

Bienaymé's more technical criticisms included a mathematical explanation of how the true mortality of a population should be calculated. In *La démographie figurée*, Bertillon calculated the ratio of deaths for a particular age group over the observed population of the beginning of the period. Bienaymé criticized this procedure on the grounds that Bertillon's denominator was static: it did not correspond to the population in which the deaths occurred except at the beginning of the period, since the size of the population diminished every time someone died. While Bertillon's mistake was not serious when applied to the adult population (mortality rates are relatively stable over the course of a year, and in a large population the effect noted by Bienaymé on age-specific mortality rates is relatively small), Bienaymé's criticism was apt with regard to infant mortality. Practically, however, the SGF data did not permit the kind of calculations which Bienaymé demanded.[39] It was on these grounds that Bertillon defended his procedure.

Finally, Bienaymé closed by criticizing Bertillon's choice of the term "*démographie*." According to Bienaymé, the Greek term "demos" referred to the people in the sense of a political body and not people as counted by the census. The term thus referred to the political development of France and not to human statistics. While the point may seem gratuitous, it can be read as a symbolic rejection of Bertillon's model of statistics.

The purpose of Bienaymé's report was thus to establish that Bertillon's book, and the other submissions that year, did not meet the academy's standards as statistics. The report did not, however, reject Bertillon's work outright. The value of *La démographie figurée*, Bienaymé explained, lay in the realm of hypotheses. While it contained no real facts, it did contain a number of suggestions which could be fruitfully pursued by true savants. For this reason the commission agreed to accord the work an honorable mention.

Rather than accept the judgment of the academy, Bertillon published a lengthy response, defending his work in the *Journal de la société statistique de Paris*.[40] In response to Bienaymé's substantive criticisms, Bertillon defended his choice of measures on practical grounds, distinguishing between the considerations of a statistician and those of a mathematician. To sustain this claim, he appealed to the work of Adolphe Quetelet and William Farr, two savants who had the advantage of being both "tested statisticians and mathematical scholars."[41] In the article Bertillon clearly articulated the differences between his conception and that of the academy. He also used the occasion to make a strong bid for a new type of alliance between administrators and scientific statisticians.

Bertillon began by forcefully rejecting Bienaymé's argument that statistics must be limited to the personal collection of data, either by private individuals or administrators, and defended the scientific value of analyses of official data. It was indicative of the failure of the academy's program to encourage private studies that Bertillon did not bother to comment on that model of statistics. Instead he compared the practice of administrative statistics with that of scientific statistics or demography. His focus on this contrast suggests that he himself defined demography in opposition to the descriptive model of administrative statistics that dominated the SGF and the Société Statistique de Paris during the 1860s. The article also highlights how he used his differences with Bienaymé to gain support from administrative statisticians.

In comparing administrative statistical practice with demography, Bertillon wrote:

> The object of official statistics is only the methodical, faithful recording of social facts, year by year, with no other concern but to sum up the facts in the same order and to separate those of different orders by pushing the analysis of these categories as far as the administrative resources allow.
>
> The statistical investigations of savants today (what I have termed scientific statistics) have for their object to compare these various values one with the other, to observe their average value, the fluctuations to which these values are subject, the law of their succession in time, place

and (amongst) the races, the natural or social influences which seem to weigh on these movements, either in order to accelerate them or to slow them down, and, with this knowledge, to predict and in consequence, to modify, to direct to our profit the future of nations.[42]

This quote reiterates the novelties introduced in Bertillon's speech of 1873. Demography or scientific statistics is defined not only as the manipulation of data to create new information (as with political arithmetic) and as the use of numbers to identify laws, but also as a practical policy tool that can be used to predict and modify future developments. While Bertillon presented the two approaches to statistics as distinct, he also emphasized their complementary character: "Moreover, these studies executed on the basis of official documents lead to another result which is no less important: that is to observe the imperfection, the omissions of official inquiries, to signal them and to indicate the improvements to which they are susceptible. As such, the scholarly investigations are like a higher and free control practiced on administrative documents for which they demonstrate the utility and oblige the progress."[43] In contrast to Bienaymé, who argued that only independent studies could be used to control the quality of official data, Bertillon proposed an exchange between administrators and savants. Administrators would provide data for use by savants, while savants, through their analyses, would control and suggest improvements in official data. As we will see, this exchange was at the core of Bertillon's program for institutionalizing demography. In any event it is interesting to note that in Bertillon's presentation, mathematical expertise was not deemed essential to scientific statistics.

Intellectually, the difference between Bertillon and Bienaymé can be ascribed to differences in their epistemological criteria, rather than to technical differences over how to calculate rates. For Bertillon, the task of statistics was to provide a (more) solid knowledge base for legislative reform. For Bienaymé, it was to arrive at certain knowledge — or rather, certain knowledge of the degree of certainty with which quantitative claims could be made. It was this difference which Bertillon referred to when he distinguished between mathematical and statistical considerations. Its importance lies chiefly in the message that Bertillon seems to have drawn from it: confronted with a clear rejection by the Academy of Medicine and the Academy of Science, he placed his lot with administrative statistics and a model of a mutually beneficial exchange between administrative statistics and social science.

Discipline Assertion as a Bid to Transform
Cognitive Boundaries

Bertillon's scientific activities in the early years of the Third Republic high-light two crucial features of the remapping of the social sciences and the constitution of social-science entities in nineteenth-century France: the im-portance of social problems and political debates for the introduction of social-science concepts and the role of public debates in diffusing new styles of reasoning. With regard to each, the analytic distinction between science and politics, or between science and the public sphere, is misleading. As my analysis shows, quasi-public debates in the academies of sciences, medicine, and moral and political sciences were a crucial forum for elaborating and diffusing statistical entities and reasoning. They were an explicitly political and scientific forum, and their participants were there by dint of their pre-sumed public and intellectual authority. In contrast to England, however, academies and the public sphere more generally were not centers of policy formation or politics.

Academic debates over depopulation and infant mortality were occa-sions for exploring a collectivist concept of population. Discussions within both the Académie des Sciences Morales et Politiques and the Academy of Medicine point to the tension between interpreting population trends as the result of contingent, historical events on different cohorts and as evi-dence of an internal dynamic, driven by the interacting forces of natality and mortality and governed by statistical laws. Differences in interpretation corresponded to differences in the nature of national statistical entities. Speakers oscillated between a view of national statistical populations as an aggregate of individuals and as holistic units. The same debates were also an occasion for the statistical education of political and intellectual élites. Broca struggled to explain to his colleagues how to interpret a statistical rate and how to evaluate documented trends.

One curious feature of the French nineteenth-century debates is the extent to which technical rather than political issues provided the focus of academic debate. A second feature is the absence of clear alliances between advocates of particular epistemological views and specific political views. In contrast to the situation in the United Kingdom, differences in how to use statistical rates did not align neatly with differences over specific policy prescriptions or even general political ideologies. This absence of clear artic-ulation may reflect the peculiar nature of depopulation as a social problem. The debates discussed above mark the introduction of depopulation into the political agenda. One of the political appeals of the issue was that it cut across conventional political and ideological lines. Monarchists, Republicans, and socialists disagreed on most things, but they agreed on the gravity of the threat of depopulation. They also agreed on the inadvisability of translating that concern into action, or so the absence of concrete legislation would seem to suggest. While French officials had focused on the care of abandoned infants under the protection of the state from the early years of thė Third Republic, it was only in 1913 that French politicians and administrators translated an almost obsessive discursive concern with depopulation into explicit legislative measures. In that year benefits took effect to encourage people to have large families, and in 1914 legislators introduced tax breaks for families with three children or more.[44] The absence of practical legislation until then lent a largely rhetorical bent to the debate. At least in the nineteenth century, the stakes in the debate over national population statistics were how the state of the nation would be represented, rather than what the nature or extent of state intervention should be.

Bertillon's attempts to gain recognition from the gatekeepers of political economy and the élite scientific academies for his version of population statistics also shed light on the meaning of disciplinary activity in the nineteenth century. Disciplinary activity was aimed at reworking the epistemological rules governing the host discipline, be it political economy or élite medicine, in such a way as to incorporate demography. Bertillon's promotion of demography called upon political economists to rework their mapping of the hierarchy between descriptive and speculative, explanatory knowledge. It called upon the Academy of Medicine to abandon its explicit exclusion of "the numerical method" from the corpus of relevant forms of knowledge. Finally, it called upon the mathematicians at the Academy of Sciences to relax the distinction between mathematics and statistics. In all three cases, it called on academicians to adopt a new model of statistics that privileged rates over absolute numbers and the identification of laws over certainty and description.

As for the social and institutional logics governing statistics, Bertillon's intellectual trajectory points to a variety of competing intellectual circles, each associated with a distinct cognitive map. Three in particular shaped the development of social statistics in this period: élite medicine, which made a clear distinction between clinical medicine and public hygiene and explicitly relegated statistics to the latter; political economy, now extended to include national administrative statistics and the Société Statistique de Paris; and finally, the newly flourishing culture of positivist medical and social science.

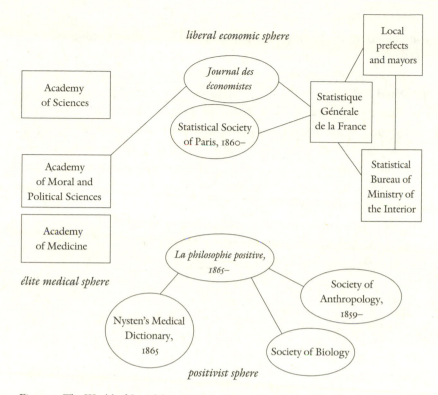

Figure 2. The World of Social Statisticians, France, 1870–1875: Social and Epistemological Spheres as Viewed from the Perspective of Bertillon's Professional Trajectories

Between 1875 and 1878 Bertillon sought recognition from all three sectors, which in each case was denied on epistemological grounds. It was only after this triple rejection that Bertillon explicitly linked his program for statistics to the active promotion of demography as a separate science.

The experiences of Guillard and Bertillon suggest an initial response to the questions of why one should establish a discipline in the nineteenth century and what nineteenth-century social scientists were asking for when they called for the recognition of a new category or project as a separate science. For both Guillard and Bertillon the turn to explicit forms of disciplinary activity was linked to the public rejection of their intellectual projects on epistemological grounds by gatekeepers of the two élite sciences authorized to discuss social life — medicine and political economy. In both cases the rejection or exclusion of Guillard's and Bertillon's projects was based on the argument that what they did was "not statistics." And in both cases subsequent calls for recognizing demography as a separate science amounted to an attempt to renegotiate the criteria of what counts as statistics, within specific institutional spheres.

Before turning to those efforts, it is helpful to move across the channel to England and to examine the fortunes of a similar intellectual and administrative project, vital statistics. In the period when Guillard and Bertillon struggled to situate and give content to demography, proponents of vital statistics successfully institutionalized a similar project in mainstream scientific and administrative bureaus. A comparison of their projects and the conditions in which they were institutionalized highlights the impact of broader institutional conditions on the diffusion of statistical reasoning and the conditions for discipline formation.

PART II

The Institutionalization

of Vital Statistics in England:

How to "Secure" a Discipline in

Nineteenth-Century England

CHAPTER FOUR

The Invention of Vital Statistics, 1830–1837

As we have seen, nineteenth-century demography consisted of a revival of the more abstract, speculative approach to statistics formerly associated with political arithmetic. In the first half of the nineteenth century this approach was reintroduced in association with problems of public hygiene and social statistics more generally. The leading formulations in the period can be found in the work of Quetelet, Villermé, and Fourier. Guillard and Bertillon drew on this tradition in the development of demography. In England, William Farr combined the same early-nineteenth-century French tradition with local actuarial techniques to produce vital statistics. But whereas in France demography broke with the public hygiene movement, in England, vital statistics retained the original association. And whereas in France demography was excluded from élite social science and administration, in England it was held up as the ideal form of statistical practice. Finally, whereas in France social statisticians struggled to apply this new form of statistics to national population statistics, in England social statisticians were singularly unconcerned by the ontological considerations which so troubled the French.

The question that concerns us next is why these differences were so pronounced. Why did French and British social statisticians take Quetelet and Villermé's project in such different directions? Why did English statisticians adopt a probabilistic interpretation of national population statistics nearly fifty years before they mastered the techniques of probability theory, and why did French statisticians resist doing so? More specifically, I want to understand what about the institutional conditions in which demography and vital statistics developed accounts for these differences in reception and intellectual development. This chapter examines the local context in which William Farr first formulated and introduced vital statistics, while chapter 5 explores the institutional arenas in which the new discipline was pursued.

These include public administration, the medical and public health movements, and the world of organized social statistics.

In contrast to demographers, vital statisticians were singularly unconcerned with disciplinary activity. Thus while Farr introduced the label of vital statistics in the late 1830s, he and his colleagues spent little time reflecting on the hierarchy of knowledge, the boundaries between disciplines, and the status of vital statistics as a science. It was only in the late 1870s that social statisticians began to invest in the type of rhetorical work that characterized the promotion of demography in France. This relative lack of concern with explicit disciplinary work in the first decades of the discipline, and this subsequent preoccupation, provide an opportunity to further explore the meaning of nineteenth-century disciplinary activity. One of the empirical challenges of the analysis is to explain why proponents of vital statistics abstained from explicit disciplinary activity during the first thirty years of their practice and why, after 1878, they suddenly began to call for recognition of their practice as a separate science, distinct from other types of politics, social science, and social statistics.

William Farr and Vital Statistics

Farr's Engagement in Public Health, 1828–1835

The stories of William Farr and vital statistics are often linked.[1] The entry for Farr in the *Dictionary of National Biography* in 1908 states that his early articles "laid the foundation of a new science."[2] Similarly, a posthumous collection of Farr's works was entitled "Vital Statistics."[3] Like Bertillon twenty years later, Farr came to statistics through public hygiene. Born in 1807 to parents of "humble circumstances," Farr was fortunate enough to have been sponsored by a local squire who financed his education and arranged for a medical apprenticeship. In 1828 Farr's benefactor died, leaving him a legacy of £500. He used his money to continue his studies in Paris, which was then the center of medical science.

In Paris Farr was introduced not only to new developments in clinical medicine but also to the new discipline of public hygiene. The latter combined the empirical study of environmental causes of illness with a call for government intervention. According to French public hygienists, statistical inquiry was a necessary preliminary to legislative reform. Farr was in Paris when Louis René Villermé delivered his first course on public hygiene at the Athenée in Paris and when the statistical journal *Annales d'hygiène* was first published. He also attended the lectures of Pierre Louis, the main advocate of the numerical method in medicine.

The July Revolution of 1830 put an end to Farr's Paris adventure. On his return to England, he moved to London. He continued his medical studies at University College in London and in 1832 qualified for a license as an apothecary. Medicine in England in the first half of the century was a highly stratified profession. Farr's degree as an apothecary and his social background made it difficult to establish a successful private practice. To supplement his income, he turned to public lecturing and medical journalism. His aim was to introduce English doctors to the scientific approach to medicine and, more specifically, to public hygiene. Although in France such appeals were received without enthusiasm, in England they found support in the movement to reform the medical profession.

From Public Health to Vital Statistics, 1835–1837

In 1835 Farr had only a vague, albeit principled, commitment to the use of statistics to measure vitality. By 1837 this ideal had become the focus of a coherent disciplinary project, which he entitled "vital statistics." One of the key intervening events was the publication of an article entitled "On the Laws of Collective Vitality" by the actuary T. R. Edmonds in 1836.[4] The article made a number of points which were to become mainstays of Farr's version of vital statistics. First, in direct opposition to the medical consensus in France, Edmonds insisted that doctors must identify the collective laws of vitality in order to understand individual health. Second, he argued that the relation between the vitality of different ages was constant and could be described by mathematical equations, or laws of vitality. Third, he stressed the contribution that doctors could make to the collection of data on the condition of those in "uneasy circumstances." Edmonds explained that while knowledge of the mortality of those in "easy circumstances" could be ascertained from the records of life insurance offices, the mortality of the poor remained a mystery. Finally, Edmonds argued for calculating mortality by reference to those who had not died (or, in today's terms, in relation to the population at risk). Only life tables combined data on deaths (by age) with information on the number of persons living at the time, thus allowing for a correct appreciation of the laws of vitality.

The reception by the *Lancet* of Edmonds's article and of subsequent contributions, most notably by Farr, underlines a number of differences in the relation between medicine, public health, actuaries, mathematics, and social statistics in England and France. In France the discussion over the numerical method at the Academy of Medicine in 1836 had ended in an absolute rejection of the relevance of statistics for medical science. In his article, Edmonds acknowledged that medical researchers might balk at his call to apply actuarial methods to medical science. The editors of the medical journal supported his position, however, and added an appeal of their own for future communications on the subject.[5] The influence of Edmonds's work on Farr's work and on vital statistics points to a more general relation between actuaries and social statisticians in England that was absent in France. Thus while in England the actuarial connection created a natural channel for diffusing mathematical developments into statistics, in France the absence of this connection buttressed the active efforts of the Academy of Sciences to police the boundary between the two types of intellectual activity.[6]

In the year after the publication of Edmonds's article, William Farr answered his call with two articles of his own. The first appeared in the first volume of his new journal, the *British Annals of Medicine, Pharmacy, Vital Statistics and General Science* (which folded after the first few issues), the second in the influential volume *A Statistical Account of the British Empire*, edited by the economist James McCulloch.[7] Like his French counterparts, Farr initially aimed to incorporate his new approach to statistics into both political economy and medicine. Each article was entitled "Vital Statistics" and contained a programmatic statement on the application of statistics to the study of vitality, a review of existing statistical sources, and a technical discussion of statistical tools and measures.

An examination of Farr's two articles affirms the influence of Edmonds's writings on his intellectual project. In the first article, Farr postulated the existence of collective laws of vitality and maintained that knowledge of them was relevant for the study of individuals. He based his argument on an analogy with the development of knowledge in the natural sciences. In a manner similar to Louis Adolphe Bertillon twenty years later, Farr went on to insist on the relevance of this knowledge for the medical profession, appealing to the desire of practitioners to "give their profession a scientific character."[8] But while Bertillon worked with a model of the population as divided between generations or age groups, strangers to one another, Farr adopted a more medical image of society. According to Farr: "Life is made up of health and sickness, in other words, the population is composed of two classes, the healthy and the sick, the living and the dying; the relation they bear to each other is the measure of salubrity."[9]

On the basis of this image Farr insisted that mortality should be interpreted as a measure or index of sickness and thus of relative health. With this rhetorical move, Farr transferred the moral and political weight of the concept of vitality to the statistical measurement of mortality. As Eyler has demonstrated, this notion — that data on mortality were a proxy for detailed knowledge of variations in the distribution of diseases and illness — was to become the cornerstone of a nationwide program of inquiry and intervention. The remainder of Farr's article was a lesson in the principles of life tables and an illustration of their value in evaluating the sickness and the health of a population.

Farr's first article on vital statistics appeared in 1837; by 1839 the project had been recognized and institutionalized, not in the arena of medicine as Edwards and Farr initially intended but in the General Registrar's Office (GRO) — the English equivalent of the Statistique Générale de la France — and in the Statistical Society of London (SSL). An examination of the situation of the GRO and the SSL in these years helps to explain their openness to the new project.

Vital Statistics and the Statistical Movement

Models of Statistical Practice

Both the Statistical Society of London and the General Registrar's Office were established in a period of widespread social and legislative reform. Social legislation and institutional innovations in this period were often initiated by adherents of social movements who lobbied public opinion. In most cases the government's initial response was to establish a royal commission or other official body of inquiry to investigate the situation and propose practical solutions. These commissions both conducted their own research and commissioned reports from a variety of local officials and savants.[10] At the forefront of the campaign to establish the SSL and GRO were provincial statistical societies and the statistical section of the British Association for the Advancement of Sciences (Section F of the BAAS). In addition, social statistics were cultivated by political economists and public health administrators. Each of these organizations and groups embodied a slightly different model for the practice of social statistics. In France statistical projects were differentiated around epistemological issues such as the grounding of the numbers in firsthand observation or the "reality" of statistical entities; in England, by contrast, distinctions were made with reference to the relation of statistics and politics. A comparison of the criteria of recognition articulated in founding statements of some of these organizations serves to identify the social and intellectual axes organizing the field of social statistics.

Viewed from the perspective of modern social science, a striking feature of the provincial societies' programs was the identity or continuity that they posited between social research or statistics and social reform. Statistics, in this model, was a problem-driven enterprise directed at clarifying policy problems and their solution. This relationship was clearly stated in the first annual report of the Manchester Statistical Society. In recounting the origins of the society, the editors ascribed it to "a strong desire felt by its projectors to assist in promoting the progress of social improvement in the manufacturing population by which they are surrounded. Its members are not associated merely for the purpose of collecting facts concerning the condition of the inhabitants of this district, as its name might seem to imply, but the first resolution entered on its minutes pronounces it to be a 'Society for the discussion of subjects of political and social economy, and for the promotion of statistical inquiries, to the total exclusion of party politics.'"[11] Thus the founders of the Manchester Society explicitly rejected a purely descriptive project for statistics. For them, statistics constituted a form of reasoned discussion on pressing social and political issues.

In contrast to the provincial societies, both Section F and the Statistical Society of London were established to pursue scientific, rather than political, goals. For both organizations the popular association of statistics and politics posed a particular problem. The challenge was whether and how to allow statistics into the organizations without threatening their scientific status. In each case the initial solution was to limit statistics to a purely descriptive, "factual" enterprise, but these more restricted criteria of statistical science proved impossible to institutionalize and were soon overturned. That said, the provincial societies and early versions of the Statistical Society of London and the BAAS differed significantly in their mapping of knowledge and criteria for what properly counted as "statistics."

The BAAS was founded in 1831. It was one of a growing number of peripatetic associations that met in different cities across the country. Provincial statistical societies tended to be led by industrialists and Dissenters, but the BAAS was the creation of traditional élites. All the founders were liberal Anglicans of the Broad Church Party, and all were active in university life (an option which, in 1831, was closed to Dissenters). Over a quarter held chairs at Cambridge, three were professors at Trinity College, Dublin, and three were at Oxford.[12] By the mid-nineteenth century the BAAS had established itself as the primary gatekeeper of British intellectual life.

The proposal to include statistics in the BAAS would seem to have originated at the third annual meeting of the association. The plan was developed and piloted by a small group of scholars based in Cambridge, including Charles Babbage and William Whewell. Adolphe Quetelet was also present at the initial planning session. Far from welcoming the proposal to create a separate section for statistics, the founders of the association held back on the grounds that statistics would introduce politics and thus "passion" (and dissension) into the annual meetings of the association. In a speech before the General Committee of the BAAS, Adam Sedgwick drew attention to the dangers posed by the original project. Although founders of the association supported an image of science as a theoretically informed, speculative enterprise, when it came to statistics they appealed to a much narrower definition: "By science, then, I understand the consideration of all objects, whether of pure or mixed nature, capable of being reduced to measurement and calculation. All things comprehended under the categories of space, time and number belong to our investigations, and all phenomena capable of being brought under the semblance of law are legitimate objects of our inquiry."[13] In the remainder of his speech, Sedgwick spelled out the rationale for his redefinition of science in terms of quantification. Thus, he continued: "Can then statistical inquiries be made compatible with our subjects, and taken into the bosom of our society? I think they unquestionably may, *so far as they have to do with matters of fact, with mere abstractions, and with numerical results*. Considered in this light they give what may be called the raw material for political economy and political philosophy; and by their help the lasting foundations of these sciences may be perhaps ultimately laid."[14] In the end, the General Committee approved the creation of a new statistical section, albeit with certain restrictions. In the mandate for Section F, statistics was limited to the collection of numerical facts. Discussion of either political economy or political philosophy was explicitly excluded.

In many ways the BAAS program was similar to the French descriptive model institutionalized in the SGF. Two important features, however, distinguished the two. These were the grounds on which the descriptive model was adopted and the institutional arrangements that were put in place to secure it. First, while in France the descriptive model was adopted on ontological and epistemological grounds—Moreau de Jonnès argued that only numbers which retained a one-to-one correspondence with reality could produce true knowledge (science) — in England the leaders of Section F imposed their model on the basis of purely strategic considerations. As Sedgwick implied later in his speech, the closest they could come to an epistemological justification was to appeal to the immaturity of statistics as a science. Second, in France intellectual gatekeepers successfully denied to the new "scientific" approach both scientific and administrative recognition, but in England their social counterparts failed to impose the authority of a purely descriptive approach.

The leaders of the association took a number of steps to limit the activities of Section F to head counting and other forms of descriptive statistics: they systematically rejected proposals from Section F (including requests for funding), made a concerted attempt to deny membership to applicants from more politically active statistical societies such as the Manchester Statistical Society and the Statistical Society of London, and decreed that statistical papers must be limited to politically neutral tables and numbers. To their dismay, their efforts failed. This inability to police the intellectual activities of Section F can be explained by the institutional dependence of the organization on public support and by popular interest in the social problems that statisticians addressed. Under public pressure, the leaders were forced to allow three members of each of the offensive societies to join, and statisticians maintained their control over the content of their papers. That said, Section F continued to uphold a more strictly "scientific" image of statistics than that of the provincial statistical societies.

To summarize, the models for statistics embodied in the mandates of the Manchester Statistical Society and the BAAS represent two extremes in what would seem to have been a continuum of different descriptive projects. The Manchester Statistical Society proposed a model of statistics as problem-driven inquiry into the condition of England. Statistics in this model involved both quantitative and qualitative data. At the other end of the continuum, the initial project for Section F was quantitative and encyclopedic. While the data were to be used by statesmen and economists, statistics itself was clearly positioned outside the sphere of science.

The Statistical Society of London

In 1833 the original members of Section F voted to found a separate scientific society devoted exclusively to statistics. Like the Manchester Statistical Society and Section F at the BAAS, the original proposal called for a strictly descriptive form of knowledge. The idea was proposed by T. R.

Malthus and seconded by the Reverend R. Jones. The object of the society was to be "the collection and classification of all facts illustrative of the present condition and prospects of Society,"[15] a statement of purpose that combined the program of Section F with the "condition of England" question. The first meeting of the Statistical Society of London was held in March 1834. It was presided over by the Marquis of Lansdowne and attended by a number of Members of Parliament, noblemen, and leading political economists.

The prospectus for the Society, which was read at the first meeting, reiterated Malthus's formulation. The remainder of the statement focused on the practical work of the society. Its goal was to aid in the collection, arrangement, and communication of statistical "facts." A central concern was to exclude opinions from the work of the society. "The Statistical Society will consider it to be the first and most essential rule of its conduct to exclude carefully all Opinions from its transactions and publications — to confine its attention rigorously to facts — and, as far as it may be found possible, to facts which can be stated numerically and arranged in tables."[16] Thus the prospectus, like the directives for Section F, confused — or rather conflated — theory and opinion. Concern to exclude opinions led the authors to exclude theoretical work from their program as well. The stricture against opinions was re-enforced by the original members' choice of motto. The symbol of the society was a wheat sheaf with the phrase *Aliis extenderum* — for others to harvest — written below. In keeping with the descriptive model for statistics, the work of the statistician was limited to collecting and communicating facts to be used by others for whatever scientific or political purposes they might wish.

Another important point in the prospectus concerned the practical character of statistical knowledge and the relation of the Statistical Society of London to the government. Whereas for the founders of the Manchester Statistical Society this aim led to a program of activism, for the early leadership of the SSL it suggested a work of coordination and cooperation with the administration. As the prospectus stated: "It will be desirable that the society should as soon as possible endeavor to open a communication with the statistical department established by Government at the Board of Trade. Without such a communication constantly kept up the Society can never be assured that it is not doing unnecessarily what the Government is doing at the same time and better. The result of such a communication would probably be that the Society would abandon to the care of the Government some part of this very extensive field of inquiry altogether and more of it partially, which would still leave a very sufficient though a less overwhelming task to the Society."[17] The original members thus hoped that the official statistical apparatus would gradually replace them as a collector of facts. Their job, like that of the myriad of voluntary organizations which were established during the 1830s, was to compensate for as of yet underdeveloped government services.[18]

During the first year of its existence, the main activity of the society was to design a printed questionnaire for collecting parish-level data. This project was in keeping with a broader conception by which the society was to be a sort of guide for private investigations. By introducing a uniform set of questions and directives, the society hoped to insure the comparability of data collected. This project would seem similar to that institutionalized in France by the Academy of Sciences. A closer examination of the implementation of this vision in the two countries, however, reveals a number of fundamental differences. In England, the project for diffusing a questionnaire was soon abandoned (for lack of response). In its place, the society appointed a number of committees devoted to specific projects or areas. During the first ten years of its existence many of these committees conducted their own firsthand research. However, they soon abandoned this work in favor of analyzing existing official data.

The Statistical Field in France and Britain: A First Consideration

The above discussion lays the basis for mapping the different models in place for the practice of statistics when Farr introduced his project for vital statistics. In France the relevant axis of differentiation was the degree of abstraction contained in the category "statistics" (thereby distinguishing between descriptive and scientific administrative styles); in England the differentiation was between systematic, comprehensive research versus problem-oriented research. The key issue was the place of "politics" in "science," with the spectrum ranging from provincial statistical societies that called openly for problem-oriented research to élite scientific organizations that attempted to protect themselves (and their knowledge) from the stigma of "politics."

These differences in the substantive criteria distinguishing statistical practices were paralleled by differences in the social base, audience, and strength of the different spheres. In France statistics was practiced in a relatively autonomous or isolated set of intellectual spheres, peopled by full-time scholars and directed at established scientific élites. In England, by contrast, statistics developed in a set of organizations populated by a mix of political, social, industrial, and municipal élites. On the one hand, different types of statistical organization directed their work toward different audiences (thereby submitting themselves to different criteria of recognition). The provincial societies spoke to newly consolidated municipal élites and the Statistical Society of London to politicians and policy makers, while Section F presented itself as a purely scientific organization (even though its annual meetings were directed at the same publics addressed by the other two types of organization). On the other hand, the private nature of these organizations rendered even the most scientific of them dependent on a broader, reform-oriented public. As a result, scientific gatekeepers were less powerful (than in France). This relative weakness can be clearly seen in the failure of the British Association for the Advancement of Sciences to limit statistics to descriptive, encyclopedic activities rather than problem-oriented research.

The initial reception of vital statistics in the late 1830s can be explained by the relative weakness of cognitive barriers to new projects and the "fit" of the project with elements of each of the different dominant models. As an intellectual project, vital statistics combined the more scientific or mathematical orientation of the "gentlemen of science" at the BAAS (as evidenced by their call for a combination of inductive methods and theoretical reflection and their search for mathematical laws) with the problem-solving orientation of the broader statistical movement. A similar project introduced in the same period in France, associated with Louis René Villermé, was condemned by the Academy of Sciences; but in England vital statistics was quickly recognized and incorporated into existing structures.

In contrasting the logics of scientific development in France and England, I am in no way suggesting that epistemological considerations were irrelevant in England or that political concerns did not inform "boundary work" in France. Instead, I wish to underline differences in the criteria of recognition and social differentiation. I argue that in France, sanctions were formulated in epistemological terms, while in England they were expressed in the language of science versus politics. And although in France intellectual control was extremely effective, in England it was relatively weak. The main differences in projects for statistics and in the criteria for recognition in France and England are summarized in later chapters.

CHAPTER FIVE

Vital Statistics as an Instrument of Social Reform

The willingness of statistical organizations to give a hearing to vital statistics can be explained both by the "fit" between Farr's political goals and those of their members and by the inability of gatekeepers to impose epistemological rules. Gaining consideration is not, however, identical with success. Public interest does not, on its own, explain how vital statistics came to be adopted as the authoritative form of statistical practice and a model to be emulated. Beyond its intellectual strength, the success of vital statistics depended on the support of two extra-scientific movements: the movement for civil registration and the medical branch of the public health movement. The political success of each of these movements contributed to the creation of an administrative infrastructure supportive of the new style of statistical reasoning. The General Registrar's Office produced and published the type of detailed, continuous information necessary for vital statistics, while the newly created public health administrative bureaus used vital statistics in the formulation of social policies, giving it an instrumental dimension absent in France.

Vital Statistics and the General Registrar's Office

Farr's "Takeover" of the General Registrar's Office

In 1833 the House of Commons appointed a select committee to investigate the existing system of parochial registration and suggest possible reforms. The meeting took place a few days after the Cambridge meeting of the BAAS. Adolphe Quetelet crossed the Channel to testify on the need to improve English population registers so as to bring them in line with those of other European states. At the same time, a variety of professional and scientific societies took up the issue. The Provincial Medical and Surgical Association agreed to send a letter to the select committee approving its work and calling for the inclusion of data on causes of death in the proposed legislation. Similarly, the medical sections of both Section F and the SSL lent their support, as did the *London Medical Gazette*. In 1834, at the height of this activity, over a thousand petitions were presented to the House of Commons and over seven hundred to the House of Lords.[1] The result was a far-reaching reform of civil registration.

The Civil Registration Act of 1836 called for the registration of births, deaths, and marriages. To assure this mandate, the act created a new bureaucracy including over two thousand registrars, a number of superintendent registrars, and a national statistical bureau, the General Registrar's Office.[2] The scope and efficiency of the statistical apparatus contrasted sharply with the situation in France, where overworked local officials with little commitment to the task and no training whatsoever were responsible for collecting and compiling statistical data. In England the GRO received individual level data; in France the Statistique Générale worked with summary statistics. And whereas in England statistical data were published weekly and available for public use almost immediately, in France private statisticians often waited for years to gain access to aggregate numbers. On the recommendation of Edwin Chadwick, William Farr was appointed compiler of statistics for the newly created central bureau.

The importance of the Civil Registration Act for the history of statistics lies not so much in the program that it specified as in the program that it made possible. Under Farr's influence, the bureau was transformed from a clearinghouse for information into an active branch of the public health movement and a base for the cultivation of vital statistics.[3] The work of the GRO centered on compiling and publishing annual, quarterly, and weekly reports. All three extended the strict mandate that Farr and his supervisor, the general registrar, had been granted.

Officially the purpose of the annual report of the register general was to inform Parliament on the state and movement of the population in the past year. Unofficially, Farr used the annual reports, and more specifically a letter to the general registrar which he attached to each one, to communicate his broader pedagogic and political message. His "letters" included lengthy discussions of selected public health problems along with explicit policy recommendations, discussions of the contribution of the GRO to current scientific debates (notably in the area of epidemiology), and lessons in statistical modes of reasoning (including the construction and interpretation of statistical rates and life tables). The reports were distributed to local public health officials and prominent politicians and reported in the popular press. They were extensively cited by both statisticians and writers for the public health movement and became required reading for a generation of statisticians.

With the quarterly and weekly reports Farr also went beyond his formal mandate. The Civil Registration Act called on local registrars to send quarterly summaries to the statistical bureau in London. This provision corresponded with the purely advisory function of the GRO. But while the authors of the act viewed the GRO as a sort of library or knowledge service for legislators, William Farr saw it as an active branch of the administration and of the movement for sanitary reform. To render his statistics effective, Farr demanded that local registrars send him weekly reports of all registration activity. Rather than keep this information for internal administrative use, Farr made it public. Every week, newspapers across the country published the mortality rates for each district. The effectiveness of this practice lay in the cultural meaning that Farr ascribed to the statistical tables.

As noted above, Farr believed that mortality statistics provided an index of the distribution of illness. He also believed that vital statistics could be used to measure the amount of preventable illness and thereby the effectiveness of local sanitary measures and of local government. One of the most impressive aspects of Farr's work was his ability to persuade local administrators, medical men, and the informed public of these connections. Local mortality statistics came to be accepted as measures of the relative salubrity of different regions and the relative effectiveness of local government.[4] This situation contrasts sharply with that in France, where the carriers of demography had no influence on the shape or content of official statistics before the late 1870s and where population statistics played a purely representative function.

Statistics as Hypothesis Testing

The last section of Farr's first letter to the registrar general of 1839 included a statistical inquiry into diseases of the towns and the open country. The study illustrates Farr's problem-oriented approach to statistical inquiry, as well as his "experimental" mode of statistical reasoning. It also demonstrates the combination of statistical pedagogy and policy propaganda, which characterized the majority of his texts. Farr's discussion projected an image of statistics as a process of hypothesis testing and methodical inquiry. In contrast with the majority of texts in social statistics, Farr's work highlighted the series of manipulations and choices involved in the quantitative study of social phenomena. This approach, which paralleled the work of Quetelet and Villermé in France and differed significantly from the descriptive approach associated with French administrative statistics, provided a model for Guillard and Bertillon in the development of French demography. A review of Farr's comparison of mortality in the town and country illustrates the main features of vital statistics as a distinct form of statistical reasoning.

Farr began his letter with a statistical demonstration that mortality in the cities was significantly higher than in the countryside. To establish this claim, he explained, it was necessary to find a (quantitative) way to distinguish between towns and the open country; in this particular study density provided a proxy for place. A mapping of the density of the different districts allowed Farr to select certain areas as representative of urban and rural conditions.[5] The next step in the inquiry was to calculate the mortality of each of these areas. Far from being a simple problem, the task involved statistical manipulation. To establish regional mortality the observer had first to establish the population living in each of the areas in question. This information was generally provided by the census, but the last census had been in 1831 and Farr's study was of mortality in 1837. It was thus necessary to project the population of 1837 on the basis of the censuses of 1811, 1821, and 1831. Rather than assume a constant rate of growth for all areas of the country, Farr calculated separately the rate of growth in cities and in the country. He then used these two rates to calculate the population of the two divisions.

Having calculated the population in 1837, Farr proceeded to calculate mortality rates for urban and rural areas in order to verify the popular conception that mortality was much higher in the cities than in the country. To do this, Farr established a number of comparisons between regions with similar absolute populations but very different densities (and thus different territorial size). He compared the general mortality in the London Metropolis with that in five southeastern counties and the general mortality of districts containing large cities with those containing only towns and villages. In both cases, the comparison confirmed popular perceptions: mortality in the more crowded districts was twice as high as in the less crowded ones.

General mortality rates could be due to a variety of causes, however. In the next step of his inquiry Farr focused his attention specifically on the effect of urban living on mortality. Data on the causes of death provided a means of separating out the different types of effect. Certain diseases, he explained, were known to flourish in insalubrious (urban) environments; they thus provided an index of the effect of urbanization. According to Farr, these diseases included what he termed the "epidemic class" and deaths directly related to occupation—his "pulmonary class."[6] Farr's analysis revealed that in those regions where the absolute mortality was low, death by epidemic diseases was less than death by pulmonary illness. In those areas where epidemic diseases equaled or surpassed mortality in the pulmonary class, absolute mortality was high.

Farr's explicit discussion of research design and quasi-experimental approach distinguished vital statistics from more descriptive forms of statistics. Vital statistics was presented as a process of epistemologically controlled inquiry, guided by hypotheses and directed at establishing or refuting theoretical arguments. Two technical tools, "standard mortality rates" and life tables, figured centrally in Farr's intellectual project.[7] A brief examination of the use which he made of them further illustrates how Farr's concept of social science as social reform infused all aspects of his work and, as a consequence, that of the GRO.

Vital Statistics as Instrumental Knowledge

The concept of a standard mortality rate, or the Healthy District Mortality Rate as it later came to be called, was directly linked to Farr's belief in the possibility of prevention and his environmentalist theory of disease. In comparing the general mortality rate of different districts, Farr identified a numerical value which distinguished between the top decile and the rest. In the 1840s one tenth of the registration districts had mortality rates of 17/1000 or less. Technically, the Healthy District Mortality Rate allowed Farr to quantify the amount of prevention possible. All those deaths above this standard level were ascribed to environmental factors and labeled "unnecessary." As Szreter points out, the genius of the concept lay in its fluidity; not only were the majority of districts by definition above the accepted level of mortality, but every local improvement raised the standard for the entire nation.[8] In 1848 legislators adopted Farr's measure as a means to arbitrate between local and central government. The Public Health Act of 1848 explicitly authorized national government officials to intervene in the local administration of public health in those areas where the mortality rate exceeded 23/1000. While this measure proved largely impractical, it did serve to consecrate Farr's use of statistics to measure the possibility of prevention.

Just as the adoption of "standard mortality rates" as an administrative tool underlines Farr's practical achievements at the GRO, his work on mortality tables underlines its serious scientific contributions. Of all the different statistical tools available in the first three quarters of the nineteenth century, mortality tables best embodied the new "scientific" style of statistical reasoning, at least with regard to population statistics. Proponents of the new style held them up as a crucial tool of inquiry, while opponents in both France and England rejected them on epistemological grounds (see below). In the course of his career, Farr constructed a number of local and national life tables. The first English Life Table was presented in the *Fifth Annual Report* to the Registrar General in 1843.[9] The report was written at a time when the mandate of the GRO was being reconsidered; the unveiling of this first life table should thus be read as a particularly strong argument in defense of Farr's scientific program for the administration.[10] Farr's use of the report to present his English Life Table illustrates a number of features of the GRO. First, it illustrates the technical prowess of the administrative apparatus that Farr had begun to develop. One of the main prerequisites for constructing a life table is the availability of detailed, reliable data on the size and the age structure of the population (generally provided by a census) and on deaths by age (which may be culled from civil registration data). In 1841 the GRO was put in charge of the decennial census. The result was that the same office was responsible for both the census and civil registration. A second consequence was that for the first time, the census benefited from an extensive network of trained technicians committed to the technical success of the operation.

Second, the report highlights Farr's views on the proper relation of mathematics and statistics. The letter of 1843 contains an extensive discussion of different ways to construct a life table.[11] In the body of the letter, Farr spelled out the steps involved in calculating the rates that made up a life table. He also provided a technical appendix in which he presented two alternative methods to extrapolate these numbers from the available data.[12] Cullen emphasizes that most readers of the report were unable to decipher the logarithms and complicated equations which figured in the appendix,[13] but their very inclusion attests to two important features of administrative statistics at the time. First, mathematical work was presented as an integral aspect of administrative statistics, and official publications were treated as a legitimate scientific texts. As Farr's report makes plain, there were no clear institutional boundaries between scientific statistics and either mathematics or administration.

A second significant feature of the *Fifth Annual Report* was the status that it ascribed to life tables as the tool par excellence of vital statistics and thus of social reform. Far from being an accepted notion, this proposal transformed the use and meaning of such tables. A life table uses an observed set of age-specific mortality rates to model the progress of a hypothetical population from birth to death. It usually begins with a population of 100,000 persons, all born in the same year, and calculates how many survive to the next year, until all of them eventually die. When Farr took over statistical production of the GRO, life tables had been used either to estimate the duration of life of a population or to fix assurance premiums. By contrast, Farr proposed that they be used for the comparative study of mortality. Unlike his French administrative counterparts, Farr saw the knowledge gained from life tables as more realistic than speculative:

> As it might be admitted, from the similarity of the human organization, that all classes of men would, *caeteris paribus*, live on an average the same number of years, it becomes important to ascertain whether this be the case; and if it be not, to what extent life is shortened in unfavorable circumstances. The Life Table answers this purpose; for it measures the duration of life, and is as indispensable in sanitary inquiries as the barometer or thermometer, and other instruments in physical research. Upon applying it in a number of well-selected cases the influence of any external cause or combination of causes can be analyzed; while without its aid and extended observation and calculation we are liable to be misled at every step by vague opinions, well-concocted stories, or interested statements, in estimating the relative duration of life; which can no more be accurately be made out by conjecture than the relative diameters of the sun, moon and planets of our system.[14]

For Farr, the scientific value of life tables lay not in the numbers themselves but in the use of the tables in comparative investigation and in their ability to test hypotheses concerning the causes of unnaturally high mortality. To illustrate his claims, Farr constructed three local life tables: one for the population of Surrey, one for the London Metropolis, and one for Liverpool. The choice of cities corresponded with his continued interest in the effect of urban living on health. Surrey, he explained, "presents a specimen of the rate at which life wastes in the country population. Liverpool is an example at the other extreme, of the effects of concentration in towns, without any adequate provision for removing the effluvia and for securing by art the degree of purity in the dwellings and atmosphere which is partially maintained by nature in an open cultivated country."[15] As Farr went on to remind his readers, before this study Liverpool was considered one of the healthiest cities in England. Farr's comparison of the three tables was designed both to document the relative health of the three cities and to indicate the type of information which only a life table could reveal.

This example illustrates how Farr incorporated life tables directly into his project for vital statistics. They provided both access to the laws of mortality which governed a particular local population — thus verifying the existence of such laws — and a tool for identifying causes. Finally, that Farr was able to construct not one table but a series of them demonstrates his success in developing an infrastructure and intellectual project which effectively married scientific inquiry and social reform.

Vital Statistics and the Medical Branch of the Public Health Movement

The appointment of William Farr as compiler of abstracts for the General Registrar's Office and the relative autonomy that the GRO enjoyed for the duration of his tenure were only some of the necessary conditions for the success of vital statistics. The success and authority of the project also depended on the cooperation of the medical profession. More specifically, it depended on the adoption of vital statistics as a resource by the medical branch of the public health movement.

In the 1830s the public health movement was divided between Edwin Chadwick's engineering approach and a medical branch under the leadership of Sir John Simon. Whereas Chadwick identified "filth" as the main cause of excessive mortality and focused on sanitation as the object of the public health movement (thus privileging the role of the engineer), Simon emphasized the role of different diseases in the elevation of mortality rates and called for disease-specific solutions (thus privileging medical men as the experts to be entrusted with the responsibility for public health). An important feature of this struggle was the support that each branch lent to different styles of statistical reasoning. The engineering branch supported a more descriptive model of statistics, while medical men supported the more abstract, quasi-experimental approach associated with vital statistics. The struggle came to a head in 1844, when representatives of each side fought out their political differences in the halls of the London Statistical Society in the guise of a debate over the choice of statistical measures. At the time, neither side had made any significant institutional progress as regards either legislative reform or administrative control. Chadwick had not yet been given control over the General Board of Health (which he directed from 1848 to 1854) and representatives of the medical branch were still far from their eventual institutional victory in 1858, when John Simon took over as medical officer under the Privy Council.

Statistical Debates: The Relation between
Technical and Political Considerations

In 1844 Edwin Chadwick submitted a methodological article to the Statistical Society of London. In his presentation Chadwick argued for the use of the mean age at death as the most accurate measure of longevity and thus of public health. Far from considering this claim peripheral to his sanitary program, Chadwick made the effectiveness of the measure a central component of his argument about the role of "filth disease" in mortality and the need to improve sewers and housing.[16] The argument was developed in his highly publicized and widely read *Sanitary Report* of 1842. In 1844 Chadwick developed the technical dimension of his argument in a lengthy paper for the Statistical Society of London in 1844, entitled "On the best Modes of Representing Accurately, by Statistical Returns, the Duration of Life, and the Pressure and Progress of the Causes of Mortality amongst Different Classes of the Community, and amongst the Populations of Different Districts and Countries."[17]

That Chadwick used the SSL to make his case reflects the authority of the institution (rather than either a provincial statistical society or Section F) in evaluating statistical claims. The article was not only accepted but chosen to be read at the next ordinary meeting of the Statistical Society of London. The paper proved highly controversial. Its presentation was the occasion of a drawn-out exchange between Chadwick and Mr. Neison, a highly respected actuary and one of the more active members of the society. Rather than continue the debate at the next meeting, the president asked Neison to prepare a written rejoinder to be included alongside Chadwick's paper in the next edition of the *Journal of the Statistical Society of London*.[18]

The debate between Chadwick and Neison centered on the choice between three different measures of mortality: a general mortality rate (deaths over population), age-specific mortality rates (deaths for a given age over the population of that age) as laid out in mortality tables, and average age of death. The first measure was clearly unacceptable, the second was favored by Neison and vital statisticians more generally, and the third was promoted by Chadwick in his *Sanitary Report*. For our purposes, the interest of the debate lies in the alternate criteria of assessment that the two sides invoked in their defense of their favored measure and in their critique of the alternatives.

Chadwick opened his paper with a criticism of the "usual" use of mortality tables. While he illustrated his remarks on the misleading nature of mortality tables with examples drawn from the Carlisle table of Dr. Milne, his remarks were necessarily also directed against Farr, who had recently published a similar set of tables. Like his French counterparts, Chadwick focused his case against mortality tables on the hypothetical, speculative character of the knowledge. According to Chadwick, two factors rendered mortality tables unreliable measures of the amount of death experienced by a locality. The first was their assumption of a stationary population. The second was the assumption that laws were sufficiently general to allow mortality tables developed on one local population to be used to evaluate the mortality of a second local population.[19]

Chadwick's argument rested on a distinction between actual observations (which were reliable) and hypotheses and mathematical calculations, which were not. As he explained: "deductions from tables, however correctly made from the experience of other towns must be, and are proved, by such experience as that hereafter cited, to be merely 'guess-work.' . . . For myself, I make it a general rule of precaution neither to receive nor adduce statistical returns as evidence without previous inquiry, wherever it is possible, into the particulars on which they are founded, or with which they are connected. I adduce them less as principal evidence, proving anything by themselves, than as proximate measures, or as indications of the extent of the operation of causes substantiated by distinct investigations."[20] In place of mortality tables, Chadwick called for using the average age of death as a measure of local mortality and thus public health. In defending this measure, Chadwick emphasized its intuitive quality. According to Hamlin, Chadwick also favored it because he believed that it could be used to distinguish between the effects of locality and those of class on mortality. At the time, the GRO did not collect information on the age of death, and Chadwick went to great lengths to personally collect data from local correspondents so as to make his case for establishing it as the preferred index.[21]

Neison's response to Chadwick's paper was by all accounts devastating. His article was a careful, systematic demonstration of the effects of age structure on the average age of death and its consequent inadequacy as a measure of public health. He also made a particularly strong argument for using life tables, thus buttressing the intellectual position which Farr had developed at the GRO.[22]

Neison began his attack with a battery of statistics demonstrating extensive differences in the age structure of different communities. The "next point of the question," he explained, "is to determine whether this circumstance will affect the *calculation of the average age* at which the respective members of an entire community die, and if so, to what extent."[23] Having established extensive variations in mortality at different ages, Neison went on to make two types of calculation. The first was a hypothetical mortality rate for a particular district of London, were it to have the age distribution of another district:

> Then in order to get quit of the objection arising from Bethnal-Green having a differently distributed population to that of St. George's Hanover-square, we shall suppose that the population of Bethnal-Green is actually transferred to St. George's Hanover-square, but influenced by exactly the same rate of mortality as that which prevails in St. George's Hanover-square, and which would be in no way altered as to its healthiness or unhealthiness, but have simply suffered a change in population, and in that respect placed under the same circumstances as the other. The result would be that the average age at death in St. George's Hanover-square, would be reduced from 1.23 years to 27.25, so that in fact the inhabitants of St. George's Hanover-square, instead of enjoying 5.42 years of life more than those of Bethnal-Green would only experience 1.45 years more than the other, as shown when the necessary correction is made for the distribution of the population.[24]

The second calculation was the hypothetical mortality rate of a district assumed to be subject to the age-specific mortality rates of another district. Neison's point was to show that two communities with the same "rate or intensity of mortality" could exhibit widely different average ages of death. Like Farr, Neison relied on a quasi-experimental manipulation of statistical indices to move beyond observation and common-sense intuitions to the underlying mortality of the community. The exercise was similar to that which Farr presented in the *Fifth Annual Report*. The main differences lay in the greater use which Neison made of this technique and the very careful pedagogic nature of his presentation.

The debate between Chadwick and Neison over the proper statistical measure highlights a number of features of the art of statistical reasoning in England relative to France. First, as noted earlier, there were no cognitive boundaries between political, administrative, and "scientific" or technical statistical issues. Second, by making a systematic attempt to manipulate statistics so as to distinguish between different causes, both men engaged in a quasi-experimental use of statistics that differed significantly from the more descriptive practice generally associated with administrative statistics. Finally, there was an alignment between competing programs for public health and alternative models for the practice of statistics.

The Success of "Medical Management"

The Public Health Acts of 1858 and 1859 marked the victory of the medical branch of public health over Chadwick's more centralized, engineering vision. Sir John Simon was appointed medical officer to the Privy Council in the late 1860s and granted extensive authority over public health, thereby institutionalizing what came to be called "state medicine" and providing vital statistics with a secure institutional base. Over the next twenty years state intervention in public health expanded significantly. The Sanitary Act of 1866 (following yet another outbreak of cholera) extended local government authority and central government supervision, while the Public Health Acts of 1872 and 1875 systematized, extended, and professionalized public health administration. One consequence of these developments proved particularly important for the subsequent history of vital statistics, namely the creation of a new occupation — that of medical officer of health — and the theory of state medicine with which it came to be associated. The project reached its culmination with the appointment of John Simon. Together with Farr, he incorporated vital statistics into the everyday workings of public health administration, thereby giving it an instrumental political function.

The idea of a medical officer of health was first suggested by Edwin Chadwick in 1842 in his *Report on the Sanitary Condition of the Labouring Population*. It was repeated in the *Report of the Royal Commission on the Health of Towns* (1844) and in the *Towns Improvement Clauses Act* (1847).[25] Like most public health measures, it was introduced at the local level and only later incorporated into national legislation. In 1846 the Town Council of Liverpool introduced a variety of sanitary regulations, including provisions for appointing a full-time medical officer of health. Liverpool's example was followed by the City of London, which appointed John Simon to the post in 1848. The Public Health Act of 1848 created the position of medical officer of health and provided for the voluntary appointment of officers; thirty-eight cities responded to the invitation.[26] The Metropolis Local Management Act of 1855 provided for the appointment of forty-eight medical officers for each district of the Metropolis. Finally, in 1856 the new officers founded the Metropolitan Association of Medical Officers of Health, thereby establishing themselves as a professional body. The goals of the organization were "mutual assistance and the advancement of sanitary science."[27]

The appointment of Simon as head of the newly created medical department in 1858 provided medical officers with a representative in the central government. In Simon's mind, the appointment authorized the development of a department which combined science (and more notably epidemiological research), administration, and policy agitation. His own description of the task, which he set for himself, captures what I earlier described as the nineteenth-century model of social science as social reform: "Confident that, if the knowledge were got, its utilization would speedily follow, we had to endeavor that all considerable phenomena of disease prevalence in the country should be seen and measured and understood with precision, — should be seen as exact quantities, be measured without fallacious admixture, be understood in respect of their causes and modes of origin; that true facts, and true interpretation of facts, with regard to the diseases of the country, and the causes producing them, should be supplied on a sufficiently large scale for political appreciation and uses."[28]

Like Farr and other administrators, Simon took advantage of his relatively vague mandate to implement his own personal program of "medical management." His "success" depended in large part on the cooperation of Farr at the GRO. Simon described their working relation thusly: "Punctually on every Monday morning, the GRO used to receive from the nine City Registrars their returns of the deaths which they had registered during the previous week . . . in their respective districts: and punctually every Monday afternoon, as soon as the GRO could spare those papers, they were placed at my disposal in a way which enabled me to complete my use of them during the evening; so that on the Tuesday mornings, when the weekly courts of the City Commission were held, I was ready with all needful particulars as to the deaths which had befallen the City population during the previous week, and with my scheme of such local inquiries as were to be made in consequence."[29] Thus Simon used the GRO's statistics in much the same manner as Farr. Rather than produce long-term, retrospective images, he transformed official vital statistics into a working tool of inquiry and propaganda aimed at medical research and the promotion of public health legislation.

The institutionalization of state medicine and the instrumental use of official statistics were complemented by a parallel set of intellectual and more specifically pedagogic developments which cemented the relation between vital statistics and state medicine. The first was the publication in 1856 of a book by Henry Wysdore Rumsey entitled *Essays in State Medicine* and the consequent engagement of the British Medical Association in the struggle between Simon and Farr. The text laid the theoretical or philosophical basis for an alternative approach to public health. Rumsey's essays emphasized the importance of medical expertise over that of sanitary engineers. There was also extensive criticism of the statistical methods which the General Board of Health had used in its sanitary campaigns.

A second, related event was the creation of the first lectureship on public health at St. Thomas's Hospital in 1856, and the appointment of Edward Headlam Greenhow to the post. According to Simon, in preparing his first courses Greenhow was immediately confronted with the inadequacy of official medical statistics, and thus the relatively weak empirical base of most public health propaganda. At Simon's urging and with Farr's cooperation, Greenhow drew on unpublished data from the GRO to prepare an extensive study of the distribution of mortality — by cause of death, by district, and by occupation. The study, which appeared in 1858 as a parliamentary report of the General Board of Health, concluded with a call for creating a central bureau responsible for the systematic study of the spread of disease.

Rumsey's and Greenhow's publications placed vital statistics at the center of a medical project for state medicine. As MacLeod argues, the boundaries between the medical department, the GRO, and the British Medical Association were never very clear.[30] Together with a number of other organizations, including the Epidemiological Society and the Medical Officers of Health Association, these entities constituted an investigative body and an effective lobby for promoting legislative reform.

Scientific Recognition

A number of symbolic acts attest to the ascension of vital statistics to the status of scientific exemplar. These include an expansion of the purview of Section F in 1856 from "Statistics" to "Statistics and Economic Science," the elimination from the motto of the Statistical Society of London in 1857 of the strictures against opinions, and the establishment of Theory and Method sections at the very successful meeting of the International Congress of Statistics in London in 1860. Finally, the inclusion of public health and vital statistics in the Social Science Association further strengthened its status as an authorized and respected form of knowledge practice.

Entry into the Statistical Society of London

The early years of the Statistical Society of London were marked by a crisis in leadership. While the general membership increased, attendance at the council meetings dropped dramatically, from thirty in the first year to twelve and thirteen in the second and third, finally leveling off at eight.[31] According to all accounts, the real problem facing the society was how to sustain a genuine intellectual program. The original prospectus specified the task of the society as the collection of "fresh statistical information" for use by the government.[32] In the early years of the society, this mandate translated into an encyclopedic program of data collection. As the authors of the original prospectus explained: "Willing agents of inquiry exist in abundance quite ready to aid in collecting materials, but few of these agents take a very wide view of all these objects of statistical inquiry and indeed few have very distinct notions about the precise information the Society may wish to collect even as to any one object. To sketch therefore distinctly by means of interrogatories, carefully and succinctly drawn, the whole outline which it is wished to fill up, is the only way to secure to the Society the full benefits to be expected from their zeal."[33] A large part of the Council's time was thus spent designing interrogatories for use by these local agents. Forms were sent to a variety of public authorities, including the police, hospitals, poor-law administrators, school boards, factory commissioners, insurance societies, landlords, newspaper editors, magistrates, and prison governors.[34] Unfortunately, few volunteers were forthcoming. Similarly, few private inquiries produced papers that the council deemed of scientific quality. The gravity of the situation can be measured by the decision of the council in 1835 not to write an annual report for the BAAS.[35]

Farr entered the SSL along with a number of new members who were recruited to strengthen the faltering society. In contrast with the existing leadership, this new cohort was younger, and many of the new members held professional positions that directly involved them in statistics in one way or another. While all were committed Whigs and social reformers, they lacked the political positions and influence of the founding members.[36] In terms of statistics, their presence was associated with the introduction of a new type of research. In contrast to local studies aimed at documenting the condition of the working classes, the new group undertook secondary analyses of official and institutional data, combining empirical work with theoretical and methodological reflection.[37] A report from the Committee of Vital Statistics of Large Towns in Scotland in 1843 demonstrates the diffusion of Farr's original project among members of the Statistical Society.

The report opened with a statement of purpose and an insistence on the policy relevance of the findings. The aims of the committee were "to identify certain physical laws in vital statistics" and to use that knowledge to guide the "legislator and philanthropist in encountering the physical evils resulting from moral causes."[38] Similarly, vital statistics was "to trace the immediate causes of changes which affect the welfare of the people, with a view to suggest such improvements as may arrest in its progress a retrograde movement in the condition of the inhabitants of large towns."[39] As these remarks indicate, by 1843 statisticians clearly associated vital statistics with the identification of laws, the search for causes, and the task of policy formulation.

The "Takeover" of the Statistical Society of London

The "takeover" of the Statistical Society of London by proponents of vital statistics was a gradual process. The first step was the creation of a journal and the assumption of control over the editorial committee. From the very beginning, proponents of vital statistics were among the loudest critics of the society's initial stricture against expressing opinions. The position was clearly stated in 1839 in the sixth annual report of the society: "It was not to perfect the mere art of "tabulating" that [the Society] was embodied: — it was not to make us hewers and drawers to those engaged on any edifice of physical science; — but it was that we should ourselves be the architects of a science or of sciences, the perfecters of some definite branch or branches of knowledge, which should do honour to ourselves and to our country, and at the same time to the distinguished men who summoned us to the labour"[40] By the early 1850s official documents reflected vital statisticians' view that statistics could not be limited to mere data collection. While not all members agreed on the place of theory and hypothesis in statistics, all agreed that official numbers had to be accompanied by interpretation and analysis. The point is particularly striking when compared with the French position that numbers should be allowed to speak for themselves.

The English position was clearly expressed at the Seventeenth Annual Meeting of the Statistical Society of London. In his opening speech Lord Harrowby noted that while statistics was an inductive science, numbers did not speak for themselves. Instead tables had to be juxtaposed with knowledge of other related facts.[41] In contrast with Moreau de Jonnès, Lord Harrowby stressed the need to include extensive commentary alongside statistical tables, so as to prevent readers from drawing "false conclusions." And whereas Moreau de Jonnès viewed tables as the end product of statistical analysis, Lord Harrowby insisted that they constituted a tool of inquiry. In the discussion that followed, other members took up the same theme, associating it directly with the debate over the place of opinions. Lord Overstone, one of the original supporters of the restriction against opinions, reversed his position and noted the danger "of accumulating facts idly and unprofitably." Turning to Lord Harrowby, he concluded: "The justice of the observations you have made has been felt by most of our Members, that figures are not necessarily statistics, that their value depends upon the manner in which they are got together, and that it is quite necessary for the deduction of a legitimate argument from them, that all the relations of their origin should be known."[42]

These quotes attest to the influence of Guy's and Neison's campaign to introduce a more experimental form of statistical practice. They also reflect the growing cost of survey studies and the improved quality of official data. Between 1843 and 1853 the membership of the society fell from 428 fellows to 371. Membership fees were the only source of income for the society, which was increasingly in debt. One of the many economies introduced was the gradual abandonment of all inquiries using paid agents.[43] At the same time, private contributions for special studies were increasingly rare. In 1849 the Twelfth Annual Report noted that only one committee had received funds for local investigations.[44] Thus by the 1850s local survey studies had largely been abandoned for detailed analyses of institutional and official statistics.

One of the markers of the abandonment of the earlier descriptive, encyclopedic model for statistics was the decision of Section F in 1856 to broaden its rubric from statistics to "Statistics and Economic Science." A second indication of this shift can be found in the vote to omit the motto "*aliis exterendum*" from the symbol on the cover of the Journal.[45] According to the official history, William Guy and the economist William Newmarch were largely responsible for proposing this change. Both were proponents of a more "scientific," "experimental" approach to statistics. Institutionally, the success of the new approach was marked by the society's acquisition of a new building in 1845 and by a subsequent invitation to the Institute of Actuaries to rent a number of rooms for itself, thus consolidating the society's link with its more mathematically oriented colleagues. In 1869 the International Congress of Statistics lent further support to the project to integrate statistics, now defined as something more than data collection — be it theory or hypothesis testing or science — and administration.

Vital Statistics and the International Congress of Statistics

In 1860 the Statistical Society hosted the fourth meeting of the International Congress of Statistics. The idea for the congress was first put forth by Adolphe Quetelet in 1851. As noted earlier, Quetelet had been instrumental in founding both Section F and the Statistical Society of London; he was also one of the main authors of the idea that social life was subject to laws which could be identified by the use of statistics.[46] For the first decade of its existence, however, the International Congress of Statistics focused almost exclusively on standardizing official statistics. It was only in 1860 that participants turned their attention to alternative forms of statistical analysis.

The same themes that had been discussed by the Statistical Society of London in the 1840s and 1850s were raised at the London meeting of the congress in 1860. These included the place of politically sensitive issues in the work of statistics, the place of mathematical analysis (and more specifically probability theory) in statistics, and the status of statistics as a science. An examination of these debates documents a clear discursive distinction between two forms of statistics, one descriptive and politically neutral, the other more "mathematical," "scientific," and explicitly "political." It also points to the introduction of a new administrative variant of the scientific approach.

While the question of whether statistics was a science was raised at the meeting of 1860, it was not discussed until 1869, when it became the focus for the creation of a new section devoted to the "Theory and Methodology of Statistics." From the very start the issue was framed in terms of a choice between two distinct projects for statistics: a descriptive or historical approach and a mathematical or "philosophic study of numbers." This formulation indicates that statisticians were aware of the tension between the two models described above. They also recognized the similarities between vital statistics and demography. In his list of authors associated with the "philosophic study of numbers," Prof. Vissering grouped together Quetelet, Villermé, Farr, and Guillard as representatives of the mathematical form.

The discussion began with a proposal that the congress should formally distinguish between "historic" statistics (or what I have also referred to as descriptive or administrative statistics) and "scientific" statistics.[47] Quetelet objected vehemently: "There would be the greatest danger in thus cutting statistics in two and in saying to the bureaus, limit yourselves to making tables. One can not make tables without understanding them, and in order to understand them, one must know the science. The greatest wrong which is made towards statistics [arises because] there is not enough science in the bureaus which are devoted to it."[48] In the course of the discussion a number of leading statisticians supported Quetelet's position, including Ernst Engel, the head of the Royal Prussian Statistical Bureau, and William Farr.[49]

In developing his point Engel took the discussion one step further. Not only were scientific considerations essential for good administrative work but, in his opinion, administrative statistics should be adapted to further the goals of science.[50] Farr, for his part, emphasized the intimate relation between "the observation of facts and mathematical deductions."[51]

On a more practical level, this insistence on the unity of statistical approaches led to a number of suggestions concerning the proposed central statistical commissions. The president, Mr. Von Baumhauer, insisted that statistical bureaus should be staffed with men who were knowledgeable in science and who continually had in mind the types of information that scientists might ask of them. Alfred Legoyt, the head of the SGF, suggested that the proposed central councils should include both legislators and men of science, thus freeing them from the tutelage of immediate administrative demands.[52]

Finally, the commitment to introduce scientific considerations into the work of administrative bureaus expressed itself in a series of concrete recommendations for the collection of official data. These included, among others, a recommendation that the birth register should include the age of both parents, their profession, and the length of their marriage. This information, Mr. Kiaer explained, would allow statisticians to study a number of as yet undocumented influences on fertility, including class differentials, early or late marriage, and the age differential between the parents. Another topic discussed was the need to introduce standard conventions for recording stillbirths.

Turning to more technical issues, the section called on administrators to publish not only averages but extreme (or outlying) values as well. The meeting concluded with a lengthy discussion on the construction of mortality tables. As we have seen, until this point only "scientific" forms of statistics, such as social physics, demography, and vital statistics, used mortality tables. Gatekeepers of more descriptive forms dismissed them as speculative, uncertain, and consequently "not statistics." In 1869 the Section on Theory and the Application of Data overturned this stricture. This move was consistent with the committee's broader embrace of a "scientific" approach to administrative statistics. Discussions focused on the administrative requirements for scientific statistics, as evidenced in the attention paid to the design of registration and census forms with categories relevant for pressing "scientific" concerns, the appointment of "scientific" advisors, and the training of lower-level administrators in the principles of statistical "science." By the late 1860s vital statistics and the associated scientific version of administrative statistics would seem to have been well ensconced in the hierarchy of sciences, at least in England. The coming decade, however, witnessed new challenges to the authority of vital statistics on both political and scientific grounds.

Institutional Expansion and Divergent Visions

Statistics and the Social Science Association

The Statistical Society of London was one of several organizations that were instrumental in forming the National Association for the Promotion of the Social Sciences, or Social Science Association (SSA) in 1858. The stated aim of the new organization was to facilitate the development of knowledge concerning pressing social questions and to combine the efforts of the many reform organizations and groups already at work. In contrast with earlier philanthropic organizations, the SSA focused explicitly on legislative reform. Public health legislation was one of its primary areas of activity, and vital statistics both benefited and suffered from its success. On the one hand, the SSA actively contributed to the legislative success of the campaign for administrative reform, a campaign which included measures to improve official statistics. On the other hand, the linkage of social science with professional activity directly challenged the authority of "amateur" social statisticians, most notably vital statisticians such as Guy and Farr.

Socially, the Social Science Association brought together leading public figures, including politicians, publicists, and intellectuals. The 139 members of the first General Committee included nineteen peers or sons of peers, twenty-seven Members of Parliament, ten fellows of the Royal Society, and several members of the leading statistical and scientific societies.[53] Annual meetings were important "civic" occasions attended by thousands of local participants and extensively reported in the national press. Outside the annual meetings, the departments functioned largely as special lobbies organized for promoting specific legislative proposals. The organization also played an important role in promoting and professionalizing social reform.[54]

The initial mandate of the SSA explicitly called for identifying statistical laws as a condition of social reform. From the perspective of vital statistics, these assertions were both reassuring and disturbing. On the one hand, they suggested that statisticians and social scientists were engaged in a common search for knowledge of the laws which guided social life and a desire to translate that knowledge into practical measures. On the other hand, the emphasis on knowledge gleaned from practical experience and the insistence on immediate action stood at odds with statisticians' concern for carefully constructed statistical inquiries. Whereas social statisticians rejected the value of "intuitions" and individual "experience" as sources of scientific knowledge, the members of the SSA seemed to be less careful about the distinction between opinion and "truth." Nor were they certain to ascribe to statistics a privileged place in the pursuit of social science.

The reactions of social statisticians to the new society indicate their misgivings. In 1865 William Guy published a paper asserting the Statistical Society's model of statistics as policy-relevant science. In closing, he explicitly opposed his claims to those of the Social Science Association: "The fact that a Society calling itself the '*Social Science Association*,' has within a few years come into existence, does not in any way invalidate our claim to have first set foot, in fact, though not in express terms, a social science; nor, if we were to lay claim on our own behalf, to the exclusive cultivation of that science, should we do any injustice to the younger society. For it is obvious that the work done by the Social Science Association, excellent as it is, is not in the nature of science. It may be described, without injustice, as a Social Reform Association, encouraging the discussion of alleged social evils, inviting publicity, and taking practical steps, by means of memorials, petitions, and deputations to men in authority, to promote legal and social reforms."[55]

Guy's depiction of the Social Science Association as a reform society committed to political lobbying is wholly consistent with the public image that the association projected and with what is known about its activities. In presenting this image, he had two aims. First, he hoped to contest the association's exclusive claim to the label "social science," thereby defending the definition of statistics as the quantitative study of all aspects of social and moral life. Second, he hoped to persuade social reformers of the necessity of statistical inquiry for their practice, thereby defending vital statisticians' insistence that social policy depended on the specifically statistical search for laws and causes. As he went on to explain: "To the members of that Association, and to all other men, we offer the services of a social and political science, slowly and painfully constructed on the basis of facts laboriously brought together, but upon the collection, arrangement, tabulation and analysis of which we bring constantly to bear the pure bright light of scientific method. We do not allege that there is no other way to social reform and improvement but this toilsome path of ours; . . . but we also know that in almost all disputed questions, our aid is invoked, because we are believed to collect, arrange and classify our facts in the true spirit of science, calmly and impartially, having as our primary object the discovery of truth by facts, and not the redress of grievances."[56]

Thus one of the effects of the creation of the Social Science Association was to put social statisticians on the defensive concerning their claims that science was essential for social reform. While this challenge was met by a turn to disciplinary activity, it also opened the way for the introduction of an alternative model for statistics. In this new version, social science was denuded of its scientific pretensions and statistics was presented as an auxiliary science or tool in the service of this new type of practice. Paradoxically, the introduction of this new axis of differentiation — between statistics as a science versus statistics as a method or auxiliary science — was reinforced by a second challenge to the method of vital statistics from a totally different institution, the Statistical Section of the British Association for the Advancement of Sciences.

Statistics, Economic Science, and Section F

The change in the mandate of Section F from statistics to "statistics and economic science" was supposed to resolve questions about the scope of statistics in favor of a broad definition that included policy formation. While the move heralded a new phase in the history of social statistics, it did not mark an end to the controversy that had surrounded the section from its creation in 1833. Instead, the change was the occasion for a new series of attacks on the place of Section F in the British Association for the Advancement of Science. Again, the issue concerned the status of statistics as a science and the proper relation between science and politics. The annual inaugural addresses from the Section F public meetings document the extent to which the attack on Section F was experienced as a challenge to a particular model of statistics associated with vital statistics, and the range of responses evoked.

The first evidence of a problem can be found in 1860 in the address by the economist Nassau W. Senior. Senior opened his speech with a comment on the "unscientific character" of the papers delivered at the meetings of Section F since the inclusion of economic science. The criticism provided Senior with an occasion to reflect on the difference between a "science" and an "art": "I need scarcely remind you that a Science is a statement of existing facts, an Art a statement of the means by which future facts may be brought about or influenced. A science deals in premises, an art in conclusions. A science aims only at supplying materials for the memory and the judgment. It does not presuppose any purpose beyond the acquisition of knowledge.

An art is intended to influence the will; it presupposes some object to be attained, and it points out the easiest, the safest, or the most effectual conduct for that purpose."[57] Senior used this definition to argue that whereas "the science of political economy" was an art, statistics was a science. The nonscientific character of Section F was thus seen as a violation of the epistemological rules of what counted as statistics.

In contrast to Senior, a number of speakers presented statistics as a method in the service of economic science. In the same year J. J. Fox delivered a paper in which he argued that social economy and political economy were sciences because they had a substantive object (the relation between man and man in the first case, man as citizen in the second), while statistics did not. Statistics, however, provided a valuable method "for the prosecution of other sciences."[58] The editor of the *Journal of the Statistical Society*, William Newmarch, attributed the most recent advances in economic science to statistics and its combination of observation and experiment.[59] Like the other speakers, Newmarch separated statistics from the identification of laws, thus depriving it of its "scientific" status. But whereas the others did so by assigning the interpretation of data, and thus the identification of laws, to other true "sciences" (most notably economic science and social science), Newmarch challenged the existence of Queteletian "laws." In what can be read as a reaction to the determinist version of statistical laws presented by Buckle in 1857, Newmarch argued: "We have heard a great deal lately of these so-called 'statistical laws.' We have heard a great deal of the Necessarian conclusions which are said to flow inevitably from the evidence of a certain class of statistical results, or 'laws.' It appears to me, with all deference, that the term 'law' as applied to any statistical result whatever, is a misapplication of the term. The utmost that Statistics can do is to express numerically the *average* result of any given series of observations of occurrences taking place under particular conditions among human beings."[60] According to Newmarch, the nature of human and social life rendered impossible the identification of predictive laws analogous to those of astronomy or dynamics.

This restriction on the power of statistical knowledge was complemented by a clear formulation of the actual power of statistics. According to Newmarch, the contribution of statistics lay in the identification of "Ultimate Statistical Units," or statistical measures of what social reformers could realistically expect to achieve. For Newmarch, Farr's "healthy district mortality rate" was such a unit, in that it provided a measure of the mortality to be expected in "a community of human beings inhabiting a country like our own and enjoying reasonable comfort." This concept gave substance to Newmarch's argument that statistics was essential for social reform, within the limits of his notion of statistics as a method.

Institutional Conditions and Styles of Reasoning: A Preliminary Discussion

Vital statistics succeeded in large part thanks to its inclusion in the agendas of the General Registrar's Office, the medical branch of the public health movement, and public health officials. This process was accompanied by a particular path of intellectual development. Under the direction of Farr and Neison vital statistics came to be associated with a problem-oriented approach and a hypothetical, quasi-experimental use of numbers. In contrast to earlier descriptive forms of statistics, proponents of vital statistics highlighted the fabricated, constructed character of statistical indices. This focus was evident in their systematic discussions of the relation between different measures of the same phenomenon (mortality) and in their open manipulation of numbers to create new statistical objects, such as rural mortality, which existed independently of a specific observed population. It was equally evident in their elevation of mortality tables to the tool par excellence of vital statistics and the use of these tables as a comparative tool.

A comparison between France and England highlights the consequences of incorporating vital statistics into national government bureaus. In England the GRO explicitly set out to produce immediately available data of high quality to private statisticians; it regularly produced mortality tables for a variety of populations and purposes. But in France such information was lacking. The SGF did not collect information on the causes of death, nor did it publish weekly or even monthly statistics on population movement by locality. Moreau de Jonnès went so far as to dismiss such tables as "fictions." The first national French mortality table was not produced until 1876, by Bertillon at the request of Quetelet.

Another striking feature of the English use of vital statistics is the way the quality of data, the style of statistical reasoning, and the political function of administrative population statistics were related. The collection of relatively reliable detailed data on births, deaths, and causes of death, and the problem-oriented, quasi-experimental, hypothesis-driven type of inquiry associated with vital statistics, were directly linked to the largely instrumental political function of vital statistics. Vital statistics developed as a tool to make the case for a medically driven program of public health, in opposition to an engineering version. Concrete statistical indices were used to arbitrate between local and central government intervention on matters of public health. This direct articulation between specific styles of statistical reasoning and specific policy agendas gave to vital statistics the backing necessary to provide for its institutionalization in official statistical bureaus.

This situation contrasts sharply with the largely representative political function of population statistics in France. As is clear from the debates over infant mortality and depopulation, in France population statistics were used to document the state of the nation. Explanations for trends were sought outside the numbers in theories of civilizational decline and patriarchal authority. This political function in turn fit with a descriptive style of statistical reasoning and a concern for the realism of statistical entities. Thus whereas English vital statisticians accepted discussions about the hypothetical, fabricated character of mortality tables as inherent features of the knowledge, French administrative statisticians saw these arguments as grounds to dismiss their scientific value altogether.

As for the scientific status of vital statistics, the different statements examined above attest both to the intellectual success of the style of reasoning embraced by Farr, Neison, and Guy and to the introduction of new fault lines. All the arguments post-1860 accepted the basic premise that a statistical social science involves a complex process of observation, experiment, analysis, and reform. Their differences concerned the unity of the project and the claims of statisticians to it. Each of the criticisms cited above challenged the jurisdiction of statistics over certain elements of vital statistics. Fox and Newmarch deprived it of a role in identifying laws and thus of its status as a science, Danson and Fox separated it from its policy component, and Fox went so far as to deny to statisticians the task of identifying causes.

Challenge is not, however, equivalent to dethronement. For every speech that called the status of statistics into question, there was another that asserted the authority of the dominant scientific administrative style associated with vital statistics. As noted above, the clearest defense of statistics was Guy's article of 1865 entitled "On the Original and Acquired Meaning of the Term 'Statistics,' and on the Proper Functions of a Statistical Society: also on the Question Whether There Be a Science of Statistics; and, if So, What Are Its Nature and Objects, and What Is Its Relation to Political Economy and 'Social Science.'" The title clearly lays out the parameters of the new debate, while its length attests to the importance which Guy attached to the subject.

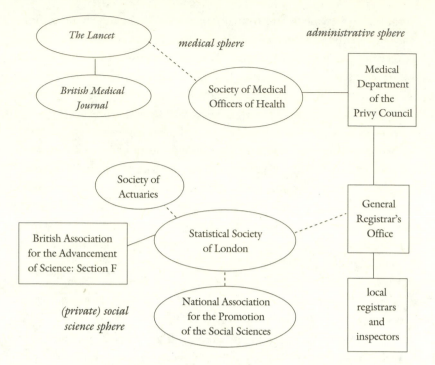

Figure 3. The World of Social Statisticians, England, 1858–1871: Social and Epistemological Spheres as Viewed from the Perspective of Farr's Professional Trajectory

As was to be expected, the text was a defense of the "scientific" "experimental" project. Like Quetelet and Bertillon, Guy defined statistics as the numerical study of all aspects of human life.

It would seem that the success of the instrumental (political and administrative) dimension of Farr's original project was paralleled by a challenge to its scientific claims. On the one hand, the institutionalization of the medical approach to public health in the Medical Department of the Privy Council, the GRO, and a myriad of professional and scientific societies, including the Social Science Association, contributed to the improvement of official statistics and the translation of statistical knowledge into a practical instrument of social reform. On the other hand, the growing importance of the social sciences as a practice elicited competing claims. The creation of the Social Science Association and the transformation of Section F signal the beginnings of a process which was to take much greater force in the following decades.

With regard to the problem of discipline formation, this development was of interest because it was the occasion for expressing disciplinary claims. As with French demography in the early 1850s and again in the 1870s, discipline formation would seem to have been associated with a bid to alter (or preserve) the place of a particular intellectual project vis-à-vis others. In France, disciplinary activity was a response to the definitive exclusion of the scientific, experimental project from élite intellectual institutions. In England, it came in response to a breakdown of the institutional infrastructure that had supported the initial establishment and recognition of the project, thus threatening the project's intellectual claims. In both cases discipline formation emerged in response to exclusion on explicitly epistemological grounds. It was only when critics of vital statistics challenged the use of numbers to identify laws that its proponents engaged in explicit disciplinary activity. Similarly, in France it was only when "demographers" were told that their technical operations could not, by definition, produce knowledge worthy of the label of statistics that they called for recognizing their project as a separate science.

PART III

The Institutionalization

of Demography in France:

How to "Secure" a Discipline

in Nineteenth-Century France

CHAPTER SIX

Discipline Formation at Last

U ntil the late 1870s social statisticians in France and England pursued their projects under a relatively stable set of institutional arrangements. In England, individual statisticians moved fairly easily between a variety of different organizations with different models of statistical practice. Statistical projects were evaluated — and thus differentiated — according to how they combined scientific and political (reform-oriented and instrumental) considerations. Relevant organizations included private statistical and scientific societies, national administrative bureaus, and organized movements for social and professional reform. The authority of vital statistics was linked to that of social science, which during this period played a central role in politics and policy formulation. In France, by contrast, the carriers of demography confronted a world divided between élite, quasi-official scientific institutions and Republican, positivist scientific societies. As we saw in part I, the boundaries between these spheres were regulated by relatively powerful gatekeepers with disciplinary maps specifying the nature of statistical knowledge and its relations to other knowledge categories or disciplines. Under the Second Empire, positivist science was excluded from power.

In the late 1870s these multilayered structures began to dissolve. In both France and England, mid-nineteenth-century forms of social science were challenged, and ultimately replaced, by new, more professional disciplinary forms. By 1885 a new order had been established. Both demography and vital statistics lost out to new contenders. The parallel celebrations of the twenty-fifth anniversary of the Société Statistique de Paris and the fiftieth anniversary of the Statistical Society of London provide a preliminary indication of the new institutional and intellectual scene. The French celebration privileged graphical and geometric methods, while the English heralded the advent of mathematical statistics. Institutionally the French event marked the reentry of mathematically trained engineers and scientific élites into the realm of social statistics (as compared to mathematics). In England, the ascension of mathematical statistics paralleled the professionalization of science, politics, and social reform in a way that marginalized amateur forms. In both countries, these developments occurred in the context of the expansion, reform, and professionalization of the civil service, the incorporation of the social sciences into higher education, and the incorporation of science into nationalist discourse.

The remainder of this book traces the emergence of these new projects for social statistics, their organizational base, and the challenges that they posed to the authority of demography and vital statistics. The discussion of French developments begins by examining the short-lived success of demography as a specialized activity. This chapter explores how it was that demography came to be institutionalized in formal organizations between 1876 and 1878 and why these specialized institutions failed to provide the type of continuity that the sociological literature on discipline formation would lead one to expect. Chapter 7 examines the incorporation of demography into élite political and administrative structures. Paradoxically, the success of the intellectual project was paralleled by the dissolution of demography as a distinct disciplinary entity, although the category persisted as a cultural resource open to appropriation and reformulation by a variety of contenders.

In England the authority of vital statistics was challenged by a more general "crisis" of political economy in the late 1870s and by alternative scientific and political projects in the early 1880s. Chapter 8 examines the attacks on statistics from historical economics and mathematical economics. Chapter 9 asks: How did mathematical statistics come to supplant vital statistics as the dominant form of practice? This question provides an opportunity to explore the introduction of more familiar, academic forms of scientific disciplines and the transformation of social statistics from a science to a method.

Before proceeding, it would seem important to make a few remarks concerning a "coincidence" in periodization. In developing these two stories, I did not set out to establish a perfect chronology whereby demography and vital statistics — or rather the intellectual and social structures supporting them — emerged, developed, and dissolved in exactly the same years. Indeed, the story of vital statistics as a distinct disciplinary category begins in the 1830s, whereas the story of demography coincides with the creation of the Second Empire in 1851. In the late 1870s, however, the institutional context for the pursuit of social statistics changed radically in both countries. A number of separate elements would seem to have contributed to this parallelism. These include changes in the relation of science and the state, generational effects, and a parallel transformation in the status and substance of political economy as a science and the place of statistics therein. The analysis that follows pays special attention to the role of each of these factors in the development of social statistics.

Problems of Social Classification

The institutionalization of demography was marked by three separate events. In 1876 Paul Broca and his colleagues founded the École d'Anthropologie as part of the Paris Faculty of Medicine, and Louis Adolphe Bertillon was given a chair of demography and medical geography. The development was undoubtedly linked to a more general reform of the medical faculty that favored the new scientific approach to medicine championed by the Paris medical élite.[1] In the following year a young scholar, Arthur Chervin, joined forces with Bertillon to create a new journal, *Les annales internationales de démographie*. Finally, in 1878 Louis Adolphe Bertillon and Émile Levasseur opened the first session of the International Congress of Demography. While Bertillon's course at the School of Anthropology involved a public presentation of his earlier project, the other two events marked the transformation of demography into a collective project and a bid to establish it as a policy science. The discussion that follows uses the congress and the journal to explore both the new collective identity of demography and the reformulations effected by these acts of institutionalization.

Analyzing these events raises questions concerning historical sources and appropriate systems of classification. Both the *Annales internationales de démographie* and the official transactions of the International Congress of Demography are prefaced by a list of participants along with some form of identification, generally an organizational or professional affiliation. What do these lists tell us about the event in question? Because the lists include the names of persons in some way associated with demography, they provide precious information concerning the social base of demography at the time or, more precisely, of people open to considering its claims. At the same time, the lists were part of the public presentation of the new science. Each name and affiliation potentially contributed to the representation that readers made of the new discipline. Since most of the people included on the lists had multiple associations, the way they were identified must also be read as a strategic attempt to project a certain image.

One approach to the data at hand would be to conduct a prosopographical study.[2] This method, however, assumes that the list of names provided by these events constituted a "scientific community," thus justifying the development of a collective profile. While this assumption may be valid for an ongoing scientific society, which held regular meetings over an extended period, it is far more dubious for a journal which only lasted seven years, much more for a one-time congress held on the occasion of a Universal Exposition. A second possibility would be to classify participants according to the way they are identified in the official congressional transactions and international journal. This approach produces a list of fourteen terms such as professor, engineer, lawyer, head of statistical bureau, etc. While this literal representation has the advantage of respecting the original categories, it is misleading on both empirical and theoretical grounds. By combining people with radically different institutional affiliations—in a period when terms such as "professor" and "lawyer" were not exclusive roles but rather descriptions of activities—it suggests a type of social proximity and inter-action which is not sustained by the data. To give but one example, pro-fessors at the Collège de France were not part of the same social group as professors at the School of Anthropology. Second, the absence of a clear articulation between this classificatory schema and the questions posed in this book and (and their accompanying theoretical framework) renders the comparisons provided by this classification difficult, if not impossible, to interpret.

A third solution, adopted here, builds on the historical analysis devel-oped thus far. In part I of this book, I identified three models for the practice of statistics: a descriptive model associated with the Prix Montyon, a second descriptive project promoted by the liberal economists, and a scientific administrative project, which was initially associated with public hygiene and moral statistics and later came to be associated with the term "demography." Between 1833 (when the SGF was formed) and 1871 (the year marking the creation of the Third Republic), these distinct approaches were adopted and promoted by different formal organizations. The first was upheld by academicians at the Academy of Science. The second was institutionalized and promoted by persons moving between the Academy of Moral and Political Sciences, the SGF, liberal economic forums of various sorts, and the Société Statistique de Paris. Finally, the more abstract, explan-atory use of statistics was initially associated with public hygiene organiza-tions and municipal administrative bureaus.[3] Under the Second Empire it was supported by positivist, Republican social science societies, most nota-bly the Société d'Anthropologie and Émile Littré's *La philosophie positive*.

This chapter explores the persistence of this tripartite division after the fall of the Second Empire and the creation of the Third Republic in 1871. If the analysis in part 1 is correct, the institutionalization of demography in 1877 and 1878 can be read as a successful attempt to overcome, or at least defy, the intellectual and organizational exclusion to which demography had been subject. But what kind of victory was it? Should the recognition of demography be understood as the entry of yet another discipline into the panoply of existing categories, or did it reflect and contribute to a broader transformation in the field? And if so, which field? The logical possibilities include statistics, social science, administrative science, and some combination of the three. In examining the institutionalization of demography, I want to establish which particular features of earlier intellectual and organizational arrangements were challenged. Which boundaries persisted and which were reworked? And how was demography transformed in the process?

The different lists of subscribers, members, and participants in the founding events of demography provide an occasion to explore continuities and changes in the organizational (rather than cognitive) clusters established between 1833 and 1871. To the extent that the tripartite structure persisted, participants at demographic events should have continued to be associated with formerly positivist Republican organizations and municipal administrative bureaus. To the extent that these structures were dissolved, specifically demographic events should have (also) included members of the national administration, scientific academies, and political economic organizations.

These questions concerning the organization of the field provide a solution to the problem of how to classify participants. Instead of focusing on specific occupations, the analysis that follows classifies individuals according to their membership in one of three institutional sectors: a liberal-administrative sector, a medical-municipal sector, and a third, residual sector. The first corresponds to the traditional institutional bases of demography, including municipal bureaus, positivist scientific societies, and public hygiene organizations, all of which were disproportionately peopled by medical men. The second sector is the realm of élite science. It includes quasi-official scientific academies, national-level administrative bureaus, and liberal economic organizations. In those cases where a mention is ambiguous (as with new organizations or professions such as engineers or lawyers which are not explicitly attached to the "High Administration"), I have included them in the residual category so as not to aggravate sectoral influence. In selecting these categories I wish to explore their relevance for the organization of social statistics after the establishment of the Third Republic and the presumed removal of explicitly political barriers to those forms of science formerly identified as "Republican."

The First Specialized Journal

The Public Image

In appearance the *Annales internationales de démographie* was an imposing publication. Each volume contained between five and six hundred pages, including articles which varied in length from ten to sixty or seventy pages and a large bibliographic section.[4] Works reviewed included official statistical publications and scholarly texts. The journal also provided extensive reports of recent conferences. Finally, it signaled upcoming events of interest, such as the Universal Exhibition of 1878 and Bertillon's course in demography.

One of the striking features of the new journal was the discrepancy between the cover page, which situated demography in the liberal-administrative sector, and the articles, which situated the new science in the medical-municipal sector. Far from amounting to false publicity, the cover page indicated the audience that the editors hoped to attract; the articles, on the other hand, represented the state of the art as it was at the time of publication.

Tables 1 and 2 reproduce the list of "principal contributors" which figured on the cover page of the new journal. While the original list was ordered alphabetically, I have divided it between French and non-French participants on the grounds that the institutional meaning of their participation was not the same. First, formally similar types of organization had very different status connotations in different countries and thus cannot be treated as comparable. Second, foreign affiliations did not carry the same symbolic weight as domestic ones among French readers. The first point worth noting is the large number of foreigners. Of the twenty-three names, fifteen, or nearly two thirds, were non-Frenchmen. The inclusion of the term "international" in the title was thus re-enforced by the identity of the "patrons" of the new science. Of these fifteen men, all except three held positions in the administration, and of those twelve, ten were the heads of bureaus of statistics in their respective countries.[5] Demography was thus clearly associated with foreign administrative statistics. This affiliation served both to confer upon it the prestige of international recognition

Table 1. Main French Contributors, *Annales de démographie internationales*, 1877

		Affiliation (as listed)
Bertillon	prof(m)	Professeur de démographie et de géographie médicale à l'Ecole d'anthropologie, Vice-Président de la ssp
Chervin (Arthur)	soc(m)	Membre du Conseil de la ssp
De Lavergne (Léonce)	acad(s)	Membre de l'Institut, Sénateur, Ancien Président de la ssp
Levasseur (Émile)	acad(s)	Membre de l'Institut, Professeur au Collège de France, Ancien Président de la ssp
Loua (Toussaint)	adm/s(s)	Chef du Bureau de la sgf, Ancien Président de la ssp
Passy (Hippolyte)	acad(s)	Membre de l'Institut, Président honoraire de la ssp
Vacher	pol(s)	Membre de la Chambre des députés, Vice-Président de la ssp
Yvernes	adm/s(s)	Chef du bureau de la Statistique au ministère de la Justice à Paris

prof = professor
soc = member of a scientific society
acad = member of a scientific academy
pol = elected official (deputy or senator)
adm = administrator

adm/s = administrator in moral scientific sector (municipal administrator, director of welfare institution, etc.)
ssp = Statistical Society of Paris
(m) = moral-scientific sector
(s) = liberal-administrative sector

and to affiliate it, at least implicitly, with the International Congress of Statistics, whose main work was the development and standardization of national administrative statistics.

The sixteen formal affiliations (associated with eight names) included positions from both the liberal-administrative sector and the medical-municipal sector. More surprisingly, political economists and administrators outnumbered more marginally identified individuals by a ratio of six to two. According to the front page of the first issue of the journal, demography was firmly situated within the network of political economy and national administrative statistics. This concern to situate demography within

Table 2. Main Non-French Contributors, *Annales de démographie internationales*, 1877

	Affiliation (as listed)	
Bodio (Louis)	adm/s	Directeur de la Statistique générale d'Italie
De Czoernig (Baron Charles)	adm/s	Conseiller intime actuel de S.M. Imp. Roy, Ancien Président de la Commission Centrale de Statistique à Vienne, Membre correspondant de l'Institut de France
Farr (William)	adm/s	Superintendant du Bureau du Registre Général des naissances, mariages et décès d'Angleterre, Correspondant de l'Institut de France, Vice-Président honoraire de la Société de Statistique de Londres
Jassens	adm (m)	Inspecteur du Service de Santé de la ville de Bruxelles, Membre du Conseil supérieur d'Hygiène publique de Belgique
Keleti (Charles)	adm/s	Chef du Bureau royal de Statistique de Hongrie
Makschiew (Alexis)	mil	Général major de l'armée Russe, Professeur de Statistique à l'Académie d'Etat-major à Saint-Pétersbourg
Mansolas (Alexandre)	adm/s	Chef de division, Directeur du Bureau de Statistique au ministère de l'Intérieur à l'Athènes
Mayr (Georges)	adm/s	Chef du Bureau royal de Statistique de Bavière
Messedaglia (Angelo)	prof	Professeur de Statistique à l'Université de Rome
Morpurgo (Émile)	pol	Député au parlement Italien
Pery (G.)	adm	Capitaine dans l'armée Portugaise, attaché à la Direction générale des travaux géodésiques au ministère des Travaux publics
Snow (Edgar)	adm/s	Superintendant du recensement de l'Etat de Rhode-Island, USA

prof = professor
soc = member of a scientific society
acad = member of a scientific academy
pol = elected official (deputy or senator)
adm = administrator
mil = military

adm/s = administrator in moral scientific sector (municipal administrator, director of welfare institution, etc.)
ssp = Statistical Society of Paris
(m) = moral-scientific sector
(s) = liberal-administrative sector

an élite social space was echoed in a two-page "Note to Our Readers," which the editor, Arthur Chervin, printed opposite the list of "principal contributors." Chervin opened by noting the favor in which demography was increasingly held by governments, administrators, and "all men who seek in good faith a scientific solution to social problems."[6] To support this statement Chervin quoted Levasseur, who explicitly situated demography within economics: "It is thanks to statistics that demography had become one of the most developed branches of economic science. It is therefore important to [use it] to understand laws and to make known the results acquired, all the while working for new acquisitions. I commend you for having founded a collection which in pursuing this triple goal will render a service to science."[7] The symbolic weight of Levasseur's backing is difficult to overestimate. Of all the names appearing on the list, his was certainly the most prestigious. In 1873 he was a professor at the Collège de France, a member of the Académie des Sciences Morales et Politiques, and a professor of political economy at both the École Libre des Sciences Politiques and the Conservatoire des Arts et Métiers. He was also a member of numerous scientific and social associations and government commissions. This range of positions and activities placed Levasseur at the center of an extensive and powerful social network which rendered his very presence a valuable social resource.[8]

To summarize, the opening page of the first volume of the *Annales internationales de démographie* presented the new science as a recognized component of establishment or élite statistics. The majority of the French "principal contributors" were either liberal economists or administrators, and almost all the foreign contributors were the heads of national statistical bureaus. A comparison of this image with that projected by the contents of the journal suggests that it corresponded more with what demography hoped to become than with what it actually was.

Image versus Content I: The Opening Articles

The first two articles of the first issue situated demography in the tradition of moral statistics, public hygiene, and the bid for a more scientific version of administrative statistics. The issue began with an eighty-two-page paper by Louis Adolphe Bertillon entitled "Movements of the Population in Various States of Europe and Notably France," a version of a paper which Bertillon had submitted to the Academy of Moral and Political Sciences in 1875. The text contained a programmatic statement for demography. It also explicitly linked the new science to Quetelet's social physics.

Bertillon's paper was followed by an equally long paper by William Farr, thereby affirming the close relation between French demography and English vital statistics.

The distinguishing feature of Bertillon's opening article was its specification of population as an object of study. Demography was presented as a science devoted to the study of abstract forces which constitute a collective entity. This ontological model was re-enforced by Bertillon's insistence that the relevant units of demography were not individual observations but rates which expressed probabilities. Thus, in his discussion of "methods and the means of execution," Bertillon wrote:

> It is important first of all to be fixed on the methods in use (since there are many), and on their respective merits and to state which we have adopted to measure the movements which we have studied. There are cases, as when it is a question of assuming the force of nations, of lives to prepare for an army, in which absolute numbers are of primary importance. However for our object, in order to appreciate the movements, their grandeur, their speed, the absolute number of deaths, of births and even of living, are without interest, when considered in isolation. It is the comparison of these births, of these deaths or these marriages with the living which furnished them over a (given) unit of time which is important; it is these relations which have recently been designated under the names of " matrimonality," "natality" and "mortality"; it is these coefficients which serve to measure the intensity of each of these movements.[9]

This ontological model supported Bertillon's claim that the true object of demography was the study of population movements rather than fixed states, which were, Bertillon explained, but a by-product ("artifice") of the movements.[10] Finally, population movements could be divided into necessary movements and contingent movements. Necessary movements, such as births and deaths, depended on internal causes and were "incessant, continuous and nearly regular," while contingent movements, such as emigration and immigration, were a result of external circumstances.

Bertillon's analysis is important because of his emphasis on the existence of collective or social facts and on the privileged position which he ascribed to population movement.[11] Until now, national population movements had been studied for what they taught about the state of the population, but in Bertillon's new formulation they became an object of interest in their own right. This definition of demography limited it in scope from a general social science to a study of population as a formal, abstract collective object.

Two other features of the founding statement deserve to be highlighted. The first is Bertillon's clear specification of the role of the demographer in developing administrative statistics: "The duty of the savant, of the demographer, is not to bow low before official figures, but, on the contrary, to criticize them so as to weigh their value, and even to modify them if there is cause; the only important point is to prove the sound foundations of one's criticism, and only to introduce those modifications which are of uncontestable legitimacy."[12] The task of the demographer was thus to criticize and correct the work of the administrator. While this vision was implicit in Bertillon's early work, and in particular in his plea for improved official data, with the foundation of demography it took a more direct form. The second feature is Bertillon's attempt to situate his article in relation to liberal economics and policy decisions, an orientation that buttressed his new, more abstract, formal model of population. While this focus clearly reflects his having originally written the text for the Académie des Sciences Morales et Politiques, it also re-enforces the image provided by the cover page of demography as an administrative, élite science.

In signaling this representation of demography, I do not wish to suggest that Bertillon "invented" or even introduced these features. Instead Bertillon, as so often in his career, would seem to have adapted his commitment to rigorous statistical inquiry to the ontological models and questions of his immediate intellectual circle. As I suggested above, Bertillon's contribution — and that of demography in general — would seem to lie in the connection that he established between a growing scientific and political preoccupation with depopulation and a more sophisticated, abstract use of numbers. The institutional or social significance of this connection was that it promised to provide the social and political backing necessary for a successful reform of administrative statistics.

Image versus Content II: Collective Confirmation

An examination of the set of articles contained in the first few volumes of the journal confirms its location in the municipal-medical sector. The contributions can be grouped under six distinct headings: population movement (the new core of demography as an intellectual endeavor), medical statistics, public hygiene, anthropology or anthropometry, social or political issues, and methodological papers.[13]

In keeping with Bertillon's program for demography, the largest set of papers (seven of twenty-four) dealt with aspects of population movement. In the other categories, there were five papers in anthropology, four in public hygiene, and one on medical statistics. These categories correspond to the three areas in which Bertillon had worked previously; they were also associated with the medical-municipal sector. Finally, two papers dealt directly with matters of social and political interest. These included a largely qualitative text on the causes of depopulation and a text on *enfants assistés*. The relative absence of explicitly political or reform-oriented texts, despite explicit calls to use social science as a guide to social policy, suggests that the move to institutionalization was accompanied by a certain restraint from direct political engagement. Finally, no papers on the theory or method of statistics figured in the first three issues. While this situation was rectified in subsequent issues, notably with the contributions of the German statistician Lexis and a number of Italians, none of these texts were by French "demographers."[14]

The image of a journal located in the areas of public hygiene, anthropology, and population movement is re-enforced by an examination of the authors. Of the twenty men contributing papers, twelve were foreigners. Of the eight French nationals, Louis Adolphe Bertillon, Jacques Bertillon, and the editor, Arthur Chervin, were the most active in directing the journal. Chervin was a young medical student at the time with little obvious relation to demography.[15] He graduated from medical school in 1878 with a doctoral thesis entitled "A Physiological Analysis of the Elements of Speech" and immediately accepted a position as director of the Institute of Stammerers in Paris, which he directed along with his uncle, Amédée Chervin. He developed a new and apparently effective method of teaching stammerers to speak which soon came to be known as the "Chervin method."[16] An analysis of his publications suggests that demography provided his first entry into the world of savants.

Jacques Bertillon, the third "journal builder," was the eldest son of Louis Adolphe Bertillon. Born in 1851, he was a year younger than Chervin.[17] He too attended the Faculté de Médecine de Paris and, like Chervin, would seem to have published his first articles in the *Annales internationales de démographie*. In contrast with Chervin, he had a presence that is easily explained. Because he grew up in a household with both Achille Guillard and Louis Adolphe Bertillon, his involvement can be seen as the act of an obedient son following his father's expectations.[18] While Jacques Bertillon was to inherit all of the formal positions which his father had acquired, he was a less innovative, more technical statistician. And while his name is still associated with the label "demography," he largely refrained from explicit disciplinary activity. Instead he made a career as a statistician, administrator, and leading pronatalist. As for the other five men, all except one were trained as medical doctors and all were marginal to both liberal economic and administrative circles. Dr. Gibert was responsible for a statistical bureau in Marseille, as was Dr. Rey in Phillippeville. Dr. Lafabrègue was an administrator in an institution for impoverished children (*enfants assistés*), while Dr. Rey was also a doctor in the French navy. Of the five, Gustave Lagneau was the closest to Louis Adolphe Bertillon, at least in profile. Like Bertillon, he was a member of the Société d'Anthropologie and published on infant mortality and population growth.

A comparison of the contributors to the *Annales internationales de démographie* with the list on the cover page points to a sharp contrast between the image which the editors hoped to project (one of demography firmly situated within the arena of political economy and administrative statistics — the élite sphere) and the work that they really did (which situated demography in the cluster of more marginal social sciences, and more notably in the network of public hygiene and anthropology). This discrepancy suggests that the "success" of demography, at least in the eyes of its promoters in 1877, lay in the ability of demography to make a place for itself within the élite spheres of government-supported science and administrative statistics. The goal was not very different from Achille Guillard's original project to colonize political economy. But whereas Guillard aimed at transforming economic theory and thus social policies, demography in the early decades of the Third Republic focused first and foremost on transforming the practice of administrative statistics. The importance of this goal in the new demographic agenda was clearly evidenced at the First International Congress of Demography, which met less than a year after the founding of the journal.

The First Specialized Congress

The First International Congress of Demography was one of thirty-two official scientific congresses to be held in conjunction with the Universal Exposition of 1878. The idea of combining the two types of event was first put forth in France in 1867; however, it was only in 1878 that the organizing committee made the congresses an official part of their program. This involvement of the administration in the classification and encouragement of science was unique to France. It can be read as a concrete expression of the official commitment to a positivist vision of science.[19] It also provided a mechanism of intellectual control. By accepting or rejecting different subjects, the administration made a public statement concerning their "scientificity."[20] The inclusion of demography in the official list thus constituted an important symbolic victory for the "new science."

A series of announcements in the first volume of the *Annales internationales de démographie* indicate that demography was initially introduced into the Universal Exposition under the heading of anthropology. A decree from the Ministry of Agriculture and Commerce authorized a request by the Société d'Anthropologie for a place in the Universal Exposition. In their call for contributions, the organizing committee of the Anthropological Society specified six categories of objects to be displayed at the event, including one devoted to "geographic maps and tables concerning ethnology, prehistoric archeology, linguistics, demography and medical geography." In the list of contact persons, Louis Adolphe Bertillon's name figured under the heading "demography or statistical studies of population, and medical geography."[21] Six months later, the second volume of the *Annnales* published a letter from the organizing committee of the "International Congress of Demography in Paris, under the patronage of the French government," inviting readers to register in a scientific congress.[22] The members of the committee included Bertillon as president, Chervin as general secretary, and Émile Levasseur as president of honor. The "general provisions" specified that the aim of the congress was to unite "*savants* from all countries who wish to discuss theoretical and practical questions concerning the progress of demography and medical geography." They also extended a special invitation to "governments, administrations and scientific societies" to send official representatives.

Like the journal, the congress, which lasted four days, can be studied and presented in a number of ways, depending on the questions one asks and the classificatory system employed. The discussion which follows uses three types of material to explore the content which the congress gave to the term "demography," and to situate demography in relation to other forms of statistical practice. These materials include the opening speeches presented at the congress, various lists of participants — including subscribers, attendees, and participants in the discussions — and documents that record the substance of the discussions. Of the three sources, only the first was wholly under the control of the organizers. By contrast, the various lists of participants provide an indication of the range of persons attracted by the label "demography." Finally, transactions from the congress itself attest to the nature of demography as represented by the meeting.

Demography as Administrative Reform

Both the honorary president, Émile Levasseur, and the president of the organizing committee, Louis Adolphe Bertillon, delivered speeches at the opening session. In a complementarity that was so close that it seems to have been planned, their talks contained identical images of demography. Both argued that demography was a distinct science associated with a single object — population — while statistics was (merely) a method. Both presented demography as a search for numerical laws and defended the compatibility of their claims with the exercise of individual free will. Finally, both closed by indicating the policy relevance of demography.

To the extent that the talks differed, the differences lay in the practical program that each man spelled out for demography. Levasseur contented himself with a general remark concerning the role of science in the material and moral progress of man, but Bertillon lingered over the practical and policy uses of demography. A striking feature of Bertillon's talk was his attempt to appeal to legislators over the heads of administrators:

> I have just signaled this act of our Assemblies as a new sign of modern times. For a long time legislators seemed in fact to be disinterested in the conservation of human life, which they had abandoned to the care of the Administration, to the police, inferior powers whose decisions are not always accepted without a murmur . . . From our days, our modern legislators, so careful to discuss, to lighten the various budgets, should have understand that there is nothing more odious, more unfruitful, more weighty than *premature* death, since the death of a man, removed in his flower, is not only cruel, it is ruinous; it is a capital which evaporates; I have evaluated [this loss] for my country and I have found that from this single point of view of hasty deaths a capital of more than a millions francs is put out. So many reasons for our legislators, following the path opened by our last Assembly, to continue to elaborate measures which lead to the relief of this painful tribute. The first of these measures it to advance inquiries in *la statistique humaine*.[23]

This statement illustrates Bertillon's adaptation of a form of reasoning which had been extensively developed in England by William Farr. Whereas Farr used statistics to evaluate the number of lives which could be saved, Bertillon assigned an economic value to these figures and argued in terms of the national interest. The mode of reasoning, however, was the same: statistics were used to measure the possibility of prevention and thus to make an argument for legislative reform. In the continuation of this statement, Bertillon went on to demonstrate extreme variations in the mortality rate between departments of France. His point was to play up the role of demography in identifying the causes of these discrepancies, so that legislators could reduce this tax (on lives) to a strict minimum.

A second feature of Bertillon's quote worth noting is the audience to which it was aimed. Throughout the four days of the congress, Bertillon continually returned to this idea that the future of demography (and statistical inquiry in general) depended on enlisting the support of legislators against the inertia or open resistance of administrators. He concluded his speech by appealing to those present to persuade legislators to recognize the needs of demography and act in its interests: "If some of us, in their respective countries, raise their voices to announce these *desiderata*, it too often happens that these isolated voices do not have enough force or enough authority to command the attention of the [governments] which solicit the envy of so many large and numerous interests. But by uniting our voices, our lights, we have a reasonable hope to be better heard by these high dispensers of good and evil."[24] This closing statement situates Bertillon's project for the congress, and thus for demography, in the context of his personal experience. It also spells out the strategy that he developed for promoting demography as a discipline. Frustrated by his two decades of effort to pressure the administration to improve official data, Bertillon turned to the congress to act where he and his father-in-law had failed.

The intellectual success of the congress can in large part be ascribed to the convergence of this project with the concerns of foreign administrators who attended. While an analysis of the situation of each of the twelve active foreign participants is beyond the scope of this book, the previous discussion on the International Congress of Statistics attests to a growing concern to introduce "scientific" criteria into administrative work. The main difference on this score between France and the other countries represented would seem to lie in the social position of the persons making this claim. In France it was largely voiced by persons outside the administration, while in other countries it was part of a bid by national-level administrators to strengthen the authority and autonomy of their bureaus. For persons such as Louis Bodio in Italy or Charles Keleti in Hungary, the term "demography" was associated with the scientific versus purely practical dimension of administrative statistics. In Germany, the unique role of "professor-bureaucrat" provided an important social base for asserting similar claims.[25]

An analysis of the content of the discussions points to a consensus concerning the use of the congress to pressure national governments into reforming administrative statistics. This aim was clearly expressed in the very practical focus of many of the discussions. The majority of sessions were devoted to designing alternative registration forms and modifying the census so as to capture phenomena of interest to "demography" or "science." These included (among others) the size of the "floating population" (those without a fixed domicile), the number of stillbirths, the inclusion in census forms of topics such as religion, wealth, and race, and the inclusion in the birth register of information concerning the length and number of marriages, the size of families, and the age of parents, so as to better identify causes of variations in natality. Another indication of the importance of this goal is the distinctions which the speakers at the congress made between the interests of the administration and those of science, the convergence of which was nevertheless a constant theme. As Bertillon explained: "Sirs, every time that we deal with the perfection of statistical inquiry, we are blocked by difficulties which, I believe, reside in the same vice: that is that the majority of the laws which rule us, of the legislative measures which facilitate social life, were almost all delivered in a period where the need to maintain the books of humanity was not felt with the same intensity as in our period."[26] The statement "the administration and science have an interest to know . . ." was evoked by a number of speakers.[27]

The need to enroll legislators in this campaign was clearly expressed by continual references to the "public powers." The possibility of seeking direct aid also came up in a discussion of the effectiveness of legal sanctions against those refusing to provide census information. Speakers from Germany, the Netherlands, and Belgium all noted the existence of such laws in their countries, although they questioned their efficacy.[28] Finally, Bertillon continued his observations on the obstacles that existing administrative categories posed by insisting on the necessity for legislative reform: "I believe that if we do not attempt, by our repeated demands, to obtain legislative measures, and not only administrative [ones], which rule statistical inquiries, we will be stopped by almost insurmountable difficulties. Things which have no control and sanction risk to be conducted with great irregularity."[29]

This review of the opening speeches at the congress and the four days of discussion confirms my argument that the campaign for demography in 1878 was a campaign to reform administrative statistics according to "scientific" criteria and "demographic" interests. This goal situates the congress in direct continuity with the Theory and Methods section of the International Congress of Statistics of 1869 and the administrative dimension of Quetelet's "social physics." In the French context, the campaign amounted to an appeal to legislators over the heads of French administrators. Viewed from this perspective, it can be seen as a response to the specifically French institutional configuration in which moral and scientific statistics were excluded from the SGF. Thus in contrast to England, where a similar campaign had been conducted fifty years earlier from within statistical and administrative bureaus, in France it was conducted by people outside the administration and outside élite science, with the symbolic support of foreign heads of statistical bureaus.

International Congresses Compared

Ten days after the first International Congress of Demography, the Société Statistique de Paris held a different conference with a similar agenda. Like the demographers, the "statisticians" also framed the official transactions of their sessions with lists of subscribers and participants. A comparison of the social composition of the two conferences provides an additional opportunity to situate demography in 1878 relative to other forms of statistics.

Initially, the Société Statistique de Paris had decided not to organize a congress in conjunction with the Universal Exposition. Its members changed their minds, however, when they learned that the Permanent Commission of the International Congress of Statistics had shifted its next meeting to Paris, so as to coincide with the exposition. The Permanent Commission was a closed meeting which brought together some of the most influential statisticians in Europe at the time.[30] As Toussaint Loua explained in his opening remarks at the conference, the organizers hoped to benefit from the presence of so many prestigious statisticians to increase the status of their organization and possibly attract new members. For the story of demography, the important point is that the decision was taken after the Congress of Demography had already been authorized.

Upon learning of this decision, Bertillon asked the society to exclude "demographic" topics from its agenda. The secretary general of the society (and head of the SGF), Toussaint Loua, objected to the request, and the society chose to disregard it.[31] The result was that the Permanent Commission was bracketed by two competing conferences. The International Congress of Demography was held from 7 to 9 July, just before the Permanent Commission convened, and the International Conference of Statistics met from 22 to 24 July, just after it adjourned. The triple event offers an institutional expression of the different groups of statisticians and forms of statistics in competition at the time.

The relatively weak position of the Société Statistique de Paris in 1878 suggests a similarity in the significance of the two congresses for their organizers. Both were public events that provided an opportunity to attract new supporters and establish a firmer organizational base. Moreover, the refusal by the leaders of the SSP to distinguish their program from that of the demography congress necessarily meant that the two events were competing for the same audience. A comparison of the participants at the two congresses thus provides a means to identify who was attracted to which label and thus to assess their relative chances that each project would succeed at establishing itself as the authoritative form of social statistics.

While the affiliations of most foreign members were similar to those mentioned in the transactions of the Congress of Demography, those of the French subscribers and members differed significantly. In addition to the affiliations mentioned in the demography list, the statisticians also included persons from political, legal, and business sectors, as well as economists. While these differences might conceivably be explained by the place of either economic or political topics on the agenda of the SSP's conference, this turns out not to have been the case: population statistics were largely privileged over financial, industrial, or juridical statistics. A comparison of subscribers to both congresses by sector sharpens this contrast. The demography congress was heavily weighted in favor of the medical-municipal sector (59 percent versus 28 percent), but at the International Conference of Statistics this ratio was reversed. Only 11 percent of the names on the list were affiliated with the traditional medical-municipal sector, while 54 percent were from the liberal-administrative sector (table 3). Curiously, an analysis of the persons actively participating in the sessions suggests that persons associated with the medical-municipal sector played a disproportionate, albeit secondary, role in the discussions. In contrast with England, politicians, administrators, and businessmen did not seem to use social statistics as a popular cultural form.

Taken together, these comparisons provide a composite picture of the relative social position of both demography and the Société Statistique de Paris in 1878. This image helps to explain why Bertillon and Chervin believed that they might succeed in their bid to establish demography as the dominant, officially recognized form of social statistics, and why they used the Congress to reformulate demography as a project for administrative

Table 3. Affiliation of Subscribers and Active Participants, International Congress of Demography and International Conference of Statistics, 1878, by Scientific Sector

	moral sciences sector	state sciences sector	sector unknown	total
International Congress of Demography	17 (59%)	8 (28%)	4 (14%)	29
active participant, International Congress of Demography	6 (67%)	1 (11%)	2 (22%)	9
subscriber, International Conference of Statistics	9 (11%)	44 (54%)	28 (34%)	81
active participant, International Conference of Statistics	5 (38%)	7 (54%)	1 (8%)	13

reform. In 1878 the Société Statistique de Paris was in a particularly weak position. The founding generation had either passed away or fallen from political favor, and the current program failed to attract either administrators or savants. At the same time, administrative statisticians such as Toussaint Loua exercised enough control over the organization so as to prevent Bertillon and the moral statisticians more generally from directing the society, let alone from influencing administrative statistics.

From the perspective of Chervin and Bertillon, the disenchantment of the government with the Société Statistique de Paris, along with more general political support for positivism, suggested that the time was propitious to launch their new science. Their resources included a developed intellectual project, their traditional organizational base in the medical-municipal sector, and the active support of foreign administrative statisticians. The interest of foreign administrators in demography can be ascribed to a number of factors, including their shared desire to introduce "scientific" considerations into administrative practice, the growing use of the term "demography" to refer to this goal in various German and Italian states (during the 1850s and 1860s), and Bertillon's international reputation as a statistician. As noted above, Bertillon's work on infant mortality was far better known outside France than within it. In addition, Bertillon had been an active participant in the International Congresses of Statistics from the time of their conception in 1853. The social network that was forged at these international meetings proved a valuable resource in the French effort to establish an institutional structure which challenged established organizational and cognitive boundaries.

Strategies of Discipline Formation

As these remarks indicate, while demography achieved many of the contemporary markers of discipline formation in the late 1870s, these achievements did not mark the recognition of the discipline by either scientific or administrative gatekeepers. Nor, curiously, did it involve a bid to gain their recognition. Instead, the formal discipline of demography directed its efforts at reforming official statistics. In some ways, this abandonment of the attempt to transform élite political economy and orthodox medicine represented a move toward differentiation. It also points to the obstacles posed by the gap between scientific vision and administrative policy. In England, social statisticians could rely on strategically placed members within the administration to adjust the production of official data to international standards and their own scientific agenda; in France, by contrast, proponents of demography and of Quetelet's project more generally did not have this luxury. They recognized that their first priority lay in the takeover of official statistics, or at least in gaining influence over them. In the 1870s they also recognized that to achieve that end they would have to circumvent the Société Statistique de Paris and the SGF. For demography in 1878, disciplinary activity meant a campaign to transform the production of data. Far from a purely administrative measure, the goal rested on a distinct approach to statistics, one which involved manipulating numbers to identify underlying statistical laws and causes.

The contrast between the public image, as represented by the cover pages of specialized demographic publications — be it the transactions of the international congress or the journal — and the substance of the project and social location of the main contributors attests to the limits of disciplinary success. The public image situates demography in the world of quasi-official science. The contents of the journal, by contrast, situate it in the world of public hygiene, anthropology and municipal (rather than national) administration. The contrast also points to the continued relevance of this organizational and intellectual distinction, despite the change in political regime. Through the late 1870s French social statistics was still organized in two distinct social and epistemological spheres: one associated with quasi-official scientific institutions and committed to a descriptive model of statistics as a secondary form of scientific knowledge, and a more marginal, positivist sphere of scientific societies committed to the scientific form of administrative statistics associated with Quetelet. To the extent that demographers gained the upper hand at the International Exhibition of 1878, that success reflected the weakness of the first of these spheres as much as the strength of demography.

These initial forays into discipline formation gave a new intellectual and social focus to the project of demography. The organization of the conference, the journal, and academic courses forced Bertillon and his companions to consolidate their intellectual agenda. Demography was presented as an abstract science, devoted to the study of population as an abstract, collectivistic entity subject to the interacting forces of mortality and natality (rather than migration). Demographic practice consisted of extensive statistical manipulation directed at identifying laws and causes and developing population policy. Previously Guillard and Bertillon had used demography to call for reforming existing scientific disciplines ranging from political economy to medicine, but after 1878 the focus of demography was on introducing a new scientific agenda into national statistical bureaus. Vital statisticians had worked to transform official statistics from a privileged position inside the administration; demography made its bid to transform administrative statistics from the world of science by creating a scientific discipline. The 1880s witnessed the incorporation of spokesmen for the demographic project into quasi-official scientific and administrative organizations and the abandonment of disciplinary activity as a strategy of intellectual promotion.

CHAPTER SEVEN

Limits to Institutionalization

The analysis of the International Congresses of Demography points to both a continuity in the basic intellectual project associated with the term "demography" and a change in orientation. As in the earlier pronouncements, demography in 1877 and 1878 was defined as a statistical science devoted to a search for underlying laws, the identification of causes, and the making of policy. In contrast with earlier formulations, demography in 1878 was explicitly oriented toward the reform of official statistics through a program of discipline formation.

From a substantive perspective, this shift in practical goals reflects the genuine obstacles that the French system of official statistics posed for statisticians. Official data were published irregularly, many years after being collected. Individual-level data were aggregated by local administrators, and summaries were sent to the central office, thus precluding careful control and further statistical manipulation. The processes of data collection were poorly monitored and official data were of dubious quality. Finally, social statisticians working in anthropology and public hygiene were frustrated by the absence of data relevant to their specific interests, such as data on the causes of death, professions, age structure, the number of children per family, the age of parents, and a variety of cultural and biological categories such as religion, race, and blood relations. As noted earlier, some of these lacunae resulted from the weakness of official statistical bureaus and their inability to introduce administrative reforms. Others, however, resulted from the dominance of liberal economists' descriptive model for statistics.

The first few years following the creation of the *Annales internationales de démographie* and the first meeting of the International Congress of Demography were marked by surprising success. The term "demography" entered the vocabulary of French statisticians, an administrative bureau was created which privileged the practice of demography, and Louis Adolphe Bertillon was elected president of the Société Statistique de Paris. These achievements constituted the limits of disciplinary expansion, however. The success of demography was inversely related to the weakness of the Société Statistique de Paris. In 1882 the society made a comeback, presenting itself as the proponent of a new version of statistics as a science, thereby challenging the distinctiveness of demography. By 1885 the Société Statistique de Paris emerged victorious and demography lost its bid for recognition as the authoritative voice of scientific statistics.

An analysis of these developments provides an opportunity to examine discipline formation in a period of institutional change. Both demography and the new program at the Société Statistique de Paris called into question the monopoly of élite scientific academies over the relation between statistics and the state and contributed to the restructuring of the field of population statistics. At the same time, these changes led to an abandonment of disciplinary claims, further supporting the argument that discipline formation had been an effort to change those criteria of recognition that had blocked the adoption of demography, rather than to achieve differentiation, specialization, or professionalization. Once those obstacles were removed, disciplinary activity no longer made sense. Finally, an examination of these developments underlines the persistence of strictures against the use of mathematics that help to account for the subsequent failure of French scholars to embrace either marginal economics or mathematical statistics.

Institutional Success: The Municipal Bureau of Statistics

A Traditional Anchorage

The revival of the Municipal Bureau of Statistics for the City of Paris is a story of institutional innovation and continuity. The innovation lay in the adaptation of an administrative statistical apparatus to the demands of anthropologists, public hygienists, and demographers. The continuity lay in the similarity in the basic orientation of the new bureau with that of the Municipal Bureau of Statistics of the First Empire. Under the direction of the Count de Chabrol and Joseph Fourier in the early nineteenth century, the bureau produced official statistical data that conformed to the highest statistical and mathematical standards of the time. Moreover, the original bureau had played a central role in the initial formulation of a scientific approach to administrative statistics. In the 1830s and 1840s, Fourier's *Recueil des recherches statistiques sur la ville de Paris et le département de la Seine* was one of the main sources of data for advocates of a more scientific approach to administrative statistics. Both Villermé and Quetelet used it to explore their interests in statistical laws and the relation of poverty and health or well-being, as did public hygienists.

Between 1816 and 1878 the Paris Municipal Bureau of Statistics underwent a series of transformations. While the "scientific" approach promoted by Joseph Fourier had been abandoned with his resignation, the bureau continued to provide population statistics on the city of Paris. Between 1817 and 1860 all six volumes of the *Recueil des recherches statistiques* were published. However, according to Faure not all these volumes were prepared by the Paris Municipal Bureau.[1] Under the Second Empire these publications were interrupted. No information on the population of Paris was published between 1856 and 1865, when the work was resumed, although the bureau itself was not reestablished. By the 1870s municipal statistics were under the jurisdiction of the Department of Cemeteries.

International developments seem to have played a role in the initiative to reestablish the Municipal Bureau. In his account of the founding of the office, Henri Le Roux, the head of the division, noted that between 1865 (the year of founding of the previous statistical bureau) and 1876 "statistical studies underwent considerable development." As he went on to explain: "Many large cities, and Brussels in particular, without concerning themselves with administrative statistics, instituted services of medical statistics, whose sole aim was to create an instrument which allowed for the observation of the state of public health and contributed to its improvement. The congresses of statistics and of hygiene observed the importance of the results obtained and . . . the Municipal Council thought that it was necessary 'in the interest of public health and of science' to give this publication an importance in relation with the resources of which the city of Paris disposed."[2] To make its case, the Municipal Council appointed one of its members, Dr. Lamouroux, to make an exhaustive report on the reorganization of Parisian municipal statistics.

In Le Roux's account, the reorganization was intended to create a statistical bureau "in the interest of public health and of science." Both aims are worth noting. On the one hand, the bureau was explicitly devoted to the promotion of science rather than administration or policy formation. On the other hand, its focus was public health rather than economics or social statistics.

On 27 February 1877 the Municipal Council voted on a number of Lamouroux's recommendations. It decided to improve the value of municipal statistics by calling on medical doctors to cooperate (by providing data on the causes of death), keeping documents up to date to reflect the progress of medical science, publishing a complete weekly bulletin, and creating a central statistical bureau which would be founded on a scientific base. Again, the resolutions of the council clearly linked the new bureau with the study of medicine and public health. They also anticipated concerns voiced at the International Congress of Demography in the following year. Having taken this decision, however, the council was slow to act. A year later, on 25 March 1877, it appointed a Special Commission on Municipal Statistics. The commission was composed of members of the council, administrators, and savants, including Louis Adolphe Bertillon (who was listed as president of the Société Statistique de Paris), Toussaint Loua (head of the SGF), and Émile Levasseur. While the commission was appointed in the beginning of 1878, it did not really begin to work until 1879, after the nomination of Senator Hérold to the position of prefect.[3]

Demography in Practice

The final report of the Special Commission on Municipal Statistics was delivered in 1879.[4] The work of the commission had been divided into three areas: topography, population, and miscellaneous (*variétés*), a category embracing those areas of social statistics not included under population. Each committee was assigned the task of reviewing the type of data and collection procedures in place and suggesting reforms. Bertillon was chosen as the reporter for the second section on population, while Loua headed the third section. The absence of a clear boundary between the two subcommissions provided yet another occasion for conflict between the two men — one the founder and main proponent of demography, the other the head of the national administrative bureau.

Bertillon's report for the section on population confirms his intention to insert demography into the mandate of the future bureau. In his report, Bertillon explicitly defined the task of the section as the development of population statistics "useful for demography." The final recommendations of the section on demography included a system to guarantee the quality of data on the causes of death (which had been approved by the Academy of Medicine) and the addition of various types of information to the birth, death, and marriage registers. According to the report, all the new bulletins (birth, death, and marriage) were to include questions concerning the religion, wealth, and profession of each respondent (including a specification of whether the respondent was an employer or a worker), and the ties of consanguinity within the family.

The death bulletins were divided into three forms, one for stillborn infants, the second for children under two, and the third for all others. In addition to the usual information, the forms for Paris were to include information on the length of marriage of a deceased spouse and the number and sex of children, dead and alive. For children's death certificates, the new bulletins asked for information concerning the profession and age of the parents, their wealth, and the type of school to which the children had been sent (secular or religious, pension or public). The birth registers for Paris were similarly expanded. The new bulletins specified the type of birth (home or hospital, midwife or doctor), the type of floor and sanitary state of the lodgings, the wealth and profession of the parents, the length of the parents' marriage, and their age and the number of other births. For respondents married more than once, the forms also inquired into the number of children from previous marriages. Finally, the new marriage forms asked the nationality of the couple and their families, the degree of instruction they had obtained, and their literacy. Widows were also asked to provide information on the length of their widowhood.

This list of items indicates the degree to which the new forms followed the prescriptions suggested at the International Congress of Demography. Two specific social problems underlay the new agenda for the Municipal Bureau of Statistics. The first was the classical problem of public health. One of the major innovations of the bureau was the introduction of a detailed system for registering the causes of death. To insure the success of the program, the commissioners turned to the Academy of Medicine for approval. The main objections raised against the proposal concerned the problem of professional secrecy and the possibility of tension between the patient's doctor and the doctor for the civil registrar. In the end these objections were overcome by a complicated administrative system whereby bulletins were sent from the mayor's office to the acting doctor, who removed his patient's name and returned the bulletin.

The second problem was France's falling birth rates. The majority of the new items on the registration forms were designed to explore the fertility behavior of French women, so as to identify the immediate cause of the observed phenomena. Was the declining birth rate due to a decline in births or infant mortality? Was it greater among married or unmarried women? Did the likelihood of losing a baby increase or decrease with the age differential of the parents? Which social groups were "responsible" for the slowing birth rate? Even the questions about the economic and cultural situation of families were directed at better understanding the factors at play in the "plague" which had struck the French population.

In addition to improving existing population registers (births, deaths, marriages), Bertillon called for two new types of publication. Following the English and Belgian practice, the new bureau proposed to publish weekly bulletins with the number of deaths by sex, age, and cause and their distribution between arrondissements of the city. This information was to be provided free of charge to all practicing doctors and other "eminent persons" interested in such matters. The second type of publication was to contain information "of use by the demographic, hygienic and medical sciences." In his report Bertillon did not indicate the form which this latter publication was to take. He did, however, insist that the information be organized to highlight its relation to social phenomena, and not simply listed indiscriminately:

> The trouble is not to make numerical tables which mention all of the facts collected, but the difficulty, is to leave those facts in combination, or in function, one with the other as they are in all the concrete phenomenon of nature and above all in demography; thus, to give an example, our "statistical notices" give us, for each case, the length of the marriage, they also tell us the number of births of each sex issued of those marriages. Should we be content, as we have been until this date, to separately add all these different findings? to state how many marriages? to calculate the average length and to add the births of each sex? In proceeding thusly, we allow the most precious elements to escape from our inquiry, that is to say: the relations that these facts have one with the other. Without doubt, one must add these marriages, but without separating them irremissibly from their length and their fecundity.[5]

Here we see the radical difference between Bertillon's conception of an official statistical publication and that of Moreau de Jonnès or even Alfred Legoyt (the two successive heads of the SGF between its founding in 1834 and 1871), and the association which Bertillon made between his method and demography. Even in his report before the Municipal Council of the City of Paris, Bertillon broached his pedagogic lessons concerning the significance of rates and the meaning of different types of numbers. His program for the Paris Municipal Bureau thus involved both adapting official statistics to the needs of "science" (under the label "demography") and introducing a new concept of statistics and statistical manipulation into the administrative process. Apparently Bertillon managed to convince the commission of the wisdom of his program, for in 1879 he was appointed head of the new Municipal Statistical Bureau. In January 1880 the first weekly bulletin was published; two years later Bertillon put out the first *Annuaire statistique de la ville de Paris*. The yearbook contained a compilation of all the data which the bureau had collected in the course of the year. In an imitation of William Farr's use of his letter to the registrar general, Bertillon prefaced the section on demography with a lengthy essay in which he discussed topics of statistical and social interest.

The above account of the founding of the Municipal Bureau of Statistics raises a number of points concerning the story of demography and the political conditions for the development of social statistics at the time. The first point worth noting is that demography was relatively divorced from organized campaigns for social reform. In England, statistics on the cause of death were introduced and perfected as the result of an organized campaign by the British Medical Association and the organized public health movement. They were among a number of concrete demands for legislative reform and provided the focus for organizing and coordinating a variety of professional and scientific societies. The reorganization of various statistical services was the result of the Civil Registration Act of 1836 and the Public Health Acts of 1848, 1865, and 1872.

In France, by contrast, administrative reform was largely the work of individual ministers (and in this case prefects). For Senator Hérold, this commitment would seem to have sprung from a diffuse positivist ideology associated with Republican politics. While the need for medical statistics was justified in term of public health and the threat of depopulation, French reformers did not include either demography or statistics in their political programs. This contrast in the place of social science in their reform agenda can be explained by differences in organization and political capacity. In contrast to England, the public hygiene movement in France was incorporated into the *conseils de salubrité,* quasi-official municipal advisory committees which were underfunded and functioned only sporadically. The first membership organizations concerned with depopulation were only created in 1896. While in England the public health movement was an important, highly organized, extragovernmental lobby group, in France it was a branch of municipal-level administration. And while in England vital statistics remained a central component of the movement's program, in France demography and even medical statistics occupied a relatively marginal place on the movement's political agenda, especially after 1848.

This difference also had consequences for the kind of support which the Municipal Bureau could hope to have from practicing physicians. As indicated in chapter 7, the success of William Farr's project for collecting medical statistics depended on the voluntary cooperation of medical doctors. That Farr obtained that cooperation can be explained by the support which he received from the popularly based British Medical Association. In France, a comparable connection was made between élite institutions. As Weisz has shown, the Academy of Medicine, based in Paris, was an élite organization largely divorced from the bulk of the profession. It is thus not surprising that the introduction of reliable data on the causes of death should have been limited to the Parisian area, where doctors were likely to be more sympathetic to the claims of "science" and the academy.

Finally, the story of the Municipal Bureau of Statistics attests both to the success of Bertillon at imposing his project for demography on the Municipal Council and the proximity of his project with that of William Farr. From this perspective, the activities of the Paris bureau can be seen to have combined the concrete proposals of the International Congress of Demography (which themselves drew on twenty years of international congresses) with Farr's program for the GRO. This connection can be seen not only in the focus on medical statistics and the publication of weekly and annual bulletins but also in the type of statistical reasoning which Bertillon introduced. In contrast with French national statistics, the Paris municipal bureau explicitly set out to develop a "scientific" project aimed at identifying laws and exploring social problems. As such the bureau embodied Bertillon's definition of demography from 1878 as the introduction of "science" into administration and a "scientific" approach to population statistics.

Limits to Institutional Success

The Fate of Specialized Institutions

In many ways the Municipal Bureau of Statistics of Paris marked the limits of institutional success. Under the direction of Louis Adolphe Bertillon and his son, Jacques, the bureau imitated the work of Farr at the GRO and provided a model for combining scientific and administrative goals in an official statistical bureau. This development was paralleled by the gradual dissolution of the specialized organizations and the absorption of demography into political economy.

The Second International Congress of Demography was held in 1880 in Florence. Rather than a full-blown international conference, the congress was a subsection of the International Congress of Hygiene. While organizers went to great lengths to establish and maintain the autonomy of the demography section, their efforts were relatively unsuccessful. Beyond the keynote speakers, most of the participants came to the demography sections by dint of their interest in public hygiene. French participants were almost all from the moral-municipal sector, and a number had never participated in statistical events in France. To the extent that foreign administrators attended, they came from municipal statistical bureaus rather than national offices.[6] Not surprisingly, the ambiguous status of the demography section pushed the organizers toward an explicitly disciplinary discourse and a more scientific orientation. In contrast to the first International Congress, which had been marked by a focus on administrative reform, the Second International Congress was characterized by methodological discussions, concern with instruction, and an explicit disciplinary discourse. Substantively, demographers abandoned the claim to the entire scope of social statistics and concentrated their efforts on population statistics.

A similar weakening or dissolution of the project occurred in the two other entities to which the label "demography" had been attached. These were the chair in the School of Anthropology and the Municipal Bureau of Statistics. In both the dilution was associated with the death of Louis Adolphe Bertillon in 1883 and the assumption of his positions by his son Jacques. In contrast to his father, Jacques Bertillon was not a discipline builder, nor did he have the charisma or drive to champion a new intellectual project. Having been trained by his father, he was a good statistician by the standards of his day. He had a finely developed sense of the significance of a statistical index, of the relation between numbers and "facts," and of the principles by which statistical rates could be constructed and manipulated. In adopting his father's positions, he implemented them with organizational and technical skill, but he did not innovate. His introductory articles in the yearbook of the Municipal Bureau of Statistics dealt with the spread of epidemic diseases, the overall state of the city, and his own research on divorce. But they lacked the rhetorical power and pedagogic dimension characteristic of both Bertillon's and Farr's writings.

Most importantly, Jacques Bertillon showed little interest in promoting demography as a separate discipline or in imposing demography on existing disciplines and forms of statistical practice. The 1883 volume of the *Annales internationales de démographie* was basically an encomium to Louis Adolphe. It contained an exhaustive account of his work and transcripts of the eulogies read at his funeral. Shortly after its publication, the journal folded. In 1883 Jacques also took over his father's course of demography at the École d'Anthropologie, but soon after he abandoned it, leading to the dissolution of the course.

Beyond questions of personality, this relative lack of interest in discipline assertion can be linked to the very different conditions in which Jacques Bertillon practiced his science. Unlike his father, he did not confront major epistemological barriers. In the years that followed, the label "demography" was gradually appropriated by more prestigious statisticians in the state-administrative sector and most notably by Émile Levasseur. In the process, demography shifted from a discipline that took a new, comprehensive approach to social statistics, and was worthy of being called a science, to a (largely descriptive) statistical study of population in the service of political economy. To understand this reorientation, it is necessary to examine the place of statistics in political economy, as evidenced in the changing fortunes of the Société Statistique de Paris.

The Société Statistique de Paris

The persistence of traditional divisions of the Third Republic was not initially auspicious for the Société Statistique de Paris. Instead, the new government distanced itself from the society, possibly because of its close links with the former regime and with theoretically oriented political economists. This general attitude can be seen in the suppression in 1870 of the national statistical bureau, the Statistique Générale de la France (SGF). While the SGF was not dismantled, it lost its autonomy. In 1872 Alfred Legoyt, the former director and permanent secretary of the Société Statistique de Paris, was asked to resign. The number of permanent members dropped to less than half of what it had been in the early 1860s.

In the following decade the society took a number of measures to open its leadership and expand its membership. As we have seen, the society was divided between administrative and "free" (or unaffiliated) statisticians, corresponding to my own analytic distinction between the liberal-administrative sector and moral-municipal sector. A campaign led by the "free" statisticians led to a reform of leadership, including the elimination of the position of permanent secretary, annual elections for the president, and the turnover of a third of the members of the council each year. In June 1872 Legoyt resigned and Toussaint Loua, the former deputy chief of the SGF, was elected general secretary for a period of three years. The election as president of the society of Dr. Lunier in 1878 and Louis Adolphe Bertillon in 1879 was a sign of the increasing openness of the society to approaches formerly associated with moral statistics, as well as to the institutional weakness of the organization during those years.

At the same time, leading administrative statisticians began to incorporate elements of demography and moral statistics into their own (revised) version of liberal statistics. Borrowed elements included the use of statistics in the identification of laws and causes, greater rigor in the use of indices (and an associated willingness to scrutinize the relation of indices to empirical referents), and an abandonment of the insistence that statistics be limited to certain knowledge. A key figure in this intellectual reorientation was Émile Levasseur. This shift did not, however, eliminate earlier differences over what counts as statistics.

In 1872 Edmond Flechey published a book entitled *Notions générales de statistique*, in which he discussed statistical findings and developments relevant for political economy. The work was reviewed for the Statistical Society by Loua, then deputy chief for the SGF and Flechey's immediate superior. Loua focused his comments on Flechey's definition of statistics, which reflected a vision of statistics as the use of the numerical method to identify laws. Loua insisted on a narrower descriptive definition. As he explained:

> This definition seems to us to be too broad, the role of statistics must be limited, in our opinion, to a representation of the facts by numerical terms which one can compare, according to the point of view, either in their simultaneous order, that is to say in space, or in their successive order, in other terms, over time.
>
> To [the domain of] statistics belongs the study of the procedures of investigation and the modes of calculation which it is proper to chose [so as] to know exactly the truth or the simple probability of the facts which it is called upon to register. As for the determination of laws which result from the relations suitable presented, it belongs to political economy to discover them and discuss them. The talent of the statistician consists in steeling sure arms which the economist knows how to use.[7]

Thus the difference between Flechey and Loua concerned the task of statistics and the division between observation and explanation. Although thirty years earlier Moreau de Jonnès had rejected the use of probabilities and mortality tables as "not statistics," by the 1870s defenders of descriptive statistics had adopted a more nuanced position. While Loua was willing to entertain reflections on the probability of observed facts, he rejected the search for laws and causes.

According to Kang, who has studied the history of the Statistical Society in detail, the turning point in the fortunes of the society with the successive elections as president of Daniel Wilson, the son-in-law of Jules Grévy, in 1882 and of Émile Cheysson in 1883.[8] With the support of Émile

Levasseur, these men personally recruited a large number of new members from among the political and economic élites of Paris. The result was a sharp upswing in membership, which now included a significant number of ministers, deputies, directors of statistical bureaus, and persons responsible for financial institutions, as well as the president of the Republic.

Under Cheysson's presidency, the Statistical Society undertook a number of organizational initiatives designed to publicize statistics and raise its status among the Parisian élites. These included a prize competition, a series of public conferences. and a campaign to create a High Commission of Statistics, which would coordinate the work of statistical departments. All three initiatives point to the desire of the leadership to broaden the society's mandate beyond data collection to a more "scientific" definition of statistics, and to establish the practical relevance of statistics. They also suggest a concerted attempt to substitute the authority of the Société Statistique de Paris for that of the Academy of Sciences in according scientific recognition, at least as concerns statistical work.

Institutional Success and the Abandonment of Disciplinary Activity

The Superior Council of Statistics

In 1885 two events marked the success of Cheysson's project for the Société Statistique de Paris. The first was the creation of the Superior Council of Statistics, which institutionalized a new relation between science and administration. The second was the twenty-fifth anniversary celebration of the Société Statistique de Paris. While the claims of the Société Statistique de Paris to represent a new "scientific" approach to statistics as an alternative to demography were never explicitly presented, the success effectively put an end to Bertillon's disciplinary project.

In a decree dated 12 May 1884, the Minister of Commerce acceded to the request of the Société Statistique de Paris for the appointment of a commission to look into the creation of a central bureau of statistics. The mandate for the preparatory commission called upon it "to [engage in the] search for uniform rules applicable to various branches of statistics, to facilitate the comparison of facts and of results, and to thus obtain a concordance between different official documents which would be as complete as possible . . . [in the forms of] classifications . . . in the use of unities and in the form of tables."[9] The preparatory commission consisted of eleven administrators and six independent statisticians. Levasseur, Block, and Chervin were among the six non-administrators, while Cheysson, Loua, and Jacques Bertillon figured among the administrators. On 19 February 1885 the commission delivered its report, and in March the Senate voted to create the Superior Council of Statistics.

In many ways the new council embodied the adaptation of a typical French administrative form to the needs of both statistics and the administration. Superior councils served to incorporate special-interest groups into the political and administrative process in a purely advisory capacity.[10] The Superior Council of Statistics effectively bypassed the authority of the élite academies as the main consultant to the government, all the while responding to the demands of Republican statisticians for a voice and filling a gap left by the dissolution of the International Congress of Statistics. Like the International Congress, the council was an advisory body devoted to developing and standardizing statistical categories across statistical bureaus. In terms of the relation of science and the state, two features of the new council were particularly striking.

The first was the inclusion of savants in an official organization. As we saw in part I, since the late eighteenth century the relation between the French state (administrators and politicians) and savants had been mediated by the French system of academies. A minister would address his questions to the relevant academy, members of the academy studied and debated the issue, and the academy then returned a consensual report to the minister with its policy recommendations. Under this system savants traditionally played a relatively passive role in the policy process, although there were obviously exceptions. With the creation of the council, savants were granted an official advisory position in a body which combined administrators and persons from the outside and which was located within the administration (under the ministry of commerce).

The logistics of this innovation proved highly controversial. After lengthy discussion over the proper balance between the "administrative element" and the "element foreign to the administration," the commission decided to assign two thirds of the positions to administrators and one third to the "foreign element." As the members explained in their report to the minister of commerce: "On the one hand, if the scientific element is in the majority, one should fear that the Council would be led by an exaggerated concern for pure science and would thus be led to take measures which were difficult to realize and incompatible with the good functioning of the services; if, on the other hand, we did provide this element with sufficient representation, the Council would only be regarded as a meeting of bureaucrats, [more] disposed to the consecration than to the reform of existing elements."[11] It was this reasoning which led the commission to recommend that the members of the council be divided two to one between administrators and scientists, to insure the proper balance between different types of criteria.

This arrangement presupposed an image of science as impractical and in tension with administrative considerations, an image largely absent from the comparable English discourse. It also indicates a curious conflation between the category of persons foreign to the administration — which included politicians, members of the Council of State, and the Revenue Court — and scientists. Thus while the discussion revolved around the contribution of the scientific and administrative elements, the final arrangement distinguished between administrators and those foreign to the administration.

The second related feature of the preparatory report was its explicit insistence on the value of science for social policy and administration. At the level of public pronouncements, the intention was clear. The report by Édouard Millard, senator and president of the preparatory commission, opened with the statement that "statistics was an essentially modern science": "No government in our day, can be un-interested in a science whose object is to investigate all the forces by which societies live. In democracies, public powers have an even greater obligation to weigh these forces, to determine their value and to apply them with order and precision."[12]

This statement was followed by a lengthy list of the policy issues which the science of statistics promised to address, including

> the defense of the country on land and on sea, the movements of the population, the instruction and education of a people and the degree of its intellectual culture, the causes of criminality, the conditions of hygiene; the state of the wealth of the land, natural or conquered, the importance of industrial creations, the transformation of economies of work and the questions which derive from them, the best means to foster communication between peoples and to transport the profits of their activity, the extent of our internal or colonial trade, the fluctuations in our general commerce; the distribution of taxes, the art, so rare, of establishing and, even rarer, of maintaining an equilibrium of finances; the revelation of neighboring countries, too often ignored, even when their frontiers border on ours, the observation of their progress which

threatens us or of their decadence which might warn us, so many subjects amongst many others, worthy of our attention and which belong to the science of statistics, such as you certainly understand, Mister minister, and such as is manifest to us.[13]

Strikingly absent from this list is a substantive policy agenda. In England the official statistical apparatus developed as a byproduct of campaigns for concrete social and professional reforms, beginning with the recognition of the rights of Dissenters and extending to sanitary reform, vaccination, and challenges to the monopoly that the medical profession enjoyed over the certification of causes of death. In France, by contrast, it seems to have been legitimated by a somewhat vague, principled commitment to "science" and a concern with the position of France vis-à-vis its neighbors. This difference is especially striking when one considers the near-absence of basic information essential for coordinated state intervention. As Kusiel has demonstrated in his study of the origins of economic planning in France, before the First World War France lacked even the minimal knowledge necessary for economic intervention, not to mention the administrative infrastructure which might have made it possible.[14] The same can be said for public hygiene and other forms of social reform.

This situation in turn explains the focus on the improvement of existing official documents. The annual report of the Superior Council of Statistics reads like a second version of Bertillon's program to reform administrative statistics, without the commitment to developing a separate science. The work of the council was divided into three sections, devoted to effecting improvements in topographical statistics, in population statistics, and in various other forms of statistics. The main focus of debate centered on basic reforms such as having the census conducted among the actual population (rather than the population of legal residence) and shifting the dates of the quinquennial census from the years ending in one and six in each decade to those ending in zero and five.

The establishment of the council thus involved a partial realization of the demographers' program. It was a symbolic acknowledgment of the role of "scientists" and "scientific" considerations in the development of administrative statistics. At the same time, however, the council rejected entreaties to reorganize official statistics and address the explicit needs of "science," as distinct from those of the administration. In contrast with the situation in England, the "needs" of the administration were those of general comparison and representation rather than administration or policy evaluation.

The result was the institutionalization of a more sophisticated version of descriptive statistics, which allowed for the existence of long-term trends, but did not provide information necessary to explore the causes of observed trends and fluctuations or monitor the effectiveness of (future) measures such as family allowances. It was only in the interwar period that the statistical infrastructure was adapted to policy and administrative needs, relegating "science," or more specifically the new science of demography, to the role of outsider.[15]

The Jubilee of the Société Statistique de Paris

The second event, the Jubilee of 1885, symbolized the intellectual reorientation in French statistics. The celebration lasted four days, each of which was devoted to a different type of statistical practice; taken together, they summarize the four types of activity associated with the label "statistics" at the time. The first day dealt with the history of the society. Demography was limited to this historical review: the term did not figure in the "scientific" papers delivered in the course of the conference, nor in the last speech of the day by Émile Levasseur, on the declining state of French natality. The second day of the jubilee was devoted to a series of talks reviewing the state of administrative statistics in different countries, the third to substantive presentations by foreign administrators and social statisticians, and the fourth to a series of talks by French statisticians. This clear compartmentalization of administrative and scientific statistics on the one hand and foreign and French statistics on the other attests to the strength of these categories in the minds of the organizers. While demographers had called for the promotion of an international intellectual project which infused science into administrative practice, the Société Statistique de Paris hardened the boundaries between the different communities and practices.

On the fourth day of the jubilee seven men presented papers. In the list of topics, economic statistics was given the place of honor, while public hygiene and medical statistics were excluded. Interestingly, the study of population movement was presented by Loua—who favored the administrative, descriptive approach. Moreover, the paper was not actually read during the conference for lack of time. While Jacques Bertillon was among the speakers that day, his contribution presented a problem in what was then classified as anthropology: it was an elaboration of his father's work on the distribution of heights within a population. Among the other texts, only those by Juglar and Cheysson attempted to transform statistics into an experimental tool. They were important chiefly because of the limits which they set for themselves. Juglar's presentation was a statistical study of commercial crises considered as periodic phenomena — a topic well within Bertillon's definition of appropriate objects for demographic study. In keeping with Bertillon's "scientific" approach, Juglar opened with a theory which he then proceeded to test and explore. His hypothesis was that the abuse of credit on the international level was at the origin of financial crises. His study explored the relations (covariations) between shifts in the circulation of capital, the discount of the effects of commerce, and the extent of gold and silver reserves.

Cheysson's article, entitled "Geometrical Statistics," was the most novel and methodologically sophisticated of the offerings. Whereas in 1878 his approach had been met with certain skepticism, in 1885 it was presented as the centerpiece of the jubilee meetings. In working with geometric curves, Cheysson went well beyond a graphic representation of numerical data. Instead he used the curves to identify the optimal balance of inputs in industrial and commercial production. At the same time, the geometric method stopped short of applying mathematics to the analysis of statistical data. It was also severely limited in the type of objects to which it was applicable. As the editor of the publication associated with the jubilee meeting noted in his summary of Cheysson's talk:

> [Geometric statistics] would not incur the same reproaches which are ordinarily made against the use of pure mathematics in economic questions, too complicated, it is said, to be held in a formula.
>
> It would definitely be a vain pretension to wish to put in equation the problems in which man is directly concerned with his wavering and diverse nature. The majority of objects on which political economics speculates allow, as Bastiat said, "neither weight nor measurement"; they do not have a "meter" and, consequently, escape from the hold of mathematics. But there exist certain objects which belong to the domain of the latter, such as prices, quantities, moneys . . . For these, graphic calculation can usefully reach them, on the condition that it is only applied to empirical data and is limited to a sort of convenient and rapid manipulation, that simplifies and shortens the operations, foresees the errors and brings out the solutions not only to the spirit but to the eyes.[16]

Thus Cheysson's foray into the experimental method was limited in two ways: it needed to avoid all attempts to apply pure mathematics to statistical observations, and its range of application was confined to clearly quantifiable things. The scientific study of human behavior was therefore defined as beyond the scope of the method. This delineation is particularly striking for what it reveals about the persistence of certain cognitive boundaries, despite the explicitly experimental character of the approach. Although demography, which had presented itself as the lodestar of an all-encompassing project for the social sciences, had failed to gain a footing in the liberal-administrative sector, Cheysson's project was more modest and consequently more likely to succeed. It also had the advantage of promising to provide very concrete practical instructions to economists concerned with solving industrial problems.

On the Demise of Demography

This brief review of the "takeover" and transformation of demography by the Société Statistique de Paris and liberal economists points to the continued importance of hierarchical relations between the liberal-administrative sector and the moral-municipal sector, the importance of policy linkages and channels of policy influence for bestowing scientific recognition, and the persistence of a primarily representative political use of statistics. Between 1878 and 1885 demographers and statisticians competed for "ownership" of the "scientific" approach to statistics. In many ways their claims were addressed not to official scientific authorities but to the government. At issue was official recognition of the "scientific" approach and the authority to specify what precisely that approach would entail.

The (short-term) victory of the Société Statistique de Paris can be attributed to the continued importance of membership in the élite academic and administrative sectors and the political relevance of economic over population issues. Between 1878 and 1885 the Société Statistique de Paris recruited leading liberal economists, employed in quasi-official state educational and scientific institutions and serving as national administrators. By contrast, demography remained rooted in medicine, anthropology, and municipal administration. Similarly, whereas the Société Statistique de Paris linked its agenda to analyzing and resolving the "workers question" and economic developments more generally, demographers coupled their call for a more abstract, experimental approach to statistics with a concern over depopulation. The issue proved particularly unsatisfactory as a channel of policy access.

While much has been written on the political import of depopulation, most scholars overlook the almost purely symbolic nature of the issue and the absence of accompanying social policy. Before the late 1890s fear of depopulation was largely limited to a relatively small intellectual élite and an equally small number of Catholics concerned with moral decadence and the breakdown of the family.[17] In addition, statisticians were unable (as they are still) to spell out the causes of the observed phenomenon and thus to agree on a course of action. Instead of demonstrating the ability of statistics to identify laws and causes and formulate social policy, technical discussions of depopulation inevitably ended in lengthy tirades concerning the decline of civilization, the rise of individualism and egoism, and the loss of religiosity. One indication of the policy (ir)relevance of the "obsession" with depopulation can be found in the failure of pronatalists to develop an organizational base until the late nineteenth century and the absence of government action until the twentieth.[18] In this context, nineteenth-century demography was necessarily unable to demonstrate its practical potential in the one area on which it had staked its public claims.

The institutional success of the Société Statistique de Paris and the creation of the Conseil Supérieur de Statistique mark the substantive victory and institutional demise of demography. They also reflect the limits of the "scientific" form of administrative statistics associated with demography. Both developments amounted to an explicit affirmation of the existence of a specifically scientific approach to statistics, formerly associated with the label "demography." Both also signify a disjuncture between analysis and policy prescription, with consequences for the technical development of statistics. Within the Société Statistique de Paris, statistics were used to inquire into the existence of laws and causes, but they retained their representative function. Numbers continued to be used to represent the state of the nation, rather than to address practical problems or implement specific policies. Bertillon had followed his English colleagues in using hypothetical scenarios to calculate the effect of proposed policy prescriptions (in this case on the potential savings in life), but members of the Société Statistique de Paris were less willing to engage in this type of statistical manipulation. Similarly, the Conseil Supérieur de Statistique introduced statisticians into the administration, but it limited their role to a purely advisory function. Again, statistics and statisticians were not directly involved in the policy process.

This limitation in the policy influence of statistics can be linked to the relatively bounded nature of scientific institutions (compared to English ones). While the monopoly of the élite scientific academies over the according of scientific recognition would seem to have loosened somewhat under the Third Republic, public outreach remained limited to explicitly scholarly venues (such as the public conferences at the Sorbonne), and scientific societies remained relatively independent of broad public audiences. True, the Société Statistique de Paris depended on élite recruitment for its revival. But that recruitment does not seem to have changed the profile of its leaders — who remained full-time scholars. Instead, the main change would seem to have come from the influx of mathematically trained engineers into statistics and most notably administrative statistics, thus affirming traditional links between state-supported grandes écoles — in this case Polytechnique — and high civil service positions.

Finally, the comparison between France and Britain suggests a close relation between the representative (political) use of statistics in France and a descriptive form of reasoning (evident in the more collectivistic, deterministic version of demography as well). This contrasts with the instrumental (political) use of statistics in England and a more experimental, probabilistic version of the "scientific" administrative style of statistical reasoning. An examination of developments in England between 1878 and 1885 suggests the importance of this difference for the subsequent development of mathematical statistics in England and its rejection in France.

PART IV

The Struggle to Retain

Disciplinary Recognition:

How to "Defend" a Discipline

in Nineteenth-Century England

CHAPTER EIGHT

The Challenge to Vital Statistics

As in France, the period 1878 to 1885 in England was marked by the emergence of new, competing forms of statistical practice and a transformation in the social and political institutions which had supported the previous order. The initial challenge began in political economy but extended to statistics. As long as the institutional arrangements that had supported vital statistics remained in place, the discipline held its ground. It was only when statistics was removed from the agendas of the public health movement and administrative agencies that it lost its position as *the* authoritative form of statistical practice. As in the previous discussion, the analysis that follows focuses on the consequences of these developments for what counted as statistics and for the meaning of disciplinary activity.

The Statistical Society of London, 1878–1885

Vital Statistics as an Institutional Ideal

Between 1878 and 1885 vital statistics reigned as the ideal form of statistical practice, and the Statistical Society of London maintained its position as the national statistical agency with the authority to grant scientific recognition. The official history of the society identifies the period 1864 to 1884 as one of "maturity." In the course of these two decades membership increased from 357 Fellows in 1863 to 530 at the end of 1873 to 860 at the society's fiftieth anniversary in 1883.[1] The *Annals of the Royal Statistical Society* attribute the increase in membership to the Prince of Wales, who in 1873 agreed to serve as honorary president. Like the SSA, the SSL undoubtedly also benefited from its role in the political and cultural consolidation of reform-minded Whig élites. This social orientation was clearly evidenced in the recruitment policy of the council, which was explicitly directed to enroll "Fellows, peers, members of Parliament and persons interested in Statistics."[2]

An examination of the reports of the council to the General Assembly and the Annual Presidential Addresses establishes the authority of vital statistics and of the "scientific approach," as it was called. The practice of delivering presidential addresses was introduced in 1869 and can be ascribed to a desire to consolidate a collective identity in the face of rapid expansion. In the first such address, William Newmarch, an economist who specialized in financial statistics, affirmed his version of vital statistics. In keeping with the English tradition, Newmarch located the specificity of the project in its combination of science and politics, rather than in a specific epistemological or disciplinary profile. For Newmarch, the contribution of statistics lay in its identification of "ultimate units," which provided a measure of what could reasonably be expected under "normal circumstances" and which served to indicate situations requiring "extraordinary measures." Farr's "healthy district" mortality rate provided an example of such a unit. Other areas in which ultimate units had been identified included pauperism and pauper relief, working-class employment, fiscal and financial statistics, and various forms of transportation.[3] The emphasis highlights the instrumental use of statistics and consequent importance of practical indices for action.

This list demonstrates that Newmarch saw statistics as a practical form of knowledge, directed at social policy. At the same time, he distinguished between statistics and political controversy. In 1871, in a review of papers submitted over the course of the preceding year, Newmarch categorized the articles as "scientific," descriptive, and political. Papers in the first category were "directed, with more or less success and completeness, to the application of the statistical method to the investigation of philosophical and political problems, and that is the highest function to which this Society can apply itself—a function which I hope will in future years occupy a greater share of its attention than perhaps has been possible down to the present time."[4] The second category of papers provided "statistical evidence on the progress and present state of special countries, enterprises and trades." In the "political" category, Newmarch explained, "we have had papers on the statistics of what may be called practical questions."[5] Newmarch clearly privileged the "scientific" form of inquiry over both the descriptive and practical forms.

Ten years later, A.H. Bailey expressed a similar preference for "scientific" administrative statistics when he agreed to second the council's annual report. Again, vital statistics was singled out as a model for the society to follow. "I would merely remark that I am glad to see that the subject of Vital

Statistics has occupied more of the attention of the members than has been the case in one or two previous sessions. I have thought sometimes that there has been some risk of this Society drifting into a political Society, seeing that the subjects which excite the greatest amount of attention here are those which are expected to come on for discussion in the Houses of Parliament."[6] Bailey's statement is interesting both because it echoes New-march's insistence on the value of practical studies, which are distanced from immediate political controversy, and for what it says about the direction of the society. That Bailey felt the need to applaud the renewal of work on vital statistics indicates that it no longer occupied the center of the society's attention, and was no longer a politically controversial or compelling issue. The quote also points to a tension between the ideal that the gatekeepers actively upheld and the actual work of the society as it moved into the 1880s.

The Challenge to Vital Statistics

The Attack on Political Economy

Of all the issues in the field of vital statistics, the relation between science and "opinion" proved most controversial. In the 1840s and 1850s it provided the main axis of scientific recognition. It also served as a principle of differentiation for distinguishing between formal organizations. Thus while most members of the Statistical Society of London (SSL) accepted Farr's model of social science as a tool of political persuasion, many kept their distance from the more explicitly political Social Science Association. Similarly, within the British Association for the Advancement of Sciences (BAAS), influential members continued to express their skepticism toward the scientificity of Section F. In the late 1870s their criticisms posed a serious challenge to the authority of vital statistics as a model of scientific and statistical practice.

The presidential addresses, delivered at the annual meetings of Section F, document concerns for the scientificity of statistics. Between 1860 and 1874 almost all the inaugural addresses touched on the scientific status of the section. The themes were similar to those voiced at the founding of vital statistics in the 1840s. Issues included the status of both political economy and statistics as a science (or not), the relation of theory and practice, and the desirability of specialization versus a single, all-encompassing social science. An early expression of this second wave of "attacks" can be found in a speech given in 1860 by the well-known economist Nassau W. Senior.

Senior explicitly questioned the scientificity of many of the papers presented before the section. As he explained, many of the section's authors had "wandered from the domain of science into that of art." The distinction, he reminded his listeners, lay in the difference between statements of facts and statements concerning "the means by which future facts may be brought about or influenced."[7] For Nassau, the importance of the boundary thus lay in the protection that it provided against the intrusion into science of politics, or the art of legislation and reform. In 1861 William Newmarch used the next annual inaugural address to respond. His speech enumerated the contributions of "economic science" to social and economic progress. In a rhetorical move which was common at the time, Newmarch credited political economy with most of the material achievements of the past twenty years. The main advances in political economy, he explained, were due to the adoption of the "experimental method," whereby observation and experiment were substituted for "deductions arrived at by geometrical reasoning." Statistics, he argued, were one of the main empirical methods available to political economy.

While Newmarch defended the status of economic science as a science and as a policy tool, he did not extend this "courtesy" to statistics. Instead he went on to suggest that statistics "alone cannot properly be described as a science": " I am bound to tell you, that in Statistics we have no such body of general laws as are to be found in other branches of inquiry, which no one hesitates to describe as science. We have, for example, in Statistics no such body of general laws as are to be found in dynamics, as are to be found in chemistry, or in physiology. But then we claim for Statistics — and it is no small claim to put forward for any branch of knowledge — that it is the application of the Experimental or Baconian method to the several divisions of inquiry which relate to man in society. We say, that where there is no careful application of the Statistical method . . . there can be but faint hope of arriving at the truth in any line of research connected with social problems."[8]

Thus while Nassau called into question the scientificity of statistics, Newmarch questioned the scope. And while Nassau insisted on a sharp distinction between science and practice, Newmarch affirmed it.

The Attack on Section F

Between 1860 and 1874 the scope, and thus the consequences, of this meta-discourse were relatively limited. In 1876, however, the situation changed. Francis Galton, then an explorer and geographer, attacked Section

F for its failure to conform to the strictures of science and called for its closure. The BAAS responded by creating a special commission to investigate his charges.

In considering this episode, it is important not to let knowledge of Galton's subsequent role as the founder of mathematical statistics influence an appreciation of his institutional position at the time. Until the mid-1860s Galton's work focused on geography and the popularization of science. In 1869 he published *Hereditary Genius*, in which he laid out his views on the transmission of intellectual and physical ability and the threat posed by the extinction of genius. The work, it should be noted, did not receive a great deal of attention at the time, nor did Galton push his point. It did, however, set a research agenda that shaped Galton's scientific work in the next decades and led him to statistics.

According to his friend, colleague, and disciple Karl Pearson, Galton used Section F to express his dissatisfaction with the state of social statistics and to promote his own mathematical approach.[9] While the mandate of the committee of inquiry was not explicitly aimed at Section F, Galton directed it that way. In a report entitled "Considerations Adverse to the Maintenance of Section F (Economic Science and Statistics)," Galton reviewed the papers presented at the meetings of Section F between 1873 and 1875. To support his call for suppressing the section, he noted that "not a single memoir treats of the mathematical theory of Statistics"; that while many of the papers dealt with "important matters of human knowledge . . . this is not of itself a title to the existence of the Section"; and that the work of the statistical section had little relation to that of other sections in the association ("This Section, therefore, occupies a peculiar position of isolation, being neither sufficiently scientific in itself, nor receiving help from the other Sections").[10]

In defense of the section, Farr pointed to the personal authority of past presidents, the importance of the topics treated by vital statistics, and the commitment of "every civilized Government in the world" to the collection of official statistics. He also noted that many eminent mathematicians and scholars in the past had turned their efforts to "the relations of the different orders of facts admitting of measurement."[11] In each case, it was the authority of those associated with statistics, rather than the actual scientific accomplishments, which were brought forth. In a second line of argument, Farr also emphasized the popularity of the section, especially among women. "It no doubt attracts many who would not otherwise become members of the Association. The Association, in advance of some other scientific bodies, admits members of both sexes, and the number of ladies has latterly ranged from 600 to 1,058. Among the 856 papers read in this section since its origin, 21 have been by ladies, amongst others by Florence Nightingale, Mrs. Grey, and Mary Carpenter."[12]

This last argument illustrates a fundamental difference between Galton's and Farr's views of statistical practice. Galton formulated his attack in terms of purely intellectual criteria; Farr presented it as a part of a democratic political practice aimed at transforming knowledge into Progress. The distinction, it is important to underline, was not one of science versus politics — Galton's concerns were as political as those of Farr — but rather of criteria of evaluation and recognition. Whereas Galton appealed to "scientific" criteria, Farr focused on the personal authority and standing of participants and on the extent of public support. As we will see, this difference can be related to two different models for the practice of statistics and two different audiences. And whereas Galton's argument foretold a narrower "scientific community" in which membership depended on displays of merit (formal credentials or recognized work), Farr spoke from the perspective of a world in which the boundaries between intellectual, economic, social, and political élites were relatively fluid and in which science was a general political and cultural resource.

The outcome of the episode was aptly summarized in 1881 by E. Grant Duff, the president of Section F. In a review of the history of the section he noted: "in the year 1876 the question was raised — and raised by a very eminent person — whether we of Section F should continue to hold our place. The attack was able; the defense was not particularly brilliant, but the goodness of our cause or the leniency of our judges carried us through, and we were adjudged to have successfully restated the reasons for our existence."[13] Section F was thus retained, Francis Galton returned to his relatively isolated search for techniques to measure the transmission of hereditary traits, and social statisticians continued their pursuit of social science as social reform. This was not, however, the end of the story. According to most histories, the importance of the attack on Section F lay in the consequences not for social statistics but for political economy.

The Defense of Vital Statistics

A striking feature of the ssl's response to the critique of Section F was its assiduous avoidance of the substance of Galton's remarks. Two texts published in 1877, immediately after the episode, exemplify this public display of "indifference": the annual presidential address of the ssl and a substantive article that Farr presented at the meeting of Section F. Taken together, they constituted a defiant affirmation of the political role of statistics.

Shaw-Lefevre's address was delivered on 20 November 1877, just after Galton's critique of Section F had been published. Rather than situate himself in the ongoing polemic, the speaker chose to reaffirm the dominant image of statistics as politically relevant scientific practice. The danger that concerned him was not political controversy but rather "philosophical seclusion." It was to the credit of the society, he asserted, that over the past forty years it had "dealt with and treated in an exhaustive manner those subjects which have occupied the public mind." Not only did Shaw-Lefevre applaud the past involvement of the ssl in public issues, but he called on his colleagues to continue in this path. Finally, he affirmed the society's "democratic" model of policy influence, whereby the collection of social knowledge was not only a step preliminary to the action of legislators and the public but also a subsequent tool of policy evaluation.

To the extent that the controversy surrounding Section F figured in Shaw-Lefevre's speech, it was in his disavowal of all disciplinary claims for statistics. He returned to the traditional distinction between statistics as the collection of facts and science as the establishment of relations between facts.[14] His opposition to science, however, was less radical than his initial statement might suggest. Having insisted that statistics was neither a theoretical nor an experimental science but rather the record of an experiment, he proceeded to assert the capacity of statistics to "suggest theories as to the causes which determine the condition of men" and to subsequently verify "theories which have been propounded":[15] "So closely allied are they, and so necessary an adjunct of social science and political economy, that it is difficult to form a table of statistics, without reference to the branch of these sciences which it illustrates; and it is still more impossible to discover statistics, without importing arguments as to their bearing upon the laws which are the objects of these sciences."[16] Thus Shaw-Lefevre's rejection of the image of statistics as a separate science did not reduce the practice to mere bookkeeping (as it would have done in France), nor did it deny the intimate relation between theory and statistical practice. Rather it figured in his discourse as an affirmation of the impossibility of separating statistics from its subject. As such, it countered Galton's call to separate practical political inquiry from science.

Shaw-Lefevre's statement of position can be read in a number of ways. First, it can be seen as evidence that an earlier tension between two models persisted: that of statistics as a science and that of statistics as a descriptive practice. Therefore it indicates that in 1877, Jevons's and Galton's work had not yet altered the range of competing models. Second, Shaw-Lefevre's formulation indicates the degree to which Farr's and Guy's scientific model had colonized the English descriptive model. In contrast with the situation in France, few active statisticians in England adhered to a model of theory-neutral statistics, and all recognized the manner in which the questions posed shaped their empirical data. Finally, the ease with which different speakers passed over the question of whether statistics was a science, and the absence of an organized debate around the issue, attest to the relative unimportance of disciplinary claims. For most of the century, English statisticians were far more divided over the boundary between science and politics than that between description, causal analysis, and theory.

Shaw-Lefevre's decision to ignore the challenge of mathematics to statistics (which Galton's criticisms introduced) was echoed in the article on the "Doctrines of Population" which William Farr presented at the next meeting of Section F. The article is noteworthy in that it marks the only time Farr set out to summarize the "scientific" achievements of vital statistics as a science (discipline). The introduction to the text promises to summarize the findings of statistics concerning the laws of population. Thus it might be expected to contain a formalization of Farr's statistical work of the past forty years. Instead, Farr uses the occasion to marshal statistical arguments against critics of public health, thus affirming the explicitly problem-oriented, practical nature of his overall project.

Farr begins his analysis with a discussion of theories of world population growth and the relation between birth rates, death rates, and population size. The first two paragraphs move from the Bible to Malthus, the real object of his discussion. The purpose of the article is to counter criticisms of public health and social reform in general. Turning to the case of England and "actual examples of the increase of population," Farr demonstrates that a reduction of the mortality rate in the more healthy districts of the country has not been accompanied by an increase in the rate of population growth, but rather by an adjustment of the birth rate. By contrast, in those areas with very high mortality rates the birth rate "no longer keeps pace," thereby leading to a decrease in overall population: "Thus within certain limits the reduction of the mortality had no absolute tendency to accelerate the natural increase of population."[17] The importance of this observation lies not so much in the theoretical implications of the debate as in the practical conclusions which follow: "Hence, at this stage of the investigation we are justified in drawing the inference: the diminution of the mortality of England by sanitary improvement is in no danger of multiplying men beyond the means of subsistence."[18] The remainder of the article is organized around a demonstration of the capacity of human populations to regulate population growth through the voluntary control of the birth rate. Statistical examples are used to counter the necessary role of wars, famines, and epidemics in population control and to defend public health programs.

The text was thus a classic example of the type of problem-oriented study which Farr and Neison had cultivated over the past decades. Each discussion was selected to add another element to a tightly constructed argument which systematically refuted a litany of possible objections. As noted above, this form contrasted sharply with the French aspiration to provide a mapping or representation of the state of society. The only indirect references to Galton's criticisms are found in the closing statement of the article, where Farr explicitly asserts the responsibility of the British Association to address social problems and thereby contribute to social progress: "It is impossible to survey the present state of the millions of populations of all ages and ranks, without feeling that problems remain for solution, which will task all the resources of the sciences the British Association cultivates."[19] Farr's determination to make the association responsible for this sort of discussion was further expressed by the striking absence of technical or methodological discussions which might have served to respond to Galton's criticisms.

While Farr's article can be read as a refusal to engage Galton's critique, it can also be seen more simply as an expression of the current preoccupations with population and population statistics. Between 1875 and 1885 a number of lengthy articles were published in the *Journal of the Statistical Society* on population statistics. Two themes characterize all these texts. The first, evident in a piece by R. Price Williams entitled "On the Increase of Population in England and Wales," is the Malthusian concern that population might overrun resources. In the increasingly urban, industrial context of the second half of the century this concern translated into studies on the relation of population and particular resources. Price Williams's study was based on a report which he had prepared for the Commission on the Coal Supply.[20] The paper attempted to predict future population in light of past trends. His analysis of changing rates of growth—rather than absolute numbers—is a sign of the accumulated savoir-faire of English statisticians and the value of the database which the GRO had built over the past decades.

A second set of papers by Thomas A. Welton, Noel A. Humphreys, and G. B. Longstaff considered fluctuations in the mortality rate, their effects on longevity, and consequences for the evaluation of existing public health problems.[21] Like Farr's paper, these studies were directed against critics who argued that mortality rates failed to establish the beneficial consequences of public health legislation. More specifically, critics focused on the observed increase in adult male mortality. Like earlier issues, this challenge to public health programs was (also) debated in technical terms. The defense of social reform was thus also an occasion to develop techniques for measuring the effect of changes in the mortality of one cohort on subsequent ones.

Conflicting Ideals

The contrast between Galton's appeal to mathematical formalization and Farr's reliance on political practice to ground the authority of statistics can be viewed as a contrast between (pure) science and politics. This perspective, however, overlooks the institutional considerations associated with both mathematical statistics and neoclassical economics. The two forms of statistics correspond to two forms, or channels, of political influence. Whereas in the middle quarters of the nineteenth century statisticians acted as members of informal networks of reform-oriented élites, in the last decades of the century they increasingly relied on their positions as university-based experts to influence the policy process. And whereas in the earlier period policy influence was mediated by the influence of statistical writings on public opinion, in the later period it was directed at politicians and professionals.

As we will see, the short-run "victory" and subsequent demise of vital statistics can be related to the persistence of the earlier, "amateur" model of political influence. In the mid-1870s the political and scientific importance of amateur scientists, in association with political reformers, protected vital statistics from an otherwise persuasive intellectual attack. By the mid-1880s, however, the reform of the civil service, the reassertion of partisan politics, and associated changes in the policy process increasingly privileged the type of specialized, university-based knowledge associated with the scientific critics of vital statistics, notably marginal economics and mathematical statistics.

In summary, the "scientific" work of the SSL between 1878 and 1885 attests to the persistence and affirmation of a problem-oriented practice in which statistics was cultivated in the service of social reform. It also indicates the growing sophistication of statisticians' conception of statistics as a practice and the dominance of the model for statistics espoused by Farr,

Neison, and Guy. By the late 1870s statistics embraced, according to most public representations, a combination of observation, classification, hypothesis, and theory. Moreover, most practitioners recognized the crucial influence of motivating questions on the nature and utility of the knowledge produced. While many statisticians rejected the claim that statistics constituted a science, all situated it in a broader sociological project and ascribed to statisticians an active role in identifying causes and specifying policy recommendations.

The seeming indifference of mainstream statisticians to the disciplinary reflection surrounding political economy during this period can be explained by the relatively minor place of statistics in the fallout from Galton's attack on Section F. As noted above, political economy bore the brunt of the attack. The indifference also undoubtedly reflects the uncertain outcome of those struggles. It was only in 1885, with the ascension of Alfred Marshall to the University of Cambridge and the establishment of economics as a university-based discipline, that neoclassical economics definitively usurped political economy as the leading economic science.[22] In the realm of social statistics, this victory was accompanied by the introduction of more mathematical approaches to economics into the Statistical Society of London. While this approach did not replace vital statistics, it provided a serious contender. Like the ascent of vital statistics thirty years earlier, the victory of mathematical statistics depended both on the intellectual viability of contending approaches and on the social and organizational resources available for their realization. Chapter 9 concludes my analysis of the transitional period of 1878–85 with an examination of changes in the political organizations that previously supported vital statistics, and their consequences for the intellectual status of the project.

CHAPTER NINE

Institutional Transformations and the Introduction of Disciplinary Specialization

The Defeat of the Mid-Nineteenth-Century Model

The optimism of the inaugural addresses delivered to the Statistical Society of London and the relatively unreflexive character of the papers submitted between 1878 and 1885 demonstrate the confidence of the organization in its model of statistics. As we have seen, the authority of vital statistics within scientific organizations rested on the resonance of its political project with a broader, educated public. During the 1870s and 1880s a number of developments weakened the direct role of the educated public in the policy process, thereby undermining the political status of vital statistics. These developments included the ongoing reform of the civil service and universities, and the creation of new types of state-based professions. While not decisive in the period under consideration, these reforms supported the emergence of neoclassical, university-based economics and mathematical statistics. They also laid the basis for new channels of policy influence, eventually dissolving the institutional arrangements that sustained vital statistics.

This chapter concludes the story of vital statistics by examining the consequences for it of these developments. As in France, the key institutional development was the transformed relation between science and the state. The subsequent intellectual development of statistics was shaped both by these changes and by the persistence of mid-nineteenth-century intellectual forms. While in France the continued monopoly of the Academy of Sciences over mathematics directed statisticians toward "geometrical statistics," in England fifty years of probabilistic, experimental forms of reasoning was an important condition for the subsequent development of mathematical statistics.

The Public Health Acts of 1871, 1872, and 1875 laid the basis for a new set of relations between knowledge experts and the government in the area of public health. MacLeod describes the period before 1870 as the "heroic years of innovation, when experts could, by force of will, make their mark."[1] During this period individual experts gained influential positions as advisors and inspectors, while the relative autonomy of many administrative departments left them relatively free to innovate and act. Similarly, Hennock argues that before 1870 the English administration was characterized by the centralization of knowledge and the dispersal of power.[2]

Both MacLeod and Hennock single out John Simon and his use of the Medical Department of the Privy Council as an example of this pattern of relations. As we have seen, during the 1860s Simon worked closely with William Farr to transform population statistics into an instrument of administrative action. The cooperation between their two departments was complemented by coordination with a variety of extragovernmental professional and scientific societies, which effectively lobbied for concrete legislative reforms. The establishment of the Royal Sanitary Commission of 1869 and the subsequent Public Health Acts of the early 1870s were due to the effectiveness of this network. Vital statistics figured both in the identification and documentation of public health problems and as an object of reform.

Ironically, the implementation of the public health laws of the 1870s was an important factor in the dissolution of the informal network of organizations which had brought about passage of the laws. Two administrative changes contributed to this development. First, the reforms entailed a major reorganization in the national administration of public health. The staffs of the Medical Department of the Privy Council, the General Registrar's Office, the Local Government Act Office, and the Poor Law Board were all placed under the authority of the newly created Local Government Board. This move severely restricted the autonomy of both Simon and Farr, placing their departments under the administrative control of the Local Government Board. Moreover, this change was paralleled by the introduction of much tighter financial controls by the Treasury, further limiting the scope of administrative initiative.[3]

Second, reorganization of the national departmental structure and reassertion of central control was complemented by the introduction of a new type of expert whose knowledge base included Farr's version of vital statistics. Until 1872 only the Metropolis required the appointment of Medical

Officers of Health. The new law required all borough health authorities to appoint "qualified" medical officers of health and allowed local authorities to do the same. While the act created over a thousand new posts, it did not implement the conditions to assure their authority. Between 1872 and the early 1890s medical officers organized to secure the jurisdiction that the Public Health Law of 1872 had accorded them. In the process, they effectively created and consolidated a new national-level profession. They also contributed to the establishment of a new form of knowledge-government relations and elevated vital statistics to a form of university-based, professional expertise. According to Hennock, medical officers of health put in place an arrangement whereby national authority was exercised on the local level indirectly through the centralization of knowledge standards for state-accredited professions. If the prior model was characterized by the centralization of knowledge, this new one was characterized by its dispersion. Tensions that were previously played out between central governmental authorities and local authorities were now between local officials and "experts."[4]

Far from being unique to state medicine, this new type of relationship was characteristic of a broad transformation in the basis of administrative authority, whereby universities served to certify civil servants. For the medical officers of health, the effectiveness of their authority on the local level, and thus of their role as the advocates of a new form of indirect centralization, depended on their claims to be more "qualified" than other contenders for the jurisdiction. In this situation, both the central government and the medical officers of health themselves had a direct interest in developing mechanisms to authorize the officers' exclusive competence.

As early as 1868 the British Medical Association established a committee to make recommendations concerning the creation of a diploma or certificate of proficiency in state medicine. The aim was to introduce public health as a specialty in the Medical Register, thus providing the medical profession with a mechanism of control over entry into the practice and raising the status of public health administrators. As noted above, this move was part of a broader campaign to give to the medical profession a monopoly over the public health jurisdictions. Before the committee had time to prepare its report, a number of figures in public health took it on themselves to develop teaching programs in the field. In 1870 William Stokes created the first diploma course in state medicine in Dublin. Shortly afterward, the Board of Medical Studies at the University of Cambridge created a new program for state medicine. The requirement imposed in 1872 to appoint "qualified"

persons to the newly created positions of medical officer of health undoubtedly spurred the development of academic programs. In 1875 Cambridge
held the first examinations for the diploma of sanitary science. Within a few
years a number of other universities developed diploma programs in state
medicine, including Victoria University (Manchester), Durham, Oxford,
Birmingham, Liverpool, Leeds, Sheffield, Bristol, and London.[5] All included vital statistics as a central component of the required curriculum.

While these courses considerably increased the body of qualified administrators, they did not automatically transform the profession. In 1886 the
qualifications were placed under the control of the General Medical Council, and holders of the diploma were entered in the Medical Register. Registration proved to be a major incentive for prospective students. In 1886
there were 263 registered public health practitioners; by 1900 their numbers
had increased to nearly 700. Finally, in 1888 Parliament passed a law requiring diplomas for all medical officers serving in districts with a population of
50,000 or over.

The introduction of formal educational credentials and registration was
in large part the work of the Society of Medical Officers of Health. One
consequence of the recognition and accreditation of the profession was to
separate public health officials from the rest of the medical profession. Thus
while the British Medical Association created a section in state medicine in
1871, the section failed to attract members. Instead, the more independent
Society of Medical Officers of Health (which was a continuation of the
Metropolitan Association) provided the main forum for discussion and
professional promotion. In 1875 four regional branches of the society were
established, in 1879 the main branch began to publish its monthly transactions, and in 1888 the society founded its own journal, *Public Health*.

The Appropriation of Vital Statistics as a Form of Knowledge

These developments influenced the history of vital statistics in two ways:
the introduction of formal instruction and a diploma of public health created an opportunity for institutionalizing formal statistical training; and the
organizational changes in the relation of the organized medical profession,
public health officials, universities, and the national administration dissolved the informal network that had previously supported the promotion
of vital statistics. In addition, these developments effectively closed down
those channels of policy influence which supported the democratic form of
instrumental practice formerly associated with vital statistics.

The campaign for a diploma of public health provided a major impetus for the publication and diffusion of textbooks. Where Continental statisticians wrote treatises on the theory and practice of administrative statistics, English statisticians invested in the production of teaching manuals. Before the 1870s the best-known and most extensive text was *A Manual of Practical Hygiene* by Edmund Parkes, a professor of military hygiene in the Army Medical School. In 1873 a number of other textbooks were produced, including the semi-official *Manual for Medical Officers of Health* by Dr. Edward Smith, assistant medical officer of the Local Government Board, and *A Handbook of Hygiene and Sanitary Science* by George Wilson.[6] By the early 1880s all three texts were in their fifth edition, and by the 1890s their eighth edition. In 1887 required reading for the diploma of public health at Cambridge included Parkes's and Wilson's texts as well as the annual reports of the General Registrar's Office and the Medical Department.

An examination of these texts, both dating from 1873, illustrates the image and approach to statistics deemed appropriate for public health officials. They document a model of statistics as practical, approximate knowledge, distinct both from mathematics and from the descriptive model still current in France at the time. These characteristics situate Parkes's and Wilson's project in direct continuity with Farr's program for vital statistics. Parkes begins his chapter on statistics by noting the role of army surgeons in producing statistical returns and the consequent necessity for a minimum of statistical knowledge. Parkes also indicates that he will refrain from entering into mathematical discussions. The first section of the chapter, "A Few Elementary Points Connected with General Statistics," discusses the importance of accuracy in identifying numerical units, problems of ambiguous classification, and the relation between true and observed means. This last point illustrates both the epistemological status of figures and the boundary between mathematics and statistics. As Parkes explains:

> The average number which is obtained is never the true mean, but is merely approximative or probable. To say the true mean had been obtained in any case, would be to say that absolute accuracy had been reached.
>
> The approximation of the probably average to the true average increases with the number of observations, and perhaps nearly in the ratio of the square root of the increase. The amount of error when an average is drawn can be determined by a rule derived from the calculus of probabilities, and is generally known as Poisson's rule. The error is exceedingly great when the number of observations are small, and in all cases (such as

mortality, curative effect of medicines, etc.) it is right to calculate the amount of error by Poisson's rule before forming any opinion as to the actual results.[7]

To illustrate his point and instruct his readers in calculating the "amount of error," Parkes provides an example from the work of the Frenchman Pierre Louis (taken from Gavarett's *Statistique médicale* of 1840). He also presents a second method involving the calculation of successive means.

The use of this example in a textbook aimed at army surgeons in 1864 provides a striking illustration of differences in the diffusion of statistical and mathematical culture in France and England during the middle quarters of the nineteenth century. In France concern with problems of error during this period was limited to general statements concerning the need for large databases. Certainly no one went so far as to suggest that statisticians should routinely *calculate* the degree of error. Instead, such calculations were relegated to the area of mathematics and excluded from everyday statistical practice. In England, by contrast, such calculations figured under the heading of "minimum statistical knowledge."

In the remainder of the chapter, Parkes signals the need to register extreme values as well as averages and raises various points concerning graphic representation. He concludes his discussion with a list of the usual indices or measures collected in public health and an illustration of some of the more recent findings concerning the relative health of the population. This discussion is complemented by a more lengthy discussion of army statistics. The subsequent editions of Parkes's manual retained the basic outlines of this chapter on statistics.

While Parkes's presentation was largely technical, Wilson's focused more on the interpretation of vital statistics and the bothersome question of how mortality statistics and public health are related. In the first edition, vital statistics figured as a subsection of the chapter entitled "Duties of Medical Officers of Health," and the discussion centered on the evaluation of an average mortality rate in light of the extreme heterogeneity of experiences within a district (notably variations by quarter or street).[8] By the fifth edition of 1883, however, vital statistics had obtained a lengthy chapter of its own. While less technical than Parkes's briefer discussion, Wilson's article laid out the main considerations which medical officers should take into account in compiling and interpreting vital statistics for their locality.

The chapter begins with a review of the different sources of such data, notably the census and registration. Parkes describes the method of interpolation which the General Registrar's Office used to calculate the base population between censuses. His account assumes that readers were acquainted with the use of logarithms, for no explanation was provided either of their significance or how to work with them. Like Parkes, Wilson also assumes that his audience will be comfortable with the discrepancy between statistical representations and "reality." In his discussion he speaks without apology of the inevitable discrepancy between the real increase of urban population between censuses and the calculated rate.

Having reviewed the production of census and registration data, Wilson turns to problems of classification, followed by a longer discussion of statistical results. Again, the discussion is characterized by a meta-reflection on different measures in use, alternative methods of calculation, and dangers to avoid. For example, he cautions against using weekly or quarterly returns to calculate an annual rate of growth, and refers the reader to Farr's lengthy technical discussion of the flaws in this method. The chapter concludes with what was by then a standard discussion of "statistical fallacies," most notably the effect of age structure on mortality rates.

Wilson's text attests to the ongoing routinization of the statistical practices that Farr had developed at the General Registrar's Office. By the mid-1870s the probabilistic status of statistical knowledge (in the sense of distance from "reality"), the techniques of how to construct a rate on the basis of the "population at risk," the distorting effects of variations in the age structure, and the use of what in France would be considered mathematical techniques to evaluate the reliability of calculated numbers had entered into the stock of established knowledge. While many medical officers of health were perhaps unable to respect all these rules in conducting a statistical inquiry, they were familiar with the concepts.

The Transformation of Vital Statistics as a Practice

From this perspective, the consolidation of the profession of medical officer of health clearly marked a victory for vital statistics. However, as Simon Szreter has pointed out, it also marked a radical change in the mode of instrumental action associated with vital statistics. This shift is clearly illustrated by changes in the publication policies of the General Registrar's Office and its involvement in the policy process.

Under Farr's direction the General Registrar's Office had come to see itself (and to be seen) as a central actor in both scientific and political progress. This image rested on the importance of statistical techniques in developing preventive medicine, and on a political context in which public outreach was an effective means of influencing policy. The GRO's publications were thus designed to reach an audience that extended from medical men and medical officers of health to "the amorphous, rate-paying constituency of untutored provincial public opinion that voted in and out local authorities."[9] Farr resigned from the GRO in 1883. In the years which followed, the office suppressed the problem-oriented letters of the general registrar in the organization's annual reports, privileged uncontroversial subjects, and focused discussion on the improvement of technical measures and indices rather than on substantive policy issues.[10] The exclusion of the broader public and of public issues from the GRO reflected broader changes in the policy process. It also contributed to the professionalization of administrative statistics by depriving unaffiliated social scientists of political influence and rewarding new forms of formally recognized technical competence.

The Passing of Amateur Social Science

This shift in the locus and nature of scientific "advising" is clearly evidenced in the decline of the Social Science Association (SSA) as a policy center between roughly 1875 and 1885. As noted in chapter 8, before this period the SSA epitomized the nineteenth-century model of social science as a form of political action. According to Lawrence Goldman, the effectiveness of the SSA stemmed from its special relation to the Liberal Party. More specifically, Goldman argues that the SSA played an important role in consolidating the social base of Gladstonian Liberalism and the working out of its program for social and administrative reform. The election of Gladstone in 1868 was accompanied by a shift in the political function of the association from informal parliament to "watchful lobbyist."[11]

The election of a Conservative government in 1874 effectively deprived the association of its informal political contacts, thereby limiting its political effectiveness. Discussions at the SSA increasingly focused on the evaluation of existing projects rather than on new initiatives. In the absence of a clear political agenda, the SSA lost much of its focus and support, experiencing a sharp drop in membership and consequent financial difficulties. In 1885 the association failed to hold its annual meeting, and in 1886 it was dissolved.

Two related trends help to explain the demise of the SSA: the revival of partisan politics, removing substantive debates on social policy from extra-political organizations such as the Social Science Association and entrusting them to political parties and Parliament; and a far-reaching reform of the civil service that effectively shifted the locus of administrative expert knowledge from amateur reformers to university-trained civil servants. According to Goldman, the decline of the association can in part be ascribed to its success. The argument is similar to that which I developed concerning the fate of Farr's program for vital statistics. Whereas in the late 1850s social questions were largely absent from the Parliamentary agenda, in the 1880s they were widely discussed. Similarly, whereas in the late 1850s and early 1860s the association led the call for the application of scientific knowledge to the solution of social ills, by the 1880s Social Science Association "amateurs" had been replaced by professional civil servants. As the *Times* noted in 1882, "The Social Science Congress is distinctly weakened by the similar gatherings of bodies that have encroached on the wide area open to it on its formation. There are the Trades Union Congress and the Health Congress; there are conferences of delegates from Chambers of Commerce and from Boards of Guardians. There are School Boards and conferences of teachers and of persons interested in prison management; and all these, while going in many respects beyond the scope of the Association, have necessarily robbed it of some of its old elements of attraction both as to men and matter."[12]

Both the declining influence of administrators such as Simon and Farr and the dissolution of the Social Science Association typify the gradual elimination from the policy process of social scientists in the nineteenth-century mold. This development was the result of a number of legislative acts. In the political arena, the Second Reform Act of 1867 tripled the electorate, while the Act of 1884 more than doubled it. For the first time in English history, working-class voters outnumbered the middle and upper classes. In the early 1870s the Conservative Party effectively challenged local control of partisan politics and introduced a new form of centralized control. The Corrupt Practices Act of 1883 outlawed many of the traditional practices that had allowed party whips to control local elections, and the reorganization of electoral districts in 1884 deprived local landlords of their traditional electoral power. These developments all served to introduce social issues into partisan politics, rendering informal social science and social reform organizations less central. At the same time, the ongoing reform of the civil service and the tightening of control over administrative departments also closed channels of access to the policy process. The Northcote-Trevylan Report of 1854 called for recruitment by examination to the civil service. While this move to depoliticize and professionalize the civil service took a number of decades to work its way out, it contributed to the gradual exclusion of amateur social scientists and reformers from policy work.

These developments effectively deprived the patronage system of much of its political influence.[13] They also put an end to the integrated, relatively consensual culture of social, political, and economic élites which had fostered the Social Science Association and transformed it into an "unofficial parliament." Each of the above-mentioned developments effectively deprived social statisticians of an important channel of access to the policy process. The organizing of medical officers of health and the reorganizing of the departmental structure eliminated the role of the social scientist as autonomous administrator, while organized parties replaced the Social Science Association and other cultural organizations as a locus for policy formulation.

At first glance the convergence of these different developments might seem to be fortuitous. Closer examination, however, suggests that they were part of a broader structural reorganization, whereby the knowledge and power shifted from an informal network of social, political, and intellectual élites with direct access to the central administration to university-trained professionals who exercised their authority directly on the local level.

Toward an Alternative Intellectual Model

The 1885 Jubilee

In 1885 the SSL celebrated its fiftieth anniversary. The celebration, which had been postponed for a year after the death of the Prince of Wales, was held a few weeks after the twenty-fifth anniversary of the Statistical Society of Paris.[14] In the opening address, Sir Rawson W. Rawson, president of the SSL and one of the founding members, situated the meeting relative to the earlier one in Paris: "Our program differs somewhat from that of the Statistical Society of Paris in the character of its papers, as the Council has judged it desirable that during the short time available for examining and discussing statistical questions, we should confine ourselves as much as possible to the history, theory and methods of statistics, and to the means of introducing greater uniformity in their exposition by international agreement."[15] Thus in contrast to the jubilee in Paris, which privileged administrative statistics, and at which the statistical facilities of each participating country were extensively reviewed, in London the focus was more "scientific." The decision to focus on "theory and methods" can be read as a deliberate attempt to shift the intellectual focus of the society for the future. The phrase also recalled the title of the similarly named first section at the Fourth

International Congress of Statistics, which was held in London in 1860 and had been devoted to a discussion of the scientific status of statistics. As noted above, a number of leading statisticians had already deplored the reticence of English statisticians in this area.

In 1869 William Newmarch identified "investigations of the mathematics and logic of Statistical Evidence" as one of the areas which "most require early attention" by members of the society.[16] Similarly, in 1881 William Hooper noted the absence of theoretical reflection among English statisticians. As we have seen, his article "The Method of Statistical Analysis" was written in the hopes of encouraging such work.[17] In his opening remarks, Sir Rawson expressed his hope that participants would use the occasion to settle "if possible, the vexed question of the legitimate claim of Statistics to be acknowledged as a science, and to come to an agreement as to its definition and limits."[18] The substantive portion of the meeting was divided into four sections. The first day was devoted to commemorating the history and past successes of the society. On the morning of the second day R. Giffen spoke on the role of statistics in formulating political issues and delivered two papers on the uniformity of national statistics. This session can be seen as the English equivalent of the French jubilee's day on administrative statistics, in that it dealt with issues which depended on governmental cooperation. It was followed by luncheon and an afternoon devoted to statistical methods. Three of the five papers on this part of the program announced the introduction of what a participant later referred to as *la haute statistique*, as if to proclaim the displacement of the mid-nineteenth-century model as authoritative.[19] The meeting ended with a session devoted to organizing a new international forum for statisticians, later to become the International Institute of Statistics. There is a striking contrast between the model for statistics represented in the first day of the meeting, which affirmed the authority of mid-nineteenth-century vital statistics, and that represented in the last two sessions, which replaced it with a new form of mathematical statistics.

The speakers at the historical section included Sir Rawson, who delivered the opening presidential address, Dr. Frederic J. Mouat, who presented a history of the society, and Dr. William A. Guy.[20] All three used the occasion to affirm the status of statistics as a science and the continued supremacy of the quasi-experimental, problem-oriented style associated with vital statistics. Mouat traced the origins of the society to the initiative of Adolphe Quetelet (the "founder" of the scientific-experimental approach), an initiative which he depicted as a reaction against the narrow limits placed on

Section F by the British Association.[21] His account presented the history of the society as a struggle of the "scientific" model against a narrower, descriptive approach. According to Mouat, Guy's speech of 1865 marked the victory of the scientific model. As he explained, it "permanently enlarged the scope and aims of the association beyond the mere collection of facts, irrespective of the use to which they are put, a view which has not since been lost sight of."[22]

Similarly, William Guy noted the progress of the society in its assumption of "the twofold function of origination of subject and interpretation of results." Like Mouat, he framed statistics in opposition to an earlier, descriptive model in which theory and interpretation had been outlawed under the heading of "opinion." Substantively, the model of statistics which both Guy and Mouat presented was that of an all-encompassing social science aimed at identifying the laws of society. The specificity of statistics, versus that of other sciences, lay in the nature of its object: "Other sciences deal with matters that are not of man's making, and over which he can exercise few or no modifying influences . . . But in the case of Statistics we are dealing with a mixed mass of facts brought about in part only by nature herself, but largely influenced by every change of custom, every constitutional reform, every freak of legislation."[23] Guy's point was both to claim the entire area of social science for statistics and to link statistical knowledge with social reform. Unlike other sciences, statistics dealt with social conditions, which once identified could be altered and improved.

A juxtaposition of the papers of Monday 22 June with those of Tuesday 23 June betrays a certain irrealism in Guy's and Mouat's image of the state of social statistics. As noted above, both men used the occasion of the meeting to defend the mid-nineteenth-century model against criticisms which had been voiced forty years earlier. Neither man acknowledged the intellectual challenge posed by more formal, abstract mathematical models for the practice of statistics. This seeming heedlessness can in part be ascribed to certain similarities in the overall conception of the two models, at least relative to the descriptive, atheoretical approach initially proposed for both section F and the SSL. Both the mid-nineteenth-century "scientific" approach and the new mathematical approach presented statistics as an experimental project involving the manipulation of numbers and the creation of new statistical objects. Both also conceived of statistics as a theoretically informed empirical endeavor aimed at investigating specific problems and shaped by its substantive ends. Finally, both insisted on the role of mathematics in identifying and exploring laws and regularities.

The similarity in these basic premises suggests that one of the reasons for the development of mathematical statistics in the last decades of the nineteenth century in England, and its absence in France, can be found in the nature of mid-nineteenth-century statistics. While Farr, Guy, and Neison failed to apply the calculus of probability to the measurement of significance, they did introduce a probabilistic interpretation of statistical data (which allowed them to negotiate the tension between individual and collective phenomena) and a principled faith in the relevance of mathematical techniques. This intellectual orientation contrasted sharply with that of France, where statisticians differentiated their work from that of mathematicians. Socially, this contrast was clearly exemplified in the near total absence of both mathematicians and actuaries from the "community" of French statisticians and the close relations between these groups in England.

The Introduction of Mathematical Statistics

Of the five papers read at the Tuesday session of the meeting of the SSL in 1885, three announced the advent of a new approach to statistics: "On Methods of Statistics," by Edgeworth, "The Graphic Method of Statistics," by Marshall, and "The Application of a Graphic Method to Fallible Measures," by Galton. The other two papers were by Price-Williams on diagrams of the population of London and by Émile Levasseur on graphic statistics, prepared at the request of the English organizers. That they had invited Levasseur — rather than Cheysson or Turquan, both of whom had explicitly worked on the development of such techniques — attests to his privileged status. Levasseur's paper provides an opportunity to contrast the state of the art in the two countries.

The opening sentences of Edgeworth's paper situate it in the same general tradition as Farr, Neison, and Guy. In the first paragraph Edgeworth reviews a number of definitions of statistics. Three, he noted, deserve attention "as respectively the most popular, the most philosophical, and that which is a fair compromise between the conflicting requirements of a good definition." The first embodied a very broad notion of statistics as numerical description, the second defined statistics as "the science of Means in general (including physical observations)," while the third, which Edgeworth favored, restricted it to the study of the "Means which are presented by social phenomena." The paper contained a reflection on the operational program which this last definition subsumed. While Edgeworth's choice was consistent with the mainstream position of the SSL, the content which he gave to it broke with previous definitions. According to Edgeworth: "The science of

Means comprises two main problems: 1. To find how far the difference between any proposed Means is accidental or indicative of a law? 2. To find what is the best kind of Mean; whether for the purpose contemplated by the first problem, the elimination of chance, or other purposes?"[24] Edgeworth's program for statistics differed from earlier models in its concern for what today would be referred to as statistical significance. For Edgeworth, the first step in any statistical study was to mathematically assess whether observed differences could be due to chance.

This difference in the weight assigned to purely technical or methodological considerations was complemented by an interest in the abstract or formal properties of statistical measures. As Edgeworth noted: "The methods of attacking these two problems which will be here considered are those of the more formal kind, those which are afforded by the pure Calculus of Probabilities, as distinguished from Inductive Logic in general.[25] In the first half of Edgeworth's article, he specified the types of problem which arose in statistical analysis and the appropriate method to ascertain the significance of an observed difference. He distinguished between comparisons of single means (situations with an objective mean) and comparisons between sets of means (most often subjective means). He then demonstrated how probability curves could be "artificially" generated in the latter case from the distribution of means and used to evaluate whether observed differences were due to chance or indicated the presence of a constant law. The two methods which he presented built on the theory of Laplace and the work of Lexis. In the second half of the article, Edgeworth illustrated different formulae and methods of calculation by reevaluating the findings of many of the main statistical studies of the preceding thirty years. He examined Bertillon's study of the distribution of heights in the department of the Doubs, Guy's studies of the influence of profession on longevity, and Neison's study of the unhealthiness of drinking. While most members of the audience had difficulty following each step of the reasoning, their remarks during the discussion indicated that all were aware of having been witnesses to a major advance in the practice of their science (art).

The next three papers dealt with graphic methods. The first, delivered by the Frenchman Émile Levasseur, presented graphics as a mode of vulgarization whose value was largely limited to pedagogy and popularization. According to Levasseur, graphics constituted a subordinate method whose role was to render knowledge more accessible to the senses.[26] The paper thoroughly reviewed various forms of visual display with little methodological comment. This lack of reflection on the relation between the tool and the substance of specific inquiries contrasted with the following paper by Marshall, who made a case for using graphic methods in analyzing the interaction of multiple causes. According to Marshall, there was necessarily a tradeoff in statistical analysis between accuracy and "ease and rapidity of observation."[27] To realize this end, Marshall suggested constructing what he termed "historical curves." He proposed a three-dimensional graphic, in which each of three parallel representations corresponded to a different aspect of social life, so that the user could easily compare changes in economic, moral, and social measures. Marshall also discussed the effect of scale on the shape of curves. Finally, the methodological section closed with a paper in which Francis Galton presented a method to express a curve on the basis of only a few ordinates. The technique, Galton explained, could be used "to test the presumed conformity of observations to the law of Frequency of Error." The text provided a technical explanation of how to construct the relevant probability curve and put the observed values in a form suitable for comparison.

Two features of these papers stand out in comparison with others delivered at previous sessions at the Statistical Society. The first, more obvious, characteristic is the innovative uses which both Edgeworth and Galton made of the calculus of probability. Until this point the call for applying mathematics — and, more specifically, the calculus of probability — was largely limited to a commonsense notion of probability (in the sense of the probability of error). Now, with Edgeworth, it was extended to developing mathematical measures of significance, and with Galton it became a tool for studying the distribution of variations. The second, equally remarkable, feature is the greater importance given to technical discussions. In contrast to Farr, who confined his methodological demonstrations to a technical appendix at the end of his papers and deliberately toned down his presentations to make them accessible to the broadest possible audience, Edgeworth and Marshall played up the mathematical, technical, and thus esoteric nature of their knowledge.

The privileging of mathematical analysis within statistics was (necessarily) accompanied by a change in the model of action associated with statistical practice. In presenting their work in its more technical forms at the jubilee of the SSL, both Edgeworth and Galton must have known that a fair proportion of the audience would fail to follow their reasoning. They also knew that some would follow and, more importantly, that others would appreciate the nature of the enterprise. In France, such a strategy risked public reprobation, but in England it was wholly consistent with the rhetorical commitment to promoting statistics as a science which drew its authority from a special relation with higher mathematics.

Toward a More "Professional" Discipline

Two developments attest to the immediate success of this specialized, professional model of disciplinary organization. The first was a spillover from the London jubilee meeting to the general sessions of the SSL and the meetings of section F. In 1885 Henry Sidgwick delivered an inaugural address at the annual meeting of Section F. His speech on "the scope and method of economic science, and its relation to other departments of what is vaguely called 'social science'" was a coherent statement of the neoclassical approach to economics. In measured tones, Sidgwick demonstrated that the image of orthodox economics, which had been so virulently attacked over the past eight years, amounted to a caricature of the works of Smith, Ricardo, and Mill. He also reformulated the debate. "The issue," he explained, "is whether operation of other motives (than the pursuit of individual interest) is enough to destroy the general applicability of the method of economic analysis which assumes that each party to any free exchange will prefer his own interest to that of the other party."[28] Finally, he refuted critics by openly affirming the importance of historical variation in the determination (and investigation) of economic conditions. The immediate effect of Sidgwick's speech was to effectively close down the ongoing debate over the status of economic science and statistics.

This development was paralleled by a similar one within the SSL. From 1885 onward Edgeworth's mathematical economics and Marshall's disciplinary strategy provided the model for statistical practice. This shift can be seen not only in the changing composition of published papers but institutionally. In 1885 the discussion at the proceedings of the fifty-first anniversary meeting concerned the criteria of future recruitment. The topic was introduced by Henry C. Burdett, who called attention to the election of "gentlemen whom he could not recognize as statisticians." Burdett called for limiting membership in the society to experts and separating them from laymen. He justified his position by invoking the society's own claims concerning the disciplinary status of statistics: "[Mr. Burdett] took a very exalted view of the worth of statistics, and claimed the President as a supporter of that view, because in his Address the President said it would be well if the anniversary could be made so important that statistics might be emphasized as a science."[29]

At first glance, Burdett's comments can be taken as an articulation of the inherent tension between the claim that social statistics constituted a science and the democratic, populist mode of instrumental action associated with the mid-nineteenth-century model. This interpretation, however, suffers from a certain ahistoricism, as it assumes that the notion of science was always associated with a specialized, professional form of practice and organization. In fact Burdett's comment attests to a shift in the model of social science. Previously, disciplinary claims in the social sciences were associated with the nondifferentiated study of society as a whole and the development of a public form of knowledge accessible to citizens, statesmen, and scientists. After 1885, however, (social) science in England assumed a narrower meaning associated with the practice of university-based specialists and far from the practice of either politicians or laymen.

Introducing a New Order:
The International Institute of Statistics

Curiously, the most important institutional expression of this new, technical, specialized project for statistics came from the international arena. Like the Paris jubilee a few weeks earlier, the London jubilee explicitly situated itself in continuity with the now disbanded International Congress of Statistics. As we have seen, this identification served both to affirm the place of Quetelet's intellectual model for statistics in the history of the SSL and to legitimate the participation of numerous foreign visitors. The Paris organizers marked this connection by devoting a full session to reports on the administrative apparatus in each of the participating countries (a practice introduced at the International Congress of Statistics), while the London organizers used their meeting to create a new international forum. To that end, the council of the society persuaded the Foreign Office to permit representatives of foreign municipal and national statistical governments to attend the jubilee meeting. As Sir Rawson W. Rawson informed his audience in the opening address, over forty foreign visitors attended, including twenty-two official delegates from eleven countries and three municipalities.

Substantively, the organizers of the London jubilee encouraged the founding of a new international organization in two ways. First, they devoted a full session to evaluating the uniformity of national statistics. While Mr. Jeans's paper asked whether such uniformity was desirable, Mr. Körösi, head of the Hungarian bureau of statistics, spelled out the precise areas in which uniformity had — and more importantly, had not yet — been achieved. His paper thus provided a working program for a future organization.

Second, the organizers asked Prof. von Neumann-Spallart to provide his analysis of the strengths and weaknesses of the previous International Congress of Statistics and to draw up a concrete proposal for a future organization. Von Neumann-Spallart's analysis of the failure of the previous congress focused on the absence of boundaries between the "lay element" and "active statisticians," the continual turnover in participation — owing largely to the large proportion of local lay participants — and the excessively close relations between the Congress and government. As he explained to the audience:

> The defects in the organization of these Congresses lie principally in the semi or wholly official relations between them and their leading members to the Governments, whereby their own independent action and the free discussion by them of the various subjects were considerably hampered. But the chief danger was the idea that the Governments should be bound by the decisions of the Congress or Permanent Commissions; and this danger was the more to be feared, as the final decisions of these assemblies could never be foreseen, and might be the result of a bare or purely accidental majority, and nothing was more detrimental to the authority of the Congresses than that they should on the one hand claim to speak authoritatively, whilst on the other hand, notwithstanding their position, their conclusions might be of no practical value, and could therefore never be carried out.[30]

The majority of von Neumann-Spallart's concrete proposals were directed at protecting the new organization from the liabilities posed by the absence of boundaries between laymen and experts and between administrators and scientists. According to von Neumann-Spallart, the new organization could take one of three forms, depending on how much weight was accorded to administrative versus purely scientific forms of practice. First, it could assume a "forcible and authoritative character," similar to the Comité International des Poids et Mesures or the International Telegraph Conference. In this case, the work of the organization would be directed at imposing concrete directives on national administrative statistics. Second, the new association could assume a "semi-official character," thereby following the example of the International Permanent Commission, which was restricted to government delegates and members of scientific societies. Finally, it could be constituted as a "free association," divested of any official character, but which would endeavor to establish a basis for the uniformity of official statistics. Von Neumann-Spallart recommended the last option. As he explained: "At first sight, it might appear that this free Association would be wanting in weight and authority owing to the absence of official cohesion. There can be no question however that its decisions would carry considerable weight owing to the great personal influence of the members of which it would be composed, and to their valuable labours."[31]

Von Neumann-Spallart's options are notable for the different criteria embodied in each. The first, "official" form derived its powers from political authority. As von Neumann-Spallart explained, "it is evident that these delegates could only be the directors of Central Statistical Commissions or Bureaus, and should be invested with full powers by their respective Governments to enable them to pass binding resolutions."[32] The second, "semi-official form" rested on the personal, informal authority of the participants. The association would be influential because it was restricted to persons with official positions or status in the scientific community. Finally, as von Neumann-Spallart stated, the third model, of "free association," rested its claims exclusively on merit and competence. In light of national developments within England, von Neumann-Spallart's proposal to create a "free association" strengthened a new model of disciplinary organization in which jurisdiction over the study of society was legitimated in purely scientific terms and institutionalized in private organizations independent of governmental control.

To protect his conception, von Neumann-Spallart presented a number of formal rules. While members were to be chosen from central statistical commissions, municipal statistical bureaus, and statistical societies, they were to participate as individuals rather than as official delegates. And all full members were to be given equal weight in the decisions of the organization. At the same time, membership was to be limited to eighty. While a small number of corresponding members, associates, and honorary members would be allowed to participate in the work of the organization, only full members would be allowed to vote. Finally, to mark the scientific (versus administrative) character of the new organization, von Neumann-Spallart suggested that it be "known by the designation of '*Institut International de Statistique*' recalling in this connection the excellent work performed by that most justly celebrated scientific body the *Institut de France*, as well as that performed by the '*Institut de Droit Internationale*,' which during its comparatively short career has won for itself so high a place in the public estimation."[33]

In 1886 the International Institute of Statistics (IIS) held its first meeting. Von Neumann-Spallart, now president of the institute, traced its scientific mission to the work of Quetelet. His aim, von Neumann-Spallart explained in his inaugural address, had been to collect data essential for identifying "the most general laws of the social body."[34] On an organizational level, the statutes of the institute conformed largely with von Neumann-Spallart's original proposal. The maximum number of full members was set at one hundred, to be chosen from among "the men of various nations who have distinguished themselves in the domain of administrative and scientific statistics."[35] The work of the institute was to be summarized in four types of publication: a trimestrial bulletin, an international statistical yearbook, special studies in international statistics, and transactions of meetings. The bulletins were to contain reports on the organization and efforts to reform official statistics in various countries, a summary of the most important results obtained by recent observations, and an international bibliography of recent publications.

The organizational principles institutionalized in the International Institute of Statistics were similar to those expressed by Marshall in his project for neoclassical economics and by practitioners of mathematical economics and statistics. In each case the pursuit of knowledge in the (social) sciences was predicated on the absolute autonomy of scientists from both the government and administration. The jubilee of 1885 can be seen as an announcement that this new model had entered into the competition for the scientific version of social reform. From the start, it was one of the main international forums for diffusing biometrics and English mathematical statistics to the international community. Before the First World War the institute provided a forum for presenting different approaches. However, by the postwar period mathematical statistics clearly won out. The task of coordinating national statistics passed to other international organizations, and the IIS devoted itself almost exclusively to the diffusion of English mathematical statistics.[36]

The Demise of a Disciplinary Form

In summary, a number of institutional developments help to explain the displacement of vital statistics and the ascent of mathematical statistics as the authoritative form of practice. Changes in the relations between the Treasury and administrative departments and between local and central government, in the departmental structure within the central government, and in the administration of state medicine all served to dissolve the extra-scientific social base which had supported Farr's project for vital statistics. Similarly, within the world of social statistics, the reassertion of partisan politics and the politicization of the "social question" were accompanied by the exclusion of social science as a forum for policy making.

On the other hand, this loss of resources was paralleled by the successful institutionalization of specialized disciplinary projects. The foundation of the International Institute of Statistics was only one of several developments which favored a specialized, disciplinary version of mathematical statistics and a radical division between "scientific" and "policy" knowledge. On the scientific side of the equation, these developments included the creation of university departments, first for economic science and much later for mathematical statistics in the form of Pearson's biometric laboratory. On the policy end, the advent of university-accredited state professions introduced a new type of relation between the administrative sector, higher education, and expertise. Social knowledge was increasingly transmitted, or at least certified, through university-based programs aimed at training technically competent administrators.

Placed in this context, the introduction of a diploma for medical officers of health can be seen as the first of several developments leading to the creation of the London School of Economics to train expert administrators. Whereas the models of social science advocated by Marshall and Galton and by Sidney Webb corresponded with these new arrangements by providing esoteric, specialized knowledge on which claims to expertise could be based, those promoted by followers of Farr and Guy were wholly inappropriate. Viewed from this perspective, the success of both mathematical statistics and specialized disciplinary forms can be explained by their "fit" with a new type of social structure in which the relation between science and the state was mediated by universities and university-based professions. In France statistics remained an amateur or at least nonspecialized activity, limited to the intellectual arena and introduced into the administration in the form of expert advisers; in England it was incorporated into basic professional training. And while in France this limited advisory role confined statistics (as compared to mathematics) to a representational function, supporting a sophisticated version of descriptive statistics, in England it led to the replacement of the previously dominant experimental project, directed at manipulating numbers to distinguish between causes, by mathematical statistics and marginal economics.

Conclusion

The Historical Argument in Review

The comparison of demography and vital statistics involves two cases in which initially similar ideas developed in significantly different directions. In France and England statisticians were aware of each other's work. French statisticians were familiar with French mathematicians' work on the application of probability theory to social statistics and with British vital statistics. Louis Adolphe Bertillon explicitly modeled his project for demography on William Farr's work at the GRO. Similarly, in England statisticians followed French developments closely (it is interesting to note that English libraries of the time had all the major French statistical publications, while French libraries did not buy English publications). Farr himself spent two years in Paris in the late 1830s attending lectures by Louis René Villermé just before he introduced his program for vital statistics.

This similarity in the stock of available knowledge contrasted with differences in the reception and development of what contemporaries referred to as "scientific" administrative statistics. In France political and scientific élites struggled with the "reality" of abstract statistical populations that aggregated over heterogeneous individuals. They worried whether such speculative knowledge should properly be called "statistics" and whether it was wise to use it in political and administrative procedures. In England, by contrast, vital statisticians diffused an atomistic, probabilist understanding of mortality statistics that fit with the widespread scholarly view of statistics as a component of a broader, theoretically informed social science.

These differences in content were associated with differences in the criteria of scientific recognition. In France scientific recognition depended on epistemological criteria; in England the acceptance or rejection of statistical claims was voiced in terms of the explicitly political character of the knowledge. Statistical knowledge in France was certain knowledge, whose scientific value rested on a one-to-one correspondence between observation and numbers. While political considerations undoubtedly also figured in the evaluation of particular claims, these considerations were not voiced in public. The strictly epistemological character of the discourse can be explained by the relative autonomy of French scientific organizations from both the public and the state. In England, by contrast, distinctions between projects and organizations depended on the balance between politics and science that they presented to the public. While epistemological criteria were (also) used to judge and sanction specific projects, the sanctions held little weight. This weakness of strictly scientific criteria can be ascribed to the dependence of private scientific societies on a broad base of public support. The result was an intellectual openness that allowed different styles of statistical reasoning and types of projects to circulate in the same set of organizations. The "victory" of one approach over another depended on the fit between the style of reasoning and the political uses that were made of it at the time.

The comparison of demography and vital statistics between 1830 and 1885 relates these differences in criteria of recognition to differences in the political use of statistics. More specifically, it contrasts a representative use of statistics in France with an instrumental use in England. In France statistics were used to document and describe the state of the population and thereby of France itself. The eventual adoption of the scientific administrative approach, associated with demography, depended on the politicizing of depopulation in the 1870s and the new collectivist concept of population that it introduced. The association of statistics with a pressing political problem did not, however, open the way to an instrumental use of statistics. This failure can be ascribed both to the traditional, representative function of statistics and to the nature of depopulation as a political problem. In contrast to issues of public health and labor unrest, concern over depopulation did not lead to concrete legislative measures. Instead the issue was largely symbolic, at least throughout the nineteenth century. The result was that depopulation did not give statisticians access to the political opportunities that might have changed their scientific practice. In the realm of statistics, the persistence of a representative function can be seen in the radical disjuncture between technical and political considerations in public debate.

But in England vital statistics led to a new, problem-oriented, instrumental use of numbers, whereby abstract entities and extensive statistical manipulation were used to discriminate between multiple causes. This style of reasoning fulfilled two related political functions: it played a central role in the efforts of public health reformers to influence public opinion, and it produced statistical indices that served to evaluate the effectiveness of existing legislation and to mediate between central and local government intervention. On the intellectual level, these uses were related to an atomistic, probabilist version of the new scientific, administrative approach, which resonated with the political ideology of Whig reformers and with incipient forms of social legislation directed at the management of risk.[1] Practically, they shaped the system of data collection (including the use of trained experts and supervisors rather than local officials in data collection and the transmission of individual-level data to the national center in London), the form of official statistical publications (as evidenced in weekly publications and the rapid transmission of information between governmental bureaus), and the development of practical indices such as Farr's healthy district mortality rate.

As for the broader social structures in which these intellectual and political differences were embedded, the comparison of demography and vital statistics reveals two quite different social worlds. In France the intellectual sphere was relatively isolated from broader social and political activities and organizations; the social sciences were fragmented and hierarchically ordered along intellectual, institutional, and political lines. In this context, the introduction and diffusion of the nineteenth-century scientific administrative approach depended on recognition from quasi-official scientific institutions. The bid for recognition led to a confrontation between the gatekeepers of an élite sphere of science and proponents of the new approach, situated in more marginal, positivist, Republican scientific organizations. The struggle was fought out at the level of contending epistemological criteria and alternative disciplinary maps that embodied different relations between mathematics, social statistics, administrative statistics, public health, and political economy. The sharp division between scientific and descriptive versions of administrative statistics deprived demographers of access to the raw data essential to realize their project. Similarly, the monopoly of the élite scientific academies over both mathematics and the relation between science and the state prevented them from realizing their promise to use numbers to identify laws and causes and to direct social policy.

In England, by contrast, vital statistics was pursued in a world characterized by the circulation and integration of different intellectual projects and types of élite (political, social, economic, and scientific) in a variety of distinct yet overlapping scientific organizations. Instead of explicit epistemological criteria (concerning the proper use of numbers), statistical organizations in England were distinguished by their model of the proper relation between statistics and politics. While organizations differed in the models they put forth, none managed to exclude political reform agendas from statistical papers. This failure to police a strict separation of statistics and politics can be related to the integration of scientific, political, economic, and social élites to the central role of these informal networks in the policy process, and to the dependence of explicitly scientific organizations on their active support.

This situation contributed to the recognition and diffusion of a problem-oriented approach to statistics. The political success of the broader social networks supporting vital statistics led in turn to the institutionalization of vital statistics in governmental administrative bureaus and to the production of official statistics suited to the scientific exigencies of the new approach. Another important factor, contributing to the success of vital statistics, was the dominant epistemological model of science as theoretically informed, hypothetical knowledge, not certain knowledge. Different conditions prevailed in France, where a distinction persisted between deductive, experimental sciences and inductive, descriptive sciences, to which statistics were relegated.

Parts I and II of this book document the adoption of demography and vital statistics as models of scientific and administrative practices; Parts III and IV examine the challenge and eventual substitution of the scientific administrative style by new forms, notably geometrical statistics in France and mathematical statistics in England. The analysis illustrates how changes in state-science relations opened the way for changes in the relevant audience and associated criteria of scientific recognition. It also shows how these changes were worked out at the level of scientific activity, as different intellectual projects competed for the backing of newly created audiences and asserted the authority of alternative criteria of recognition.

The comparison between France and England also illustrates two types of dynamics. In France the political victory of the Republicans in the late 1870s was accompanied by an ideological commitment to promoting positivist science. Defeat in the Franco-Prussian war was explicitly blamed on the weakness of French science. This political context opened the way for incorporating "foreign" or non-administrative elements into the administration, albeit in an advisory capacity. The Conseil Supérieur de Statistique enabled private statisticians to gain direct access to the administration, thereby breaking the monopoly of the academies over policy influence and the awarding of scientific recognition, at least with regard to population statistics.

It did not, however, alter the basic French bureaucratic model, in which expertise was located in government institutions of higher education (the *grandes écoles*) and recruitment was almost exclusively internal. Instead the 1870s and 1880s were marked by the takeover of the statistical movement by graduates of the École Normale Superieure and Polytechnique, such as Levasseur and Cheysson. The result was the incorporation into statistics of many key substantive elements of demography, along with an abandonment of the distinct disciplinary endeavor. At the same time, the Academy of Sciences retained its monopoly over higher mathematics, thereby reenforcing earlier obstacles both to a more probabilistic version of administrative statistics and to the newly emergent, mathematical forms of statistics and economics. The French rejection of both Walras's version of marginal economics and English mathematical statistics before the First World War both attest to the force of this cognitive boundary.

In England the relevant structural changes were more radical and the intellectual consequences more extreme. As Galton's challenge to vital statistics illustrates, intellectual arguments could not on their own unseat vital statistics as the authoritative form of practice. Instead, the victory of mathematical statistics depended on the dissolution not only of the public health networks supporting vital statistics but of the very form of political influence and type of policy process that had empowered the networks. In the last quarter of the century, the "statesmen in disguise"—the informal networks of scholars, industrial élites, and reformers that had shaped social policy—were replaced by active political parties, university-based social science, and a reformed civil service linking university education with bureaucratic recruitment.

For vital statistics the relevant developments were the creation of a new administrative role, that of medical officers of health, in association with a new university program in state medicine. Similarly, the establishment of marginal economics as a university-based discipline served to elevate high mathematics and esoteric expertise at the expense of the more popular discourse associated with political economy, thereby clearing the way for the victory of mathematical statistics over vital statistics. In this context, vital statisticians' distinctive mix of science and politics ceased to provide the scientific recognition and access to the policy process that it had done previously.

In concluding this historical overview, it is perhaps helpful to resituate these findings in the broader comparative literature on France and England, or rather, Britain. Existing scholarship has highlighted differences in national styles of reasoning and forms of statism. As noted in the Introduction, Ian Hacking and Ted Porter have both underlined a contrast between Prussian statistics and French and British statistics. Their analyses contrast the Prussian rejection of statistical laws (as nonexistent) with the French and British commitment to document and use them as tools of governance. Both scholars explain this contrast in terms of political representations. More specifically, they link the Prussian rejection to a holistic conception of the nation, such that aggregated data points say nothing about collective phenomena. Similarly, they associate the French and British engagement in statistics with their liberal view of the polity, such that political sovereignty rests on the will and interests of "the people." Statistics, in this latter vision, provides a tool to "know" "the people."

The comparison of vital statistics and demography documents a significant difference between French and British statistical styles, at least with regard to national population statistics. Far from challenging Hacking's and Porter's analysis, it points to the existence of two distinct liberal forms, relating to two distinct forms of statism. As noted earlier, Jepperson has argued that while both France and Britain offer examples of liberal states at the level of corporatism — that, in both countries individuals rather than corporate groups are conceptualized as the relevant political actors — they differ in the representation and role of the state. France exemplifies strong statism, Britain and the United States weak statism.[2] Concretely, this analytic contrast translates into differences in how the nation is represented — as conflictual or consensual — in the relation between the state (administration and politics) and civil society, and in the location of expertise.

The contrast between statist and anti-statist polities corresponds to a number of the key institutional differences, highlighted by the comparison of demography and vital statistics. At the same time, the comparison suggests a number of refinements or nuances to the basic analytic distinction. In nineteenth-century France statisticians, administrators, and politicians struggled with the assumption of homogeneity contained in national statistical representations. But whereas political discourse focused on the contest between monarchists and republicans, between social orders, between peasants and bourgeoisie, and between clericals and anti-clericals, statistical discourse focused on the conflict between individuals with radically different life experiences, between people born at different moments in time, in different conditions. The late-nineteenth-century Republican ideology of solidarity, it should be noted, responded to and built upon this latter depiction of society. The representation is at once liberal, in the sense of focusing on individuals rather than corporate orders or categories, and conflictual, in the sense of rejecting any automatic adjustment of interests. In England similar groups of experts displayed the individualist view of society that Hacking and Porter ascribe to liberal regimes and that Jepperson associates with noncorporate anti-statism. As Farr's work illustrates, mid-nineteenth-century statisticians genuinely believed that public knowledge would create a shared, consensual public opinion that would motivate politicians to act in the public interest.

As for the relation of the state and civil society and the location of bureaucratic expertise, there too Jepperson's distinction between statism and anti-statism illuminates the institutional contrasts documented in this book. The comparison of demography and vital statistics highlights two distinct political uses of population statistics, an English instrumental use and a French representative use. This contrast can be related to differences in the relation of civil society and the state, and to the location of bureaucratic expertise. In both countries, a new, explicitly scientific style of administrative statistical reasoning emerged as part of a private statistical movement. In England the new social statisticians (*cum* scientists, *cum* reformers) were integrated into an informal network of élites that transcended the boundary between state and civil society, serving alternately in administrative bureaus, as advisors to politicians, and as members of municipal and national scientific societies. As the case of William Farr illustrates, they benefited from the recruitment of bureaucratic expertise from the public sphere and the weakness of boundaries between state and society.

In France, on the other hand, statisticians faced a highly centralized state system in which bureaucratic expertise was located in state-supported educational institutions and recruitment was almost exclusively internal to the state system. As outsiders, people like Bertillon and his fellow demographers had little or no access to the policy process. Their only input was through contributions to the scientific work of the different élite academies. Far from political organizations, the academies served to authorize, publish, and at times encourage scientific research through the medium of prizes. Nor was the French state eager to act on social legislation, at least not during the mid-nineteenth century. One of the striking contrasts between France and England was the relative paucity and decentralization of social legislation for much of the nineteenth century in France, most notably in areas of public health. Both factors, I would argue, contributed to the largely representative use of national population statistics throughout the nineteenth century. Under the Third Republic, this political function was considerably strengthened by the adoption of positivist science as a central ideological tenet.

With regard to national styles, the contrast between demography and vital statistics clearly corresponds with findings in other areas of science. A number of historians contrast the concrete, pragmatic British approach to science with the more abstract, philosophically informed Continental style.[3] One contribution of this book is its exploration of how this difference in "high science" was expressed at the level of administrators and practicing statisticians, and the specific institutional arrangements that supported and fostered it. Far from a simple "trickle-down" effect, the commitment to particular hierarchies of epistemic criteria was accompanied by cognitive maps, whereby different forms of knowledge were assigned different roles in the production of knowledge. In both France and Britain opponents of a specifically scientific approach to statistics framed their criticisms in terms of an auxiliary role for statistics vis-à-vis "true" sciences.

The comparison of types of statism in France and Britain, and their consequences for criteria of scientific recognition and for styles of statistical reasoning, highlights the contribution of medium-term institutional analysis to the comparative historical analysis of science. For the most part, the history and sociology of statistics, and science more generally, have been divided between two temporal regimes. On the one hand, specific knowledge claims have been explained by short-term, contingent events and negotiations; on the other hand, long-term national styles, or epistemes, have been related to equally long-term institutional forms. By contrast, the analysis developed here exemplifies a third type of analysis, focused on the impact of medium-term institutional logics on the development of scientific styles.

In the course of the nineteenth century, both France and Britain were subject to similar macro-level historical developments. Both countries experienced industrialization, significant social unrest, extensions of the franchise, growth of the state bureaucracy, expanded higher education, and stronger links between university education, state bureaucracy, and industrial development. That said, these long-term processes proceeded at different paces in the two countries and assumed different forms at different moments in time. In England, for example, the move from patronage politics to a more meritocratic system occurred in the last decades of the century, at precisely the moment when proponents of a more mathematical approach to political economy and statistics challenged earlier nineteenth-century forms. The expansion of the university system directly contributed to both these developments. In France, by contrast, the three processes proceeded separately. Meritocratic recruitment to the civil service was introduced in the late eighteenth century with the creation of the grandes écoles. The expansion of higher education and of the links between universities and industry in the 1880s and 1890s had little to no impact on the location or nature of bureaucratic expertise, nor did it contribute to the expansion of state bureaucracy and the scope of government intervention. And none of these processes decisively influenced the contest between alternative statistical forms, at least not in the middle quarters of the nineteenth century.

Nor should the persistence of particular institutional arrangements for ten, twenty, or even thirty years be taken as evidence of deep structures. In both France and Britain some of the most relevant institutional features for the development of statistical reasoning were related to medium-term political conditions. In France, the emergence of demography in the first decade of the Second Empire undoubtedly colored its intellectual development. In the 1850s the political regime rendered virtually impossible the type of professional, reform-minded, scientific culture associated with the Social Science Association in England. A half-century later this was no longer so, as evidenced by the reform activities of the social scientists *cum* reformers at the Musée Sociale.[4] At the same time, the loosening of those constraints, first with the relaxation of political control in the 1860s and later with the creation of the Third Republic, did not overturn the basic distinction between marginal and élite recruitment. The substantive program associated with demography "succeeded" in part because it was adopted by statisticians, reformers, and administrators with élite scientific credentials. Similarly, in England the influence of private Whig reformers and social scientists in the third quarter of the century was directly tied to an exceptional period of British politics, in which partisan and ministerial activity was particularly weak. The demise of the "unofficial parliament," as Lawrence Goldman has called it, was directly linked to a reassertion of specifically British political institutions.

Discipline Formation Reconsidered:
The View from a Nineteenth-Century Case Study

This historical analysis provides elements for a more general theory of discipline formation. As noted in the Introduction, my aim was to use these two historical cases to develop a theoretical framework that could be used to explain not only the success or failure of particular attempts at discipline formation (as is usually done) but also the timing and form of the activity. The second aim was to develop an analytic concept of discipline formation that drew attention to the impact of macro- and meso-level institutional structures on the content of intellectual styles. This second goal rested on the national, long-term character of styles, suggesting that they are indeed influenced by national institutional forms, and on the widespread agreement among scholars that disciplines figure at the intersection of intellectual and institutional developments.

The examples of demography and vital statistics suggest an initial distinction between intellectual or research projects and disciplinary activity.[5] Instead of assuming that disciplinary activity is necessarily directed at creating a fully autonomous professional discipline, I began my study by asking about the type of changes — intellectual and institutional — that proponents of demography and vital statistics hoped to introduce through their engagement in disciplinary activity. Doing so meant adopting a heuristic definition of disciplinary activity as any activity associated with the introduction of a new disciplinary category. Relevant activities and events included the rhetorical call for recognition from existing scientific authorities, one-time events such as articles or conferences, more lasting organizational forms such as specialized journals or congresses, and the institutionalization of the new science in a set of permanent organizations responsible for training, accreditation, and the award of scientific recognition.

My approach builds on the premise of heterogeneity, central to studies of disciplinarity, which treats disciplines as practices linking technical, rhetorical, conceptual, and social elements.[6] But whereas such studies focus on micro-level logics, my aim was to link the study of disciplinary activity and boundary work to the broader institutional structures in which they were pursued. With nineteenth-century statistics, discipline formation would seem to have been related to the assertion of epistemic authority, and the relations between the state, civil society, and science. More specifically, disciplinary activity varied with the relative autonomy of the scientific sphere, the relative authority of scientific gatekeepers, and the political and social functions that specific types of knowledge were called upon to fulfill. These relation proved particularly important in determining the criteria of disciplinary recognition and the form that disciplines assumed (comprehensive or specialized). Finally, disciplinary activity proved an important process in the reworking of those same relations between state, civil society, and science.

Demography and vital statistics offer a number of instances of disciplinary activity and an equal number of moments in which disciplinary activity could (logically) have occurred but did not. In either event the timing would seem to have been related to explicit attempts by scientific (rather than political) élites to discredit the project on epistemological grounds. Scientific work can be criticized on a number of grounds, depending on who decides what counts as knowledge and by what criteria. For most of the middle quarters of the nineteenth century, vital statistics was judged by the manner in which it combined scientific and political considerations. More specifically, critics worried about the place of "opinions." While statisticians organized to combat these criticisms, they did not link their defense to explicit disciplinary activity. It was only when scientific gatekeepers attacked the epistemological basis of their knowledge, dismissing it as "not science," that vital statisticians did engage in an explicit campaign of disciplinary activity. This finding contrasts sharply with the usual view of discipline formation as directed at establishing autonomous professional communities, with their own specialized criteria and mechanisms of recognition. However, it confirms Henrietta Kuklick's observation that disciplinary claims tended to be asserted in periods of insecurity and defensiveness concerning the field's legitimacy,[7] and Steve Fuller's argument that a discipline forms "*not* by taking out a clear domain for itself, but rather by successively failing to control some *other* body of knowledge."[8]

The comparison of France and England suggests that the criteria according to which disciplines are defined and recognized vary with broader institutional conditions. In France, state support for élite scientific academies and the relative isolation of science and scientists from the policy process, except as individuals, served to privilege intellectual or scientific considerations in the granting of scientific recognition. Demographers defined and distinguished themselves by their particular style of statistical reasoning, and opponents challenged them on the same grounds. In England, by contrast, political spokesmen and municipal élites effectively overruled the judgments of scientific gatekeepers, and vital statisticians successfully weathered scientific attacks by mathematical statisticians.

This contrast highlights the relation between the political or social function that knowledge is supposed to serve and the form and content of disciplinary activity. In France, comprehensive disciplines were associated with a diffuse representative use of social knowledge and the exclusion of statisticians from the policy process. More specifically, demography only gained a serious scientific hearing when it came to be seen as essential for identifying and treating depopulation. In England, the initial, more populist, practical nature of vital statistical knowledge fit with the dependence of the new discipline on popular public support for its standing *within* the scientific community and its incorporation into the central administration. Similarly, the technical, narrower character of the knowledge was related to its instrumental use in formulating and implementing specific policies as the specialized expertise of new professions such as medical officers of health.

In my analysis of both demography and vital statistics, disciplinary activity would seem to have been directed at transforming the dominant criteria of recognition. With demography, the activity initially entailed an attempt to transform political economy into an inductive statistical science, and later an attempt to transform administrative statistics from a descriptive to an abstract, prescriptive "science." With vital statistics, the activity entailed defending traditional definitions of statistics as a democratic form of knowledge, directed at shaping public opinion in the face of challenges from a new, professional, mathematical form. For both demography and vital statistics, disciplinary activity sought to alter the very criteria by which the scientific project had been judged wanting. For both, the form that discipline formation took—a comprehensive science aimed at redefining Republican social science or a narrower, semi-professional project aimed at supporting the practice of social reformers and later public health administrators—reflected the institutional context in which the disciplinary activity took place.

Finally, the (limited) success of both demography and vital statistics contributed to broader processes of social transformation. The success of the demographers' program to insert scientific considerations into administrative practice led to the inclusion of scholars, as experts, in the formal administrative process. The creation of the Superior Council of Statistics was a major institutional innovation, giving second-tier statisticians direct access to the administrative and policy processes. In England, the success of vital statistics (and paradoxically its demise as a popular, comprehensive form of knowledge) directly contributed to the professionalization of public health reform and the introduction of university-based credentials for professional training.

This analysis is relevant to more general reflections on disciplines and discipline formation for two reasons. First, disciplines are never only epistemological or discursive communities, but always combine epistemological, political, institutional, and practical criteria in the attribution of recognition. And second, the weight of different criteria varies depending on the social structures in which the science is practiced. Crucial institutional factors include the relative autonomy of the scientific field, the structure of the field (hierarchical or more egalitarian, fragmented or integrated), the strength of the gatekeepers, and the relation between scientific and political fields (science and the state). The examples of demography and vital statistics highlight the special importance of savants' access to the policy process, the political function of social-science knowledge, and the nature of the policy process (that is, whether dominated by partisan, bureaucratic, or informal élites).

In the place of an often commonsensical identification of disciplines with a (nonexistent) ideal of scientific communities as autonomous, epistemological groups or as purely political, institutional entities, this book suggests that it is worthwhile to examine historical variations in how institutional structures support certain criteria of recognition over others, and the impact of discipline formation on the affirmation or transformation of those same institutional structures. We need to do this not only to understand discipline formation as a sociological phenomenon, but to move toward a more adequate sociology of knowledge, linking "ideas" and "institutions," "science" and "politics," agency and structure, in a way that helps to explain variations in seemingly similar forms of knowledge, the influence of national intellectual traditions, and the complex interaction between epistemological, political, and institutional considerations on the development of "scientific" knowledge.

NOTES

Introduction

1 Bertillon, "Des diverses manières de mesurer la durée de la vie humaine," 53.

2 The research for this book focuses exclusively on England. While many of the scientific and political processes and institutional arrangements that I examine extended equally to all of Britain, others differed, most notably those concerning specific administrative arrangements and the policy process. For the purposes of this book, my claims will thus be restricted to England.

3 Furner, *Advocacy and Objectivity*.

4 For a discussion of the recent date of these distinctions, their tenuous relation to actual practices, their historical origins in the United States in the cold war, and their ideological character, see Mirowski and Sent, "Introduction."

5 For classic examples see MacKenzie, *Statistics in Britain, 1865–1930*, Shapin and Schaffer, *Leviathan and the Air-Pump*, and the contributions to Barnes and Shapin, *Natural Order*.

6 The association of statistics and survey work is largely a product of postwar developments. Before the Second World War, social survey research was used to generate a number of types of analysis, including in-depth case studies and various forms of qualitative exploration. It was only with the war and the establishment of survey research centers equipped to conduct large-scale social surveys that social statistics and survey work came to be identified as two sides of the same activity. In England in the early part of the century, members of statistical societies set out to conduct their own surveys. However, by the 1840s most had abandoned the task. In France survey work by followers of LePlay developed separately from social statistics. Nineteenth-century social surveys are the object of a number of excellent studies. For an Enlightenment view of social surveys in Britain see Bulmer, Bales, and Sklar, *The Social Survey in Historical Perspective, 1880–1914*. For a more radical approach, focused on the role of social science in general and social surveys in particular in social exclusion, see Yeo, *The Contest for Social Science*, chapter 3. Analyses of the French experience can be found in Elwitt, "Social Reform and Social Order in Late Nineteenth-Century France," Savoye, "Les débuts de la sociologie empirique," Desrosières, "L'ingénieur d'État et le père de famille," Desrosières, "L'opposition entre deux formes d'enquête,"

and Horne, *A Social Laboratory for Modern France*. For a discussion of the convergence of survey work and statistics in the postwar period see Converse, *Survey Research in the United States*, and Platt, *A History of Sociological Research Methods in America, 1920–1960*.

7 The term "era of statistical enthusiasm" would seem to have first been used in a chapter heading by Westergaard, *Contributions to the History of Statistics*, chapter 13. Ian Hacking, *The Taming of Chance*, 2–6, used the concept of "the avalanche of numbers" to describe a parallel phenomenon. Both terms have since entered into the general vocabulary and are evoked in most texts on the period. Together they capture the novelty as well as the dramatic shift in the quantity and circulation of numerical descriptions at the time.

8 Kudlick, "The Culture of Statistics and the Crisis of Cholera in Paris, 1830–1850."

9 There are a number of excellent histories of Napoleonic statistics. See notably Bourguet, *Déchiffrer la France*, and Perrot and Woolf, *State and Statistics in France, 1789–1815*.

10 The relation of government statistics and liberal regimes has been extensively documented. It is one of the basic premises of Theodore Porter's authoritative history of nineteenth-century statistics. It also figures centrally in Foucault's account of governmentality as a nineteenth-century form of social control. For more detailed case studies on the role of official statistics, and more specifically the census, in the consolidation of the liberal nation-state see Curtis, *The Politics of Population*, Patriarca, *Numbers and Nationhood*, and Anderson, *Imagined Communities*, chapter 10.

11 This point has been made by a number of authors. Porter notes that in the nineteenth century the defining issue in discussions over the application of probability theory to social regularities was the relation of the individual and the collectivity, rather than the measurement of uncertainty. Porter, "Statistics and Statistical Methods," 242. The conceptual problem of homogenization is clearly laid out in Desrosières, "The Part in Relation to the Whole."

12 See notably Jepperson, "Political Modernities," and Schofer and Fourcade-Gourinchas, "The Structural Contexts of Civic Engagement," and the references therein.

13 In one of the more influential statements of this argument, Porter links the emergence of modern quantitative statistics with that of the social sciences in general. Both were associated, he suggests, with a new conception of "society" as distinct from and prior to the state. Porter, *The Rise of Statistical Thinking, 1820–1900*, 26–27. Miller and Rose, "Governing Economic Life," 185–86, develop this concept of governmentality, with reference to technologies of knowledge such as statistics.

14 This argument is central in cultural theories of the state; see notably Abrams, "Notes on the Difficulty of Studying the State (1977)," and Corrigan and Sayer, *The Great Arch*. For influential discussions of the role of the social imaginary and

the census in particular in the construction of colonial and postcolonial states see Anderson, *Imagined Communities*, and Kohn, *The Age of Nationalism*.

15 Cullen, *The Statistical Movement in Early Victorian Britain*.

16 For a clear development of this argument in the context of public health statistics see Szreter, "The GRO and the Public Health Movement in Britain, 1837–1914."

17 For an analysis of the grandes écoles and their role in the development of French science see Fox and Weisz, *The Organization of Science and Technology in France, 1808–1914*.

18 For a discussion of the role of scholars and science in the expression of otherwise censored political opposition see Nord, *The Republican Moment*, 34, and Weisz, *The Emergence of Modern Universities in France, 1863–1914*, chapter 2.

19 The nonspecialized, nonprofessional character of nineteenth-century disciplines is clearly illustrated in Andrew Warwick's study of mathematical physics at Cambridge, *Masters of Theory*.

20 Historical epistemology begins from the premise that basic epistemological categories such as cause, explanation, and objectivity are historically variable and can be studied in the same way as other types of scientific claims. For a systematic formulation of the program and its goals see Daston, "Reply to James Chandler's Commentary on 'Marvelous Facts and Miraculous Evidence.'" Defining works in the field include Poovey, *A History of the Modern Fact*, Davidson, *The Emergence of Sexuality*, Daston, "Objectivity and the Escape from Perspective," and Porter, *Trust in Numbers*. Within sociology, Margaret Somers has adopted the term "historical epistemology" to refer to the changing meaning of core concepts of social theory such as agency and structure. Somers, "Where Is Sociology after the Historic Turn?"

21 The literature on the interplay between university-based research, industry, and government is extensive and expanding rapidly. For the moment three conceptual models dominate the discussion: the concept of Mode 2 knowledge as developed in Gibbons, Limoges, Schwartzman, Scott, and Trow, *The New Production of Knowledge*, and Nowotny, Scott, and Gibbons, *Re-thinking Science*; Etzkowitz's and Leydesdorff's model of the triple helix as developed in Etzkowitz, "The Entrepreneurial University and the Emergence of Democratic Corporatism," Leydesdorff, "Emergence of a Triple Helix of University-Industry-Government Relations," and Leydesdorff, "The Endless Transition: A Triple-Helix of University-Industry-Government Relations"; and Funtowicz's and Ravetz's more philosophically informed discussion of post-normal science as presented in Funtowicz and Ravetz, "The Emergence of Post-Normal Science." While most observers accept that these relations are changing, at least in certain spheres, many reject the novelty of these accounts of the changing relations of science and society. For arguments about continuity between nineteenth-century forms and recent developments see Shinn, "Change or Mutation?," Pestre, "Regimes of Knowledge Production in Society," and Pestre, *The Evolution of Knowl-*

edge Domains. Both authors note that scientific disciplines have historically been situated at the interstices of the university, industry, government, and various publics and suggest that the model of autonomous disciplines is specific to the decades since the Second World War.

22 Weingart, "From 'Finalization' to 'Mode 2,'" and Godin and Gingras, "The Place of Universities in the System of Knowledge Production," both note the persistence of disciplinary form and university-based research within new emergent forms of knowledge production.

23 My thanks to Steve Fuller for drawing my attention to these examples.

24 Godin and Gingras, "The Place of Universities in the System of Knowledge Production."

25 The use of events to study the interaction between structure and agency has been proposed by a number of scholars. See notably Griffin, "Narrative, Event-Structure Analysis, and Causal Interpretation in Historical Sociology," Sewell, "Historical Events as Transformation of Structures," and Abbott, "From Causes to Events."

26 Latour, *Science in Action*, chapter 4.

27 This call for a meso-level institutional analysis to flush out the context in which more micro-level negotiations and credibility contests occur builds on Daniel Kleinman's work on knowledge production at the interstices of science, industry, and government in the contemporary period. See for example Kinchy and Kleinman, "Organizing Credibility."

28 Eyler, *Victorian Social Medicine*, and Szreter, "The GRO and the Public Health Movement in Britain, 1837–1914."

29 Armatte, "Une discipline dans tous ses états."

30 For a persuasive exposition of the argument see Goldman, *Science, Reform and Politics in Victorian Britain*.

31 As Desrosières explains, "What is needed is a more complete institutional and sociological table of the places where statistical knowledge was being developed. But the historical research already undertaken on these questions . . . in general bears only on partial elements of these contexts, and views them from vastly different perspectives. Accordingly, there is a risk that the comparisons will be biased, attributing much importance to a certain aspect solely because it is well documented. A context of comparison must be established before an actual comparison is conducted, but naturally this concerns more than just description or historical research." Desrosières, *The Politics of Large Numbers*, 150.

32 The problem of "success" and "failure" informs many studies of individual disciplines. For examples in the social sciences see the contributions to Oberschall, *The Establishment of Empirical Sociology*, and Soffer, "Why Do Disciplines Fail?" For a discussion of schools of thought from a similar perspective see Mac-Laughlin, "Why Do Schools of Thought Fail?," and Collins, "The Transformation of Philosophy."

33 The intellectual development of the Sociology of Scientific Knowledge (SSK) can

be traced through its key journal, *Social Studies of Science*, and a number of edited collections that survey the field. See for example Biagoli, *The Science Studies Reader*, and Jasanoff, Markle, Petersen, and Pinch, *Handbook of Science and Technology Studies*. For relatively recent overviews of the field see Hess, *Science Studies*, Fuller, *Science*, and Shapin, "Here and Everywhere."

34 A number of authors decry the neglect of disciplines and call for their reintroduction as an object of historical inquiry. See for example Rosenberg, "Toward an Ecology of Knowledge," Kohler, *From Medical Chemistry to Biochemistry*, 1, and McCormmach, Editor's Foreword, ix–x. Notable exceptions to this neglect from within SSK include Edge, *Astronomy Transformed*, and Clarke, *Disciplining Reproduction*.

35 David Cahan, in his overview of institutional studies for his edited collection on nineteenth-century science, explicitly notes the paradoxical relation between the widespread historiographic expression of interest in scientific institutions and the paucity of actual studies. Cahan, ed., *From Natural Philosophy to the Sciences*, 291. Exceptions that treat nineteenth-century French and English science include Cardwell, *The Organisation of Science in England*, Fox and Weisz, *The Organization of Science and Technology in France, 1808–1914*, Russell, *Science and Social Change, 1700–1900*, and Paul, *From Knowledge to Power*.

36 Rosenberg, "Toward an Ecology of Knowledge." Illustrations of this general approach can be found in Kevles, *In the Name of Eugenics*, Kohler, *From Medical Chemistry to Biochemistry*, and, more indirectly, Turner and Turner, *The Impossible Science*.

37 Gieryn, "Boundaries of Science," established boundary work as a central problematic in the study of disciplines and science more generally. The concept has generated a large number of case studies and extensive discussion. See for example the articles in Messer-Davidow, Shumway, and Sylvan, *Knowledges*, and the 1995 issue of *Social Research*, "Defining the Boundaries of Social Inquiry."

38 Abbott, "Things of Boundaries."

39 On the use of disciplinary histories and the canon to authorize specific disciplines see Graham, Lepenies, and Weingart, eds., *Functions and Uses of Disciplinary Histories*, and Levine, *Visions of the Sociological Tradition*.

40 The use of metaphors to authorize scientific claims has been widely discussed in SSK, notably by feminist scholars. See for example Hallyn, *Metaphor and Analogy in the Sciences*, Keller, "Gender and Science," and Martin, "The Egg and the Sperm." Gaziano, "Ecological Metaphors as Scientific Boundary Work," extends this focus to an analysis of discipline formation.

41 For a Bourdieusian version of the analysis of disciplines in terms of process see Cambrosio and Keating, "The Disciplinary Stake."

42 Early readers of this manuscript were uncomfortable with the failure of these "disciplines" to assure the conditions for their own continuity and my consequent failure to conclude my story with the creation of more permanent twentieth-century forms. While one could write the history of nineteenth-

century statistics from the perspective of twentieth-century developments, it would be a different story that would not address the questions posed here concerning national styles of reasoning or the nature of disciplinary activity in the nineteenth century. Examples of long-term histories of demography that exclude the nineteenth-century activity labeled "demography" at the time include Fournier, "La démographie comme discipline," Glass, "Some Aspects of the Development of Demography," Ramsden, "Mapping Populations and Population Science," and Vilquin, "La naissance de la démographie."

43 The term "disciplinarity" refers to the organizing logic of disciplinary, rather than other organizational logics, such as those of the profession or the department. For a full discussion of the concept and its implications see the contributions to Messer-Davidow, Shumway, and Sylvan, *Knowledges*, and Klein, *Crossing Boundaries*.

44 The argument that nineteenth-century disciplinary activity cannot be equated to professionalization in the sense of the creation of autonomous, self-regulating corporate bodies and specialized identities has been made by a number of authors. See for example Porter, "Gentlemen and Geology," and Kuklick, "Boundary Maintenance in American Sociology."

45 This focus on rules as the constitutive element of structure is a central component of structuration theory. For a discussion of this point see Sewell, "A Theory of Structure: Duality, Agency, and Transformation."

46 For a programmatic statement on historical epistemology by one of the authors most closely associated with it, see Daston, "Reply to James Chandler's Commentary on 'Marvelous Facts and Miraculous Evidence.'"

47 This approach is consistent with Whitley's distinction between specialties, research areas, and disciplines. Whereas the term "specialties" refers to collectivities with a shared commitment to a set of research practices and "research areas" to a community committed to a particular explanatory model and definition of a phenomenon, the term "discipline" describes "the application of a particular set of scientific values to some domain or field of 'reality'" such that it comes to order that reality. In this definition "discipline sets the frame within which specialty concerns are developed and research areas formulated." Whitley, "Umbrella and Polytheistic Scientific Disciplines and Their Elites," 473–74. Whitley's formulation underlines the special relation between disciplinary activity and the meta-criteria by which knowledge comes to be recognized as such. Whereas Whitley is concerned to identify and document the disciplinary distribution of epistemic criteria, my own work focuses on the struggles and negotiations surrounding their introduction and maintenance.

48 Vissering, "Limites de la statistique," 9–10.

49 For a discussion of the popular, nonspecialist character of nineteenth-century political economy see Tribe, "Political Economy to Economics via Commerce." Lawrence Goldman makes a similar argument with regard to the Social Science Association in Britain, suggesting that it is better seen as an element of popular

culture rather than as an academic discipline. Goldman, *Science, Reform and Politics in Victorian Britain*, 319.

50 Key contributions to the field include Krüger, Daston, and Heidelberger, eds., *The Probabilistic Revolution*, Stigler, *The History of Statistics*, Porter, *The Rise of Statistical Thinking, 1820–1900*, Daston, *Classical Probability in the Enlightenment*, Gigerenzer et al., *The Empire of Chance*, and Hacking, *The Taming of Chance*.

51 The concept of styles of reasoning builds on A. C. Crombie's analysis of styles of thinking in science. Crombie identifies six distinct styles that mark the history of modern science. These include (1) the method of postulation, as exemplified by the Greek mathematical sciences, (2) experimentation, (3) the hypothetical construction of analogical models, (4) ordering by comparison and taxonomy, (5) statistical analysis of regularities of population and the calculus of probabilities, and (6) the historical derivation of genetic development. From the perspective of scholarly work on science, historical epistemology marks a break both from the more classical assumption of the unity of scientific knowledge (and an associated essentialist, universalistic, and rationalist construct) and from the more recent focus on the diversity and contingency of scientific knowledge (based on an often anti-sociological, constructionist position). In their place, it offers a means to explore the long-term history of science without sacrificing the gains of a radical historicist position. For a concise exposition of the concept of styles of reasoning, in general and with regard to statistics more specifically, see Hacking, "Statistical Language, Statistical Truth and Statistical Reason," and Hacking, "'Style' for Historians and Philosophers." The concept has also been extensively discussed in a special 1991 issue of *Science in Context*. See notably Daston and Otte, eds., *Styles in Science*.

52 This movement from a "subjectivist" to a "frequentist" interpretation of probability theory provides the focus for many of the key histories of late-eighteenth- and nineteenth-century statistics, in particular those that privilege mathematical statistics. See notably Gigerenzer, *The Empire of Chance*, Daston, *Classical Probability in the Enlightenment*, and Hacking, *The Emergence of Probability*.

53 The question explicitly frames Porter's excellent study on the history of nineteenth-century statistics. It also underlies, to a greater or lesser extent, the key texts on the history of statistics published in the course of the 1980s (see note 50, above).

54 The argument that mathematical statistics and administrative statistics only came together after the Second World War is a central organizing theme of Desrosières, *The Politics of Large Numbers*.

55 Stigler, *The History of Statistics*, 7–8.

56 This argument concerning the accumulation of discrete components of what was to become a new style of reasoning is most clearly developed in Hacking, *The Taming of Chance*. In contrast, Porter organizes his narrative around the circulation of concepts between the social sciences and natural sciences. Porter, *The*

Rise of Statistical Thinking, 1820–1900. Desrosières combines elements of different types of explanation by tracing in separate chapters the parallel development of administrative and mathematical statistics. Desrosières, *The Politics of Large Numbers.*

57 Lécuyer, "Probability in Vital and Social Statistics," clearly identifies the carriers of Quetelet's project as Farr in Britain and Bertillon in France.

58 Hacking, "Nineteenth Century Cracks in the Concept of Determinism."

59 Porter, "Lawless Society," and Hacking, "Prussian Numbers, 1860–1882."

60 The emergence of "society," "the social," and "the social body" as distinct entities has been widely discussed. Porter traces the concept back to Malthus and his analysis of population laws as independent of state action. Porter, *The Rise of Statistical Thinking, 1820–1900*, 26. From a political perspective, the concept of "the social" has been associated with expansion in the scope and nature of state intervention in the everyday lives of individuals. See notably Donzelot, *L'invention du social*, Dean, *The Constitution of Poverty*, and Steimetz, *Regulating the Social.* For an analysis of the role of statistics in the discursive constitution of "the social body" see Poovey, *Making a Social Body.*

61 This contrast is especially striking given the multiple "discovery" of mathematical economics by Jevons in England and Walras in France. For an interesting discussion of the timing of these discoveries in terms of changes in physics see Mirowski, *More Heat than Light.* Schabas argues that mathematization played a central role in Marshall's disciplinary strategy. It served both to differentiate marginalist economics from political economy and to authorize the incorporation of the new discipline into the élite university curriculum. Schabas, "Mathematics and the Economics Profession in Late Victorian England," and Schabas, "Alfred Marshall, W. Stanley Jevons, and the Mathematization of Economics." Whereas Marshall and his colleagues were extremely successful at gaining scientific recognition, carriers of a similar "mathematical" form of economics in France were systematically excluded from political economy in particular and the category of recognized social sciences more specifically. This exclusion is evidenced in Walras's failure to make a career in France and in the very critical reception that his work received at the hands of French academicians. In 1900 the socialist economist Charles Gide explicitly noted the exclusion of mathematics from French economics. For a discussion of French developments see Breton, "L'économie politique et les mathématiques en France, 1800–1940."

62 The classical discussion of individualistic and holistic forms of theorizing can be found in Dumont, *Essays on Individualism.* The expression of this distinction in Continental and Anglo social and statistical theory is underlined by Desrosières, *The Politics of Large Numbers*, 96–101. Similarly, Bryant provides an interesting analysis of the differences between French and American forms of positivism. Bryant, *Positivism in Social Theory and Research.* The British individualistic tradition of social theory has been discussed by Stephan Collini in his biography of Hobhouse, *Liberalism and Sociology.*

63 Useful studies on France and England include Gille, *Les sources statistiques de l'histoire de France*, Le Mée, "La statistique démographique officielle de 1815 à 1870 en France," Higgs, *A Clearer Sense of the Census*, Wrigley, *Nineteenth-Century Society*, Dupâquier and Dupâquier, *Histoire de la démographie*, and Glass, *Numbering the People*. For a somewhat older overview of administrative statistics, including France and England, see Westergaard, *Contributions to the History of Statistics*.

64 In addition to the literature cited above, histories of the production of census data tend to focus on North America and on the United States in particular. This is partly due to the politicization of racial classifications. See notably Anderson, *The American Census*, Anderson and Fienberg, *Who Counts?*, Skerry, *Counting on the Census?*, and Nobles, *Shades of Citizenship*. Within this general genre, a number of studies focus on one or another type of official statistics. For a more sociological perspective see Alonso and Starr, *The Politics of Numbers*.

65 One of the main contributions of the linguistic and cultural turns lay in the analysis of representations as social practices essential to the analysis of power relations and historical processes. For a discussion of these historiographic developments as they influenced the practice of history and the social sciences see Biersack and Hunt, *The New Cultural History*, Chartier, *Cultural History*, and Clark, *History, Theory, Text*.

66 The seminal texts on the role of the census in specific and official statistics more generally in the construction of the modern state and colonial powers include Anderson, *Imagined Communities*, Cohn, "The Census, Social Structure and Objectification in South Asia," and Cohn, *Colonialism and Its Forms of Knowledge*. There is an enormous literature on the construction of nationalism and national identity that builds upon these works and develops them in a variety of directions.

67 For a discussion of the implications that the concept of biopower has for the history of statistics see Hacking, "Biopower and the Avalanche of Printed Numbers."

68 This role of statistics in the creation of new social hierarchies is a central theme in much of the literature on statistics and representation. See notably Poovey, *Making a Social Body*, Scott, *Gender and the Politics of History*, and Cole, *The Power of Large Numbers*. For an especially sophisticated analysis of the articulation of official statistical forms, social history, and the history of statistics, see Szreter's study of the role of fertility statistics in elaborating the official classification system and class differences in early-twentieth-century Britain, *Fertility, Class and Gender in Britain, 1860–1940*.

69 Hacking, *Representing and Intervening*. For a discussion of the relevance of this point to the history of statistics see Curtis, *The Politics of Population*, 27–28. Scott, *Seeing like a State*, on the state's use of statistics and plans to reshape social relations, provides a nice illustration of how representations serve as an object of political action.

70 Thévenot, "Rules and Implements," provided the original statement of this approach. The article is difficult; for a clearer exposition see Desrosières, "How to

Make Things Which Hold Together." Curtis's use of the term is particularly illuminating. Curtis, "Social Investment in Medical Forms."

71 Curtis, *The Politics of Population*, Desrosières, *The Politics of Large Numbers*, Patriarca, *Numbers and Nationhood*, and Szreter, *Fertility, Class and Gender in Britain, 1860–1940*.

72 Eyler, *Victorian Social Medicine*, and Coleman, *Death Is a Social Disease*. There is a large literature on public health and public hygiene. Studies on France in the first half of the century are mentioned above. The literature on the second half of the century is much less developed, especially for the Second Empire. The definitive work on public hygiene during the Third Republic is Murard and Zylberman, *L'hygiène dans la République*. For the French case see also Ackerman, *Health Care in the Parisian Countryside, 1800–1914*, Faure, "The Social History of Health in France," Lilienfeld, "Times, Places and Persons," and Rollet-Echalier, "La politique à l'égard de la petite enfance sous la IIIe république."

The English public health movement has been much more carefully studied than the French. As with the French material, a number of biographies and social histories help to illuminate aspects of the public health movement. In addition to Eyler's work on Farr, other key works include Eyler, *Sir Arthur Newsholme and State Medicine, 1885–1935*, and Lewis, *Edwin Chadwick and the Public Health Movement, 1832–1854*. Simon, *English Sanitary Institutions*, offers a useful contemporary overview of public health institutions. Contributions to an understanding of health care policy and practices can be found in Szreter, "The GRO and the Public Health Movement in Britain, 1837–1914," Rosen, *A History of Public Health*, Porter and Porter, "The Politics of Prevention," Hardy, "Public Health and the Expert," MacLeod, *Government and Expertise*, and Brand, *Doctors and the State*.

73 See for example Desrosières, "Official Statistics and Medicine in Nineteenth-Century France."

74 Most historians of demography date the discipline as having been founded in the 1930s in the United States and Britain and during the Second World War in France. Key events include the appointment of Lancelot Hogben to a chair of social biology at the London School of Economics in 1930, the creation of the Population Council in the United States, and the creation in 1945 of the Institut National d'Études Démographiques in France.

There are a number of excellent critical histories of twentieth-century demography. Most focus on political, ideological, and technical constructions of fertility and the relation between demography as a discipline and either eugenics or international development in the United States. See notably Grebenik, "Demography, Democracy, and Demonology," Greenhalgh, "The Social Construction of Population Science," Hodgson, "Demography as Social Science and Policy Science," Hodgson, "Orthodoxy and Revisionism in American Demography," and Ramsden, "Carving up Population Science." From the perspective of discipline formation, twentieth-century demography remains an interesting case in light of its situation between academic departments, research centers, and policy institutes. For older, more conventional accounts directed at establishing the scientific status of the discipline see Ryder, "Notes on the Concept of a Population," Hauser and Duncan, *The Study of Population*, and Notestein, "Demography in the United States." A more international perspective is provided in Szreter, "Demography, History of."

Histories that adopt a more conventional intellectual-history approach and thus trace the origins of the discipline to eighteenth-century political arithmetic, either implicitly or explicitly, include Behar, "Malthus and the Development of Demographic Analysis," Glass, "Some Aspects of the Development of Demography," Dupâquier and Dupâquier, *Histoire de la démographie*, Horvarth, "De Christophe Bernoulli à Achille Guillard," and Riley, *Population Thought in the Age of the Demographic Transition*. Important recent contributions to the history of the twentieth-century discipline in France and Britain include Rosental, *L'intelligence démographique*, and Szreter, *Fertility, Class and Gender in Britain, 1860–1940*.

Exceptions to the general neglect of nineteenth-century French demography include a few French "internalist" histories, focusing on the techniques and methods employed by French demographers in the nineteenth century. Like earlier accounts of mathematical and official statistics, these works are directed at identifying whether and in what way earlier statisticians "got it right." While valuable contributions in their own right, none of these accounts recognize contemporaries' own engagement in a contest between different versions of administrative statistics and quantitative social science. Dupâquier, "La famille Bertillon et la naissance d'une nouvelle science sociale." A notable exception to this effacement of the social and cognitive organization of nineteenth-century social statisticians can be found in Armatte's history of nineteenth-century French statistics, in which he maps out the variety of statistical projects in circulation in the course of the century. This book builds upon and develops that analysis by situating the dynamics between alternative projects in their institutional context. Armatte, "Une discipline dans tous ses états."

75 See notably Cullen, *The Statistical Movement in Early Victorian Britain*, and Goldman, *Science, Reform and Politics in Victorian Britain*.

76 Westergaard, *Contributions to the History of Statistics*.

77 Woolf, "Statistics and the Modern State," 598.

78 Desrosières, *The Politics of Large Numbers*, chapter 5.

79 Cole, *The Power of Large Numbers*, and Poovey, *Making a Social Body*.

80 The preparations and transactions of each congress were published, often in two or more languages. Unfortunately, no single library or archive has a complete set of transactions. For the location of these publications see Brian, "Bibliographie des comptes rendus officiels du congrès international de statistique (1853–1878)."

CHAPTER 1 The "Invention" of Demography

1 Alphonse and Bertillon, *La vie et les oeuvres du Docteur L.-A. Bertillon*.

2 Guillard, "Nécessité de constater l'âge des décédés."

3 Guillard was not original in his focus on this problem. The topic was the major issue among statisticians at the time. For a discussion of the development of French official statistics during this period, and the absence of data on the age structure of the population, see Le Mée, "La statistique démographique officielle de 1815 à 1870 en France."

4 Guillard, "De la statistique des naissances."

5 Joseph Garnier's position on population is developed in numerous articles in the *Journal des économistes*. See Garnier, "De la statistique des naissances," Garnier, "Observations sur le principe de population," and Garnier, "Population." For a detailed discussion of the views of liberal economists on population issues see Spengler, "French Population Theory since 1800," and Charbit, "Du malthusianisme au populationnisme."

6 Garnier, "De la statistique des naissances," 194–95.

7 For a systematic discussion of these positions and individual variations see the edited collections by Breton and Lutfalla, *L'économie politique en France au XIXe siècle*, and Gide and Rist, *Histoire des doctrines économiques*.

8 Le Van-Lemesle, "La promotion de l'économie politique en France au XIXe siècle," 286–87. The success of this strategy is evidenced by the fact that in a period when almost all other social sciences were disbanded, the economists received only one official warning and three threats, in 1854, 1855, and 1857. The dates are important because they indicate that in 1853, when Guillard submitted his manuscript, liberal economists were in a very delicate position. Both Guillard's insistence that economists transform their discipline to render it more autonomous and scientific and his case against the liberal account of the causes of poverty were in direct contradiction with the disciplinary strategy in place at the time.

9 For a discussion of Say's position on the use of statistics see Ménard, "Trois formes de résistance aux statistiques," and Breton, "La place de la statistique et de l'arithmétique politique dans la méthodologie économique de Jean-Baptiste Say."

10 Lutfalla, "Le 'journal des économistes,'" 499–500.

11 Arena, "Joseph Garnier," 115.

12 Nicolet, *L'idée républicaine en France, 1789–1924*, 283–85.

13 Guillard, "Statistique humaine," 367.

14 Ibid., 3.

15 Guillard, *Éléments de statistique humaine*, xxv.

16 Ibid., xviii.

17 Ibid., 327.

1 This account of the events surrounding the founding of the Statistical Society of Paris is largely taken from Kang, "Lieu de savoir social."

2 Ibid., 64–68.

3 Moreau de Jonnès, *Éléments de statistique*, 130–38.

4 For an analysis of the relation between medical statistics and the SGF see Desrosières, "Official Statistics and Medicine in Nineteenth-Century France."

5 In 1849 Legoyt published a series of articles defending state centralization and decrying the moral degeneracy and lack of patriotism of the people. These positions help explain his appointment under the Second Empire. See Legoyt, "De la réforme ministérielle et administrative," and Legoyt, "De la centralisation administrative."

6 Chevalier, "Travaux de la société de statistique de Paris," 1.

7 Kang, "Lieu de savoir social," 149.

8 Guillard, "Démographie." Theodore Porter describes Wappäus as "a statistician of the old school, writing in 1859 when a new tradition of university statistics based on numbers and dedicated to the solution of social problems was just beginning to take hold." Porter, *The Rise of Statistical Thinking*, 179. One can assume that Wappäus used Guillard's book to express his dissatisfaction with a broader set of developments which threatened his position at home.

9 Bertillon, "Démographie." The *Dictionnaire* was one of the main organs for the promotion of the new medico-scientific approach. Jacques Léonard goes so far as to describe it as a machine de guerre. Léonard, *La médecine entre les savoirs et les pouvoirs*, 81.

10 The history of physiology during this period has been treated extensively. For developments in France see Lesch, "The Paris Academy of Medicine and Experimental Science, 1820–1848," Tiles, "The Normal and Pathological," Pickstone, "How Might We Map the Cultural Fields of Science?," Holmes, "The Intake-Output Method of Quantification in Physiology," and Coleman, "The Cognitive Basis of the Discipline."

11 For a good general statement of this ideology see the introduction to Dechambre, *Dictionnaire encyclopédique des sciences médicales*.

12 Bertillon, "De quelques eléments de l'hygiène, dans leur rapport avec la durée de la vie," 4.

13 Ibid., 5.

14 Ibid., 717.

15 For an analysis of debates surrounding the reception of mortality tables in France and England see Schweber, "Controverses et styles de raisonnement."

16 Claude Bernard transformed physiology, positioning it at the top of the hierarchy of medical sciences, while Louis Pasteur "invented" bacteriology.

17 Léonard, *La médecine entre les savoirs et les pouvoirs*, chapters 8–10. For a discus-

sion of the impact of the new scientific medicine on medical education see Weisz, "Reform and Conflict in French Medical Education, 1870–1914."

18 Bertillon's talk is described in Latour, "Bulletin sur la séance de l'académie de médecine, Paris, le 19 février 1858." For a discourse analysis of Bertillon's work on infant mortality see Cole, *The Power of Large Numbers*, 149–56.

19 See for example Bertillon, "De la mortalité parisienne."

20 Bertillon, "Des diverses manières de mesurer la durée de la vie humaine."

21 Ibid., 53.

22 See Plessis, *The Rise and Fall of the Second Empire, 1852–1871*, 4.

23 For an account of the founding of the Paris Society of Anthropology see Hammond, "Anthropology as a Weapon of Social Combat in Late-Nineteenth-Century France," and Williams, "Anthropological Institutions in Nineteenth-Century France." The subsequent turn to more radical science and politics is also discussed in Harvey, "Evolutionism Transformed." For an analysis from the perspective of a radical member of the society and its only woman see Harvey, *Almost a Man of Genius*.

24 Broca, "Histoire des travaux de la société d'anthropologie (1859–1863)," ix.

25 Broca and Bertillon originally met in 1851 during a campaign to have the sentence against their colleague and teacher A. Deville commuted. It should be noted that for a period Bertillon, Broca, and Auguste Comte all had homes on the same street in Paris, rue Monsieur le Prince. The Faculty of Medicine and thus the rooms for the School of Anthropology (founded in 1878) were also situated on the same street.

26 Bertillon's use of the binomial distribution to establish the existence of racial groups is also discussed in Brian, "Des courbes qui parlent dans un brouhaha de chiffres."

CHAPTER 3   The Reinvention of Demography

1 Lavergne, "Note sur le dénombrement de la population de 1856."

2 For a review of French theories of depopulation, including the period before 1871, see Spengler, *France Faces Depopulation*.

3 Morel, "Traité des dégénérescences physiques, intellectuelles et morales de l'espèce humaine et des causes qui produisent ces variétés maladives." For a discussion of the concept of degeneracy in French thought see Walter, "What Became of the Degenerate?," and Pick, *Faces of Degeneration*.

4 Legoyt, "De la prétendue dégénérescence physique de la population française."

5 Charbit, "Du malthusianisme au populationnisme," 34–35.

6 Ibid., 43–45.

7 "Discussion sur la mortalité des enfants," 80.

8 For a history of the wet-nursing industry in France see Sussman, *Selling Mothers' Milk*. For an account which highlights the role of statistical knowledge in the

discourse surrounding infant mortality see Cole, *The Power of Large Numbers*, chapter 5.

9 "Discussion sur la prétendue dégénérescence de la population," 569.

10 "Discussion sur la mortalité des enfants," 358–62.

11 One of the main concerns of the Academy of Science with regard to statistics was to limit the practice to pure data collection by private citizens. Echoing the position of Jean Baptiste Say and others, the commission of the Prix Montyon of Statistics insisted that official data were far too unreliable to be recognized and used in true scientific work. For an analysis of the academy's restrictions on the practice of statistics during an earlier period see Brian, "Le prix Montyon de statistique à l'académie royale des sciences pendant la restauration."

12 "Discussion sur la mortalité des enfants," 358–59.

13 "Discussion sur la prétendue dégénérescence de la population," 561.

14 Ibid., 795.

15 Ibid., 852.

16 Lécuyer, "Probability in Vital and Social Statistics."

17 For a discussion of the place of public hygiene in the French Association for the Advancement of Sciences see Renneville, "Politiques de l'hygiène à l'AFAS."

18 Bertillon, "La population française," 45.

19 Ibid., 46.

20 Ibid.

21 Ibid., 64.

22 Bertillon, *La démographie figurée de la France*.

23 It should be noted that Toussaint Loua, the new head of the SGF, also published a collection of graphic representations in the same year. Loua, *Atlas statistique de la population de Paris*. For a discussion of the use of graphic representation in nineteenth-century statistics see Brian, "Des courbes qui parlent dans un brouhaha de chiffres," and Palsky, *Des chiffres et des cartes*.

24 Bertillon, *La démographie figurée*, 2.

25 "Prix Victor Cousin."

26 Levasseur, "Démographie figurée de la France, ou étude statistique de la population française: Mortalité," 674.

27 Garnier, "Rapport fait au nom de la section d'économie politique sur le concours relative au mouvement de la population," 311.

28 Ibid.

29 Ibid.

30 Broca, "Rapport sur les travaux de statistique de M. le docteur Bertillon," 98–99. The first national bureau of statistics was established in 1800 with the creation of the First Republic. It was closed in 1811 by the emperor for failing to provide statistics of immediate practical utility. It was not until 1835, with the creation of the Statistique Générale de la France, that France regained a national-level bureau of statistics. For a history of these developments see Perrot and Woolf, *State and Statistics in France*.

31 Broca, "Rapport sur les travaux de statistique de M. le docteur Bertillon," 98–99.

32 Ibid., 99–113.

33 Bertillon, *Exposé des travaux scientifiques du Dr. Bertillon*.

34 Ibid., 14.

35 Schiller's biography of Paul Broca focuses on his career as a medical researcher; as such, the account provides little information on either Broca's work as an anthropologist or his political involvements. It does, however, document his medical credentials and explains why he was accepted in the Royal Academy of Medicine while Bertillon was rejected. Schiller, *Paul Broca*.

36 In the eighteenth and nineteenth centuries prizes were one of the primary mechanisms for distributing scientific recognition in France. For a discussion of prizes and their role in the development of French science see Crawford, "The Prize System of the Academy of Sciences, 1850–1914." For an account of the history of the Prix Montyon during the first half of the nineteenth century see Brian, "Le prix Montyon de statistique." The discussion which follows builds on Brian's analysis of the influence of the academy on statistical practice.

37 Bienaymé, *Prix Montyon de statistique*, 817.

38 Ibid., 822–24.

39 My thanks to Noël Bonneuil for this point.

40 Bertillon, "Mouvements de la population."

41 Ibid., 245.

42 Ibid., 248.

43 Ibid.

44 For a detailed history of pronatalist and family legislation see Talmy, *Histoire du mouvement familial en France*. For a history of policies and practices directed at the protection of infants see Rollet-Echalier, "La politique à l'égard de la petite enfance sous la IIIᵉ république."

CHAPTER 4 The Invention of Vital Statistics

1 For an excellent biography of William Farr which focuses on the relation between his scientific and political work see Eyler, *Victorian Social Medicine*.

2 "William Farr," Dictionary of National Biography.

3 Farr, *Vital Statistics*.

4 Edmonds, "On the Laws of Collective Vitality."

5 The footnote by the editors reads as follows: "So far are we from regarding discussions on the laws of mortality as foreign to our pages, that we invite communications on the subject; promising, however, to use minute care to prevent opinions (whatever we may publish) from obscuring or uselessly supplanting facts and principles." Ibid., 8.

6 The profession of actuaries has been much more extensively studied in Britain than in France. See notably Alborn, "A Calculating Profession," and Porter, *Trust in Numbers*, chapter 5.

7 Farr, "Vital Statistics," and Farr, "Vital Statistics, or, the Statistics of Health, Sickness, Diseases, and Death"

8 Farr, "Vital Statistics," 354.

9 Ibid.

10 The first such commission was created in 1833. Between 1833 and 1835 twenty-eight new commissions were appointed to inquire into such topics as the poor laws, factory conditions, the Irish poor, religious instruction, and population statistics. Noted in Elesh, "The Manchester Statistical Society," 63.

11 Cited in ibid., 33.

12 Morrell and Thackray, *Gentlemen of Science*, 25.

13 Cited in Hilts, "Aliis Exterendum," 34.

14 Ibid.

15 Cited in McCrosty, *Annals of the Royal Statistical Society, 1834–1934*, 11.

16 Ibid., 22.

17 Ibid., 25.

18 Ironically, it was not government departments which replaced the SSL as a source of information and expertise, but the SSL which attracted official statisticians, frustrated by the limitations of the official apparatus. In 1834 the Statistical Department of the Board of Trade was only two years old. As Lucy Brown has indicated, ten years later government officials did not know much more about the state of the economy or about the condition of England than they had before the department was established. While the reasons for this failure are beyond the scope of this book, the fact of its failure is important in that it sent government administrators to the SSL in search of resources which the state failed to provide. For a discussion of the Statistical Department of the Board of Trade see Cullen, *The Statistical Movement in Early Victorian Britain*, chapter 1, and Brown, "The Board of Trade and the Free Trade Movement."

CHAPTER 5 An Instrument of Social Reform

1 Cullen, *The Statistical Movement in Early Victorian Britain*, 50.

2 Ibid., 29–30.

3 The relation between the General Registrar's Office and the public health movement is the topic of an issue of the *Journal of the Social History of Medicine* (December 1991). See most notably Szreter, "Introduction," and Goldman, "Statistics and the Science of Society in Early Victorian Britain." The work of the GRO is also discussed in Cullen, "The Making of the Civil Registration Act of 1836," and Higgs, "A Cuckoo in the Nest?"

4 Szreter, "The GRO and the Public Health Movement in Britain, 1837–1914," 436–37.

5 *First Annual Report of the Registrar-General*, 76.

6 Ibid., 77.

7 Eyler devotes an entire chapter to the place of these tools in Farr's work. Eyler, *Victorian Social Medicine*, chapter 4.

8 As Szreter explains: "Not only did [Healthy Districts] refer to an indisputably realistic target, but also to one that was insidiously dynamic. Rather than merely measuring dispersion from the national average, this established the more exclusive and therefore inherently more progressive standard of the optimal as the norm for emulation. The great majority of the nation's local authorities would always be indicated as deficient according to this standard. Furthermore, provided at least some parts of the country could continue to achieve improvements, this small minority could then be relied upon continually to raise the level of performance by which all the others were judged." Szreter, "The GRO and the Public Health Movement in Britain, 1837–1914," 439.

9 *Fifth Annual Report of the Registrar-General*, xvii.

10 Cullen, *The Statistical Movement in Early Victorian Britain*, 38.

11 *Fifth Annual Report of the Registrar-General*, xviii–xix.

12 Ibid., 161–79.

13 Cullen, *The Statistical Movement in Early Victorian Britain*, 40.

14 *Fifth Annual Report of the Registrar-General*, xxiv.

15 Ibid.

16 Chadwick's role in the social reform and public health movements has been extensively analyzed. See most notably La Berge, "Edwin Chadwick and the French Connection," Finer, *The Life and Times of Sir Edwin Chadwick*, Lewis, *Edwin Chadwick and the Public Health Movement, 1832–1854*, and Hamlin, *Public Health and Social Justice in the Age of Chadwick*. For an analysis of his use of statistics see Hanley, "Edwin Chadwick and the Poverty of Statistics."

17 Chadwick, "On the Best Modes of Representing Accurately, by Statistical Returns, the Duration of Life and the Pressure and Progress of the Causes of Mortality, amongst Different Classes of the Community and amongst Populations of Different Districts and Counties."

18 "Minutes of the Council," 9 March 1844.

19 Ibid.

20 Chadwick, "On the Best Modes," 8.

21 Ibid., 9. For a discussion of the political stakes at play in Chadwick's commitment to determining the average age of death see Hanley, "Edwin Chadwick and the Poverty of Statistics."

22 Neison, "On a Method Recently Proposed for Conducting Inquiries into the Comparative Sanatory Condition of Various Districts."

23 Ibid., 43.

24 Ibid., 44.

25 For a history of medical officers of health see Simon, *English Sanitary Institutions*, chapter 12, and Hardy, *Public Health and the Expert*.

26 Simon, *English Sanitary Institutions*, 268.

27 Hardy, *Public Health and the Expert*, 130.

28 Simon, *English Sanitary Institutions*, 291.

29 Ibid., 249.

30 MacLeod, "The Anatomy of State Medicine," 208.

31 Cullen, *The Statistical Movement in Early Victorian Britain*, 87.

32 Cited in McCrosty, *Annals of the Royal Statistical Society, 1834–1934*, 25.

33 Ibid., 26.

34 Abrams, *The Origins of British Sociology, 1834–1914*, 19.

35 Cullen, *The Statistical Movement in Early Victorian Britain*, 89.

36 Ibid., 92–94.

37 Harold Westergaard in his history of statistics establishes a similar association between vital statistics and a theoretically more sophisticated, mathematical program for social statistics. In the opening paragraph of a chapter devoted to vital statistics and theory in the Congress period, he explains that "theoretical problems were to a great extent engendered in vital statistics. It is impossible to describe the evolution of vital statistics without entering upon theory." Westergaard, *Contributions to the History of Statistics*, 208.

38 Ibid., 150.

39 Ibid., 152.

40 Cited in McCrosty, *Annals of the Royal Statistical Society, 1834–1934*, 52.

41 "Seventeenth Annual Meeting of the Statistical Society of London, Session 1849–1850," 98.

42 Ibid., 105.

43 McCrosty, *Annals of the Royal Statistical Society, 1834–1934*, 79.

44 "Twelfth Annual Report of the Statistical Society of London, Session 1845–46," 98.

45 McCrosty, *Annals of the Royal Statistical Society, 1834–1934*, 85.

46 Adolphe Quetelet is generally recognized as the author of the "scientific" administrative style of reasoning. For discussions of his work and role in the transformation of social statistics see Hilts, *Statist and Statistician*, Porter, *The Rise of Statistical Thinking, 1820–1900*, and Hacking, *The Taming of Chance*.

47 "Théorie de la statistique et application des données statistiques," 36.

48 Ibid., 38.

49 For a discussion of the work of Engel and the Prussian Bureau see Hacking, "Prussian Numbers, 1860–1882."

50 "Théorie de la statistique et application des données statistiques," 11.

51 Ibid., 40–41.

52 Ibid., 44.

53 Rodgers, "The Social Science Association, 1857–1886," 284.

54 Historians offer a number of complimentary interpretations as to the social function of the Social Science Association. In what may be considered the definitive study of the association, Goldman presents it as an important extrapartisan forum for policy formation in a period when partisan politics was particularly weak, as well as a force for professionalizing and rationalizing the civil service.

Goldman, *Science, Reform and Politics in Victorian Britain*. Abrams depicts the association as an expression of the nineteenth-century British moralistic tradition of ameliorism. Abrams, *The Origins of British Sociology, 1834–1914*, 31–52. Finally, Yeo argues that the association contributed to the consolidation of middle class professional culture. Yeo, *The Contest for Social Science*. For a discussion of the association's role in promoting health reform, see Huch, "The National Association for the Promotion of Social Science."

55 Guy, "On the Original and Acquired Meaning of the Term 'Statistics,' and on the Proper Functions of a Statistical Society," 402.

56 Ibid.

57 Senior, "Opening Address of Nassau W. Senior, Esq., as President of Section F (Economic Science and Statistics) at the Meeting of the British Association, at Oxford, 28th June, 1860," 357.

58 Ibid., 331.

59 Newmarch, "The Progress of Economic Science during the Last Thirty Years," 453.

60 Ibid., 459.

CHAPTER 6   Discipline Formation at Last

1 The close relations between a new medico-scientific élite based in Paris, municipal politics, and Republicanism have been documented by Bernard Brais in his analysis of Bourneville. Brais, "Désirée Magloire Bourneville and French Anticlericalism during the Third Republic."

2 Shapin and Thackray, "Prosopography as a Research Tool in History of Science."

3 Contrary to the image of France as a centralized strong state, social services during this period were still highly decentralized. In contrast to England, the national state had yet to begin to assume responsibility for the social welfare of its population. Instead problems of poverty, public health, and child welfare were largely administered at the local level by a mixture of private and public authorities. As the following discussion indicates, most of the municipal administrative positions mentioned in the lists of members involve directing social services, thus justifying their inclusion under the heading of a "moral science sector."

4 The original volumes were published in three trimestrial issues. These later became shorter and more frequent.

5 The three non-administrators in the group included two professors of statistics, Messrs. Makschiew and Messedaglia, and one politician, Mr. Morpurgo, who was a deputy to the Italian parliament. Of the two administrators who did not serve in statistical bureaus, Mr. Janssens was an inspector in the health service of Brussels and a member of the Council of Health, while Mr. Péry was the head of a bureau of geographic works for the Ministry of Public Works in Portugal.

6 Chervin, "A nos lecteurs."

7 Ibid.

8 Levasseur's central position in a number of élite scientific, reform, and administrative institutions is described in the many biographical statements published
during the course of his career and on the occasion of his death. A list of Levasseur's publications was taken from the catalogue of the National Library. The
entries under Levasseur's name cover over forty pages, far more than for any
other statistician mentioned in this book.

9 Bertillon, "Mouvements de la population dans les divers états de l'Europe et
notamment en France," 15.

10 Ibid., 3.

11 The inconsistencies in his discussion of the relations between causality and different types of regularities suggest that these are better taken as a statement of
orientation than as a worked-out theoretical position.

12 Bertillon, "Mouvements de la population dans les divers états de l'Europe et
notamment en France," 15.

13 The focus of this analysis on the relative place of studies of population movement
or dynamic demography has led me to place purely descriptive articles on the rate
of infant mortality under the heading of public hygiene. This choice can be
justified because all the articles were written by medical doctors and active hygienists and framed accordingly. Papers on marriages between blood relations
were grouped under the heading of anthropology, largely because they were
written in response to recently translated texts by Darwin. The one topic which
did not easily fit under any of these headings was a paper by Jacques Bertillon on
divorce which I removed from the sample.

14 Another striking omission from the *Annales internationales de démographie* is
economic topics. None of the papers published dealt with financial, commercial,
or industrial statistics or the conditions of social or economic organizations such
as workers' cooperatives or insurance companies.

15 "Arthur Chervin," *Dictionnaire de biographie française*.

16 The Institute of Stammerers was subsequently renamed the Chervin Institute in
his honor.

17 For a brief biographical statement on Jacques Bertillon and further references see
Kang, "Lieu de savoir social," xlvii.

18 Jacques Bertillon's "obedience" can be contrasted with the behavior of his younger brother, Alphonse, who after a rather tempestuous education — during
which he was consistently expelled from school — went on to "invent" an anthropometric method to identify criminals (the famous "Bertillon method") and to
play a somewhat infamous role in the Dreyfus affair. Like that of Jacques, Alphonse's involvement in statistics must be attributed to the training he received
from his father, given the absence of formal instruction in either statistics or
empirical methods of inquiry at the time.

19 For a discussion of the place of science and positivism in the new Republican
ideology see Nicolet, *L'idée républicaine en France, 1789–1924*, chapter 8.

20 For a discussion of French international congresses see Rasmussen, "Les congrès internationaux."

21 "Exposition International de 1878 à Paris," 309.

22 "Congrès international de démographie à Paris," *Annales internationales de démographie*, 97–98.

23 "Congrès international de démographie," 317–18. The official transcript of the meeting was also reproduced in full in the *Annales internationales de démographie* 2 (1878).

24 "Congrès international de démographie," 319.

25 Hacking, "Prussian Numbers, 1860–1882."

26 "Congrès international de démographie," 327. The content of the discussions reveals a consensus concerning the use of the congress to pressure national governments into reforming administrative statistics. This aim was clearly expressed in the very practical focus of many of the discussions. Most sessions were devoted to redesigning registration forms and modifying the census so as to capture phenomena of interest to "demography" or "science." These included (among others) the size of the "floating population" (those without a fixed domicile), the number of stillbirths, data on topics such as religion, wealth, and race, and data concerning the length and number of marriages, the size of families, and the age of parents, which if included in the birth register would aid in identifying the causes of variations in natality.

   Another indication of the importance of these practical goals is the distinctions which the speakers made between the interests of the administration and those of science. A constant theme was the contemporary convergence between the two. As Bertillon explained: "Sirs, every time that we deal with the perfection of statistical inquiry, we are blocked by difficulties which, I believe, reside in the same vice: that is that the majority of the laws which rule us, of the legislative measures which facilitate social life, were almost all delivered in a period where the need to maintain the books of humanity was not felt with the same intensity as in our period."

27 See for example the statement by Mr. Janssens in "Congrès international de démographie," 491.

28 Ibid., 333.

29 Ibid., 327.

30 The Permanent Commission of the International Congress of Statistics was a decision-making body created in 1872 to ensure the international, scientific character of the Congress and oversee the implementation of its work . Its members included the heads of official statistical bureaus and statisticians who had attended three International Congresses of Statistics as official delegates. For an account of the mandate of the commission and the reasons for its creation see Séménow, "Congrès international de statistique," 6–9.

31 Kang, "Lieu de savoir social," 215.

1 Kang, "Lieu de savoir social," 304.

2 Le Roux, "Les travaux de la commission de statistique municipale de Paris," 228.

3 A prefect was the official representative of the national state at the departmental level. Nothing in Senator Hérold's biography explains his support for statistics. The only connection would seem to be his firm commitment to the Republic and a general legal background. His active efforts on behalf of the Municipal Bureau of Statistics would thus seem to illustrate the importance of the emergent Republican ideology for promoting social statistics during this period.

4 "Nouvelle organization du bureau de statistique municipale de la ville de Paris."

5 Ibid, 509.

6 The one notable exception was the participation of Émile Cheysson, then a young engineer-administrator and graduate of the prestigious École Polytechnique.

7 Loua, "Notions générales de statistique," 172.

8 Kang, "La société de statistique de Paris au XIXᵉ siècle," 83.

9 "Proceedings of the Fifty-first Anniversary Meeting," 427.

10 My thanks to Paul-André Rosental for this point. For a discussion of the political function of superior councils in general see Rosanvallon, *Le peuple introuvable*, 261–65, and the discussion in Rosental, *L'intelligence démographique*, 22.

11 "Proceedings of the Fifty-first Anniversary Meeting," 436.

12 Ibid., 428.

13 Ibid.

14 Kuisel, *Capitalism and the State in Modern France*, chapter 1.

15 For a discussion of how census categories were modified in the interwar period to monitor the costs of social legislation, and more specifically of family policy and the neglect of "scientific" considerations, see Rosental, *L'intelligence démographique*, 210.

16 Cheysson, "La statistique géometrique," 136.

17 According to Talmy, the main proponents of the need to combat depopulation were members of organized Christian movements of various kinds who identified the declining birth rate with moral decadence and the breakdown of the family. Talmy, *Histoire du mouvement familial en France*. Among social scientists, these two strains came together in the work of the Le Playists, of whom Cheysson was a leading member.

18 The first pronatalist organization was established in 1896 under the leadership of Jacques Bertillon. While Bertillon's dual role as spokesman for demography and head of a political movement could have been expected to produce the type of technical and political articulation that proved to be so fruitful in England, it did not. Some striking features of the organization from the perspective of demography were its failures to use the movement as a vehicle for statistical education, to

enable the problem of depopulation to generate technical innovations, and to support campaigns for improving official data. As for the government, it was only in 1902 that it ceded to the call for creating a commission of inquiry into the problem and only in 1914 that the second such commission managed to influence legislative action, most likely because depopulation had become associated with French military defeat.

CHAPTER 8 The Challenge to Vital Statistics

1 McCrosty, *Annals of the Royal Statistical Society, 1834–1934*, 105.

2 Ibid.

3 Newmarch, "Inaugural Address on the Progress and Present Condition of Statistical Inquiry," 361.

4 Newmarch, "Report of the Council for the Financial Year Ended 31st December, 1870, and for the Sessional Year Ended with June, 1871," 240.

5 Ibid., 241.

6 "Proceedings of the Forty-sixth Anniversary Meeting,"418.

7 Senior, "Opening Address of Nassau W. Senior, Esq., as President of Section F," 357.

8 Ibid., 457.

9 Ibid., 347–48.

10 Galton, "Considerations Adverse to the Maintenance of Section F," 471.

11 Farr, "Considerations, in the Form of a Draft Report, Submitted to Committee, Favourable to the Maintenance of Section F," 473.

12 Ibid., 473–74.

13 Duff, "Address of the President of Section F," 657.

14 Ibid.

15 Farr, "On Some Doctrines of Population," 571.

16 Ibid., 572.

17 Ibid., 571.

18 Ibid.

19 Ibid., 579.

20 Williams, "On the Increase of Population in England and Wales."

21 Humphreys, "The Recent Decline in the English Death-Rate and Its Effect upon the Duration of Life," Longstaff, "The Recent Decline in the English Death Rate Considered in Connection with the Causes of Death," and Welton, "On Certain Changes in the English Rates of Mortality."

22 England was one of the first western European countries to incorporate economics into the university curriculum as a separate discipline. By the mid-1880s Cambridge and Oxford had nine lecturers on political economy. In the course of the 1890s the new discipline was institutionalized, as it acquired its own journal (the *Economic Journal*, 1891), the London School of Economics was formed in 1895, and the Economic Tripos was introduced at Cambridge in 1903. For an account of

the institutionalization of economics as a new academic discipline see Kadish, *The Oxford Economists in the Late Nineteenth Century*, Schabas, "Mathematics and the Economics Profession in Late Victorian England," and Maloney, *Marshall, Orthodoxy and the Professionalization of Economics*. These organizational developments were accompanied by an explicit disciplinary discourse concerning the relation between economic science and the natural sciences, most notably physics.

CHAPTER 9 Institutional Transformations

1 MacLeod, *Government and Expertise*, 9.
2 This model of central local relations was clearly outlined by John Stuart Mill in *Representative Government*. According to Mill, "power may be localized, but knowledge, to be most useful, must be centralized." Cited in Hennock, "Central/Local Government Relations in England," 40.
3 Szreter, "The GRO and the Public Health Movement in Britain, 1837–1914," 455–56.
4 Hennock, "Central/Local Government Relations in England," 42.
5 For an account of the development of formal instruction in public health see MacLeod, "The Anatomy of State Medicine," 221–25.
6 Brand, *Doctors and the State*.
7 Parkes, *A Manual of Practical Hygiene*, 466.
8 Wilson, *A Handbook of Hygiene and Sanitary Science*, 394–420.
9 Szreter, "The GRO and the Public Health Movement in Britain, 1837–1914," 452.
10 Ibid., 453.
11 Goldman, "The Social Science Association, 1857–1886," 126.
12 Cited in ibid., 129.
13 Ibid., 437–41.
14 The Statistical Society of Paris moved back the dates of its meeting so as to allow French and English statisticians to participate in the two events.
15 Rawson, "Address of the President, Sir Rawson W. Rawson, K.C.M.G.," 6.
16 Newmarch, "Inaugural Address on the Progress and Present Condition of Statistical Inquiry," 359.
17 Hooper, "The Method of Statistical Analysis."
18 Rawson, "Address of the President, Sir Rawson W. Rawson, K.C.M.G.," 6.
19 "Discussion," Jubilee Volume 1885, 266.
20 A final paper of the day was delivered by Alfred de Foville who delivered a somewhat literary discourse entitled "Statistics and its Enemies."
21 Mouat, "History of the Statistical Society of London," 16.
22 Guy, "Statistical Development," 44.
23 Ibid., 77.
24 Edgeworth, "Methods of Statistics," 183.
25 Ibid.
26 Levasseur, "La statistique graphique," 219.

27 Marshall, "On the Graphic Method of Statistics," 251.

28 Sidgwick, "Economic Science and Statistics," 607.

29 "Proceedings of the Fifty-first Anniversary Meeting," 346.

30 Von Neumann-Spallart, "Résumé of the Results of the International Statistical Congress," 304.

31 Ibid., 305.

32 Ibid., 304.

33 Ibid., 306.

34 Von Neumann-Spallart, "La fondation de l'institut international de statistique," 4.

35 Ibid., 17.

36 Desrosières, *The Politics of Large Numbers*, 155.

Conclusion

1 The focus on the relation of risk and social legislation is informed by Foucault's concept of governmentality. For an overview of the concept and its use in analyzing social legislation see Gordon, "Governmental Rationality," and Castel, "From Dangerousness to Risk." For detailed empirical studies see Ewald, *L'état providence*, and Castel, *From Manual Workers to Wage Laborers*.

2 Jepperson, "Political Modernities."

3 The contrast between British and Continental scientific styles has been explored in a number of domains. The classical statement that has informed much subsequent work can be found in Crombie, *Styles of Scientific Thinking in the European Tradition*. These differences have been documented by Mary Jo Nye in chemistry, Nye, "National Styles?," by Joan Richards in geometry, Richards, "Rigor and Clarity," and by Marion Fourcade-Gourinchas in economics, Fourcade-Gourinchas, "Politics, Institutional Structures and the Rise of Economics." In the area of nineteenth-century social research, Raymond Williams contrasts British and Continental discourse on social problems, Williams, *Politics and Letters*, 113–14.

4 Horne, *A Social Laboratory for Modern France*.

5 This distinction is quite standard in the literature on discipline formation. For two examples, from radically different theoretical positions, see Ben-David and Collins, "Social Factors in the Origins of a New Science," and Lenoir, "Disciplinary Boundaries and the Rhetoric of the Social Sciences."

6 Messer-Davidow, Shumway, and Sylvan, *Knowledges*, 3.

7 Kuklick, "Boundary Maintenance in American Sociology," 204.

8 Fuller, "Disciplinary Boundaries and the Rhetoric of the Social Sciences," 192. For a more general discussion of the concept of style and its use in the history of science see Crombie, *Styles of Scientific Thinking in the European Tradition*, Daston and Otte, *Styles in Science*, Hacking, "'Style' for Historians and Philosophers," Nicolson, "National Styles, Divergent Classifications," and Wessely, "Transporting 'Style' from the History of Art to the History of Science."

BIBLIOGRAPHY

Primary Sources

Alphonse, Jacques, and Georges Bertillon. *La vie et les oeuvres du docteur L.-A. Ber-tillon*. Paris: G. Masson, 1883.

"Arthur Chervin." *Dictionnaire de biographie française*, ed. J. Balteau, M. Prévost, and J. C. Roman d'Amat. Paris: Letouzey et Ané, 1959.

Bertillon, Louis Adolphe. "De quelques éléments de l'hygiène, dans leur rapport avec la durée de la vie." Faculté de médecine, thèse pour le doctorat en médecine, présentée et soutenue le 6 août 1852, Paris.

———. "Démographie." *Dictionnaire de médecine, de chirurgie, de pharmacie, des sciences accessoires et de l'art vétérinaire, d'après le plan suivi par Nysten*, ed. E. Littré, P. H. Nysten, and C. Robin. Paris, 1865.

———. "Des diverses manières de mesurer la durée de la vie humaine." *Journal de la société de statistique de Paris* 7, no. 3 (1866): 45–65.

———. "De la mortalité parisienne: Croissante selon les morts, décroissante selon les ministres." *La philosophie positive: Revue dirigée par É. Littré et G. Wyrouboff*, 1869, 445–57.

———. *La démographie figurée de la France: Ou, étude statistique de la population fran-çaise avec tableaux graphiques traduisant les principales conclusions: mortalité selon l'âge, le sexe, l'état-civil, etc. etc. en chaque département et pour la France entière comparée aux pays étrangers*. Paris: G. Mason, 1874.

———. "La population française." *Association française pour l'avancement des sciences: Compte rendu de la 2ème session, Lyon 1873*. Paris, 1874.

———. *Exposé des travaux scientifiques du Dr. Bertillon, candidat à la place vacante à l'académie de médecine dans la section des associés libres*. Paris: A. Parent, 1875.

———. "Mouvements de la population dans les divers états de l'Europe et notam-ment en France." *Annales de démographie internationale: Recueil trimestriel de travaux originaux et de documents statistiques et bulletin bibliographique spécial* 1 (1877): 161–211.

Bienaymé, Jules. *Prix Montyon de statistique (concours de l'année 1876): Comptes rendus des séances de l'académie des sciences* 84 (1877): 817–25.

Broca, Paul. "Histoire des travaux de la société d'anthropologie (1859–1863)." *Mémoires de la société d'anthropologie de Paris* 2 (1863–64): vii–li.

———. "Rapport sur les travaux de statistique de M. le docteur Bertillon." *Bulletin de l'académie de médecine*, 2d ser., 4 (1875): 97–113.

Chadwick, David. "On the Best Modes of Representing Accurately, by Statistical Returns, the Duration of Life, and the Pressure and Progress of the Causes of Mortality . . ." *Journal of the Statistical Society of London* 7 (1844): 1–40.

Chervin, Arthur. "A nos lecteurs." *Annales de démographie internationales* 1 (1877): 1.

Chevalier, Michel. "Travaux de la société de statistique de Paris." *Journal de la société de statistique de Paris* 1 (1860): 1–7.

Cheysson, Emile. "La statistique géometrique." *Journal de la société de statistique de Paris: Le 25ᵉ anniversaire*, 1865, 135–41.

"Congrès international de démographie." *Annales de démographie internationales* 2, no. 5 (1878): 97–99.

"Congrès international de démographie, tenu à Paris, les 5, 6, 7, 8 et 9 juillet 1878." *Annales de démographie internationales* 2 (1878): 300–519.

"Congrès international de démographie, tenu à Paris, les 5, 6, 7, 8 et 9 juillet 1878: Comptes rendus sténographiques publiés sous les auspices du comité central des congrés et conférences." Paris: Imprimerie Nationale, 1879.

Dechambre, Amédée. *Dictionnaire encyclopédique des sciences médicales, publié sous la direction de MM. les Drs. Raigé-Delorme et A. Dechambre*. Paris: Masson, 1864–89.

"Discussion, Jubilee of the Statistical Society of London." *Journal of the Statistical Society of London*, jubilee edition (1885).

"Discussion sur la mortalité des enfants." *Bulletin de l'académie de médecine* 32 (1866–67): 89–113, 165–95, 227–86, 335–40, 351–421.

"Discussion sur la prétendue dégénérescence de la population." *Bulletin de l'académie de médecine* 32 (1866–67): 547–601, 617–80, 741–824, 839–91.

Edgeworth, F. Y. "Methods of Statistics." *Journal of the Statistical Society of London*, jubilee edition (1885): 181–217.

Edmonds, T. R. "On the Laws of Collective Vitality." *Lancet* 2 (1834–35): 5–8.

"Exposition internationale de 1878 à Paris: Exposition des sciences anthropologiques." *Annales de démographie internationales* 1 (1877): 308–18.

Farr, William, Esq. "Considerations, in the Form of a Draft Report, Submitted to Committee, Favourable to the Maintenance of Section F." *Journal of the Statistical Society of London* 40 (1837).

———. "Vital Statistics." *British Annals of Medicine, Pharmacy, Vital Statistics and General Science* 1 (1837): 353–60.

———. "Vital Statistics, or, the Statistics of Health, Sickness, Diseases, and Death." *A Statistical Account of the British Empire*, ed. J. R. McCulloch (1837).

———. "On Some Doctrines of Population, a Paper Read in Section F of the British Association at Plymouth in August Last." *Journal of the Statistical Society of London* 40 (1877): 568–81.

———. *Vital Statistics: A Memorial Volume of Selections from the Reports and Writings of*

William Farr, ed. Noel A. Humphreys. London: Offices of the Sanitary Institute, 1885.

Fifth Annual Report of the Registrar-General of Births, Deaths, and Marriages in England. Great Britain Parliamentary Papers (1843).

First Annual Report of the Registrar-General of Births, Deaths, and Marriages in England. London: Longman, 1908.

Galton, Francis. "Considerations Adverse to the Maintenance of Section F . . . Submitted by Mr. Francis Galton to the Committee Appointed by the Council to Consider and Report on the Possibility of Excluding Unscientific or Otherwise Unsuitable Papers and Discussions from the Section and Proceedings of the Association." *Journal of the Statistical Society of London* 40 (1877): 468–73.

Garnier, Joseph. "De la statistique des naissances." *Journal des économistes* 36 (1853): 193–95.

———. "Observations sur le principe de population par MM Passy, Dunoyer, Villermé, Guizot, Léon Faucher et Lord Brougham." *Journal des économistes* 35 (1853): 428–39.

———. "Population." *Dictionnaire de l'économie politique*, ed. C. Coquelin and M. Guillaumin. Paris: Guillaumin, 1854.

Gide, Charles, and Charles Rist. *Histoire des doctrines économiques*. Paris, 1909.

Guillard, Achille. "De la statistique des naissances; dans ses rapports avec la question générale de population." *Journal des économistes* 36 (1853): 184–95.

———. "Nécessité de constater l'âge des décédés." *Journal des économistes* 35 (1853): 272–74.

———. "Statistique humaine: Conservation des enfants, naissances frustranées." *Revue du XIXᵉ siècle*, 1854, 367–76.

———. *Éléments de statistique humaine; Ou, démographie comparée, où sont exposés les principes de la science nouvelle, et controntés, d'après les documents les plus authentiques, l'état, les mouvements généraux et les progrès de la population dans les pays civilisés*. Paris: Guillaumin, 1855.

———. "Démographie (Lois de Population)." *Journal de la société de statistique de Paris* 2 (1861): 277–88.

Guy, William Augustus. "On the Original and Acquired Meaning of the Term 'Statistics,' and on the Proper Functions of a Statistical Society: Also on the Question Whether There Be a Science of Statistics; And, if So, What Are Its Nature and Objects, and What Is Its Relation to Political Economy and 'Social Science.'" *Journal of the Statistical Society of London* 28 (1865): 478–93.

———. "Statistical Development, with Special Reference to Statistics as a Science." *Journal of the Statistical Society of London*, 1885, 72–83.

Humphreys, Noel A. "The Recent Decline in the English Death-Rate and Its Effect upon the Duration of Life." *Journal of the Statistical Society of London* 44 (1883): 188–224.

Langstaff, G. B. "The Recent Decline in the English Death-Rate Considered in Connection with the Causes of Death." *Journal of the Statistical Society of London* 47 (1884): 221–58.

Latour, Amédée. "Bulletin sur la séance de l'académie de médecine, Paris, le 19 février 1858." *L'union médicale: Journal des intérêts scientifiques et pratiques, moraux et professionels du corps médical* 12 (1858): 65.

Lavergne, Léonce de. "Note sur le dénombrement de la population de 1856, suivie d'observations." *Séance et travaux de l'académie des sciences morales et politiques* 39 (1857): 213–26.

Legoyt, Alfred. "De la centralisation administrative." *Revue administrative*, 3d ser., 4 (1849): 493–98, 613–34, 669–706.

———. "De la réforme ministérielle et administrative." *Revue administrative*, 3d ser., 4 (1849): 3–24.

———. "De la prétendue dégénérescence physique de la population française comparée aux autres populations européennes." *Journal de la société de statistique de Paris* 4, no. 2 (1863): 316–38.

Le Roux, Henry. "Les travaux de la commission de statistique municipale de Paris." *Journal de la société de statistique de Paris*, 1880, 228–33.

Levasseur, Émile. "Démographie figurée de la France, ou étude statistique de la population française: Mortalité." *Académie des sciences morales et politiques* 104 (1875): 674–79.

———. "La statistique graphique." *Journal of the Statistical Society of London*, jubilee edition (1885).

Loua, Toussaint. "Notions générales de statistique." *Journal de la société de statistique de Paris* 13 (1871–72): 171–73.

———. *Atlas statistique de la population de Paris*. Paris, 1873.

Marshall, Alfred. "On the Graphic Method of Statistics." *Journal of the Statistical Society of London*, jubilee edition (1885), 251–60.

McCrosty, H. W. *Annals of the Royal Statistical Society, 1834–1934*. London, 1934.

"Minutes of the Council." Paper read at the Statistical Society of London, 1843–44.

Moreau de Jonnès, Alexandre. *Éléments de statistique: Comprenant les principes généraux de cette science, et un aperçu historique de ses progrès*. Paris: Guillaumin, 1847.

Morel, Benedict Auguste. *Traité des dégénérescences physiques, intellectuelles et morales de l'espèce humaine et des causes qui produisent ces variétés maladives*. Paris: J. B. Bailliere, 1857.

Mouat, Frederic J. "History of the Statistical Society of London." *Journal of the Statistical Society of London*, jubilee edition (1885), 14–50.

Neison, F. G. P. "On a Method Recently Proposed for Conducting Inquiries into the Comparative Sanatory Condition of Various Districts, with Illustrations, Derived from Numerous Places in Great Britain at the Period of the Last Census." *Journal of the Statistical Society of London* 7 (1844): 40–53.

Newmarch, William. "The Progress of Economic Science during the Last Thirty Years: An Opening Address by William Newmarch, F. R. S . . . at the Thirty-first

Annual Meeting of the British Association for the Advancement of Science, at Manchester, 4th–11th September, 1861." *Journal of the Statistical Society of London* 24 (1861): 452–53.

———. "Inaugural Address on the Progress and Present Condition of Statistical Inquiry, Delivered at the Society's Rooms, 12, St. James's Square, London, on Tuesday, 16th November, 1869." *Journal of the Statistical Society of London* 32 (1869): 357–85.

———. "Report of the Council for the Financial Year Ended 31st December, 1870, and for the Sessional Year Ended with June, 1871, Presented at the Thirty-seventh Anniversary Meeting of the Statistical Society . . ." *Journal of the Statistical Society of London* 34 (1871): 236–46.

"Nouvelle organization du bureau de statistique municipale de la ville de Paris: Rapport à la commission de statistique municipale." *Annales de démographie internationale* 3 (1879): 483–557.

"Prix Victor Cousin, section d'économie politique et finances, statistique." *Séance et travaux de l'Académie des Sciences Morales et Politiques* 13 (1866–67): 438–39.

"Proceedings of the Fifty-first Anniversary Meeting." *Journal of the Statistical Society of London* 48 (1885): 346.

"Proceedings of the Forty-sixth Anniversary Meeting." *Journal of the Statistical Society of London* 43 (1880): 418.

Rawson, W. Rawson. "Address of the President, Sir Rawson W. Rawson, K.C.M.G., at the Opening of the Jubilee Meeting of the Society, Monday, 22nd June, 1885." *Journal of the Statistical Society of London*, jubilee edition (1885), 2–13.

Séménow, P. "International Statistical Congress." *Congrès international de statistique: compte-rendu de la huitième session à St.-Pétersbourg*. St. Petersburg: Trenké et Fusnot, 1872–74.

Senior, Nassau. "Opening Address of Nassau W. Senior, Esq., as President of Section F (Economic Science and Statistics) at the Meeting of the British Association, at Oxford, 28th June, 1860." *Journal of the Statistical Society of London* 23 (1860): 357–61.

"Seventeenth Annual Meeting of the Statistical Society of London, Session 1849–1850." *Journal of the Statistical Society of London* 15 (1851): 97–107.

Sidgwick, Henry. "Economic Science and Statistics: The Address of the President of Section F of the British Association, at Fifty-fifth Meeting, held at Aberdeen, in September, 1885." *Journal of the Statistical Society of London* 48 (1885): 595–616.

"Théorie de la statistique et application des données statistiques, séance du lundi 6 septembre." *Congrès international de statistique à La Haye, compte-rendu des travaux de la septième session, seconde partie*. The Hague: Nijhoff, 1870.

"Twelfth Annual Report of the Statistical Society of London, Session 1845–46." *Journal of the Statistical Society of London* 9 (1846): 97–99.

Vissering, S. "Limites de la statistique." *Congrès international de statistique à La Haye, septième session du 6 au 11 septembre 1869* The Hague: Nijhoff, 1869.

Von Neumann-Spallart, F. X. "Résumé of the Results of the International Statistical

Congress and Sketch of Proposed Plan of an International Statistical Association." *Journal de la société de statistique de Paris*, jubilee edition (1885), 284–306.

——. "La fondation de l'institut international de statistique." *Bulletin de l'institut international de statistique* 1 (1886): 1–32.

Welton, Thomas. "On Certain Changes in the English Rates of Mortality." *Journal of the Statistical Society of London* 43 (1880): 65–94.

"William Farr." *Dictionary of National Biography: From the Earliest Times to 1900*. London: Oxford University Press, 1908.

Williams, R. Price. "On the Increase of Population in England and Wales." *Journal of the Statistical Society of London* 43 (1880): 462–508.

Wilson, George. *A Handbook of Hygiene and Sanitary Science*. 5th ed. London: J. and A. Churchill, 1883.

Secondary Sources

Abbott, Andrew. "From Causes to Events: Notes on Narrative Positivism." *Sociological Methods and Research* 20, no. 4 (1992): 428–55.

——. "Things of Boundaries." *Social Research* 62, no. 4 (1995): 857–82.

Abrams, Philip. *The Origins of British Sociology, 1834–1914: An Essay with Selected Papers*. Chicago: University of Chicago Press, 1968.

——. "Notes on the Difficulty of Studying the State (1977)." *Journal of Historical Sociology* 1, no. 1 (1988): 58–89.

Ackerman, Evelyn Bernette. *Health Care in the Parisian Countryside, 1800–1914*. New Brunswick, N.J.: Rutgers University Press, 1990.

Alborn, Timothy L. "A Calculating Profession: Victorian Actuaries among the Statisticians." *Science in Context* 7, no. 3 (1987): 433–68.

Alonso, William, and Paul Starr. *The Politics of Numbers*. New York: Russell Sage Foundation, 1987.

Anderson, Benedict R. O. G. *Imagined Communities: Reflections on the Origin and Spread of Nationalism*. Rev. ed. London: Verso, 1991.

Anderson, Margo J. *The American Census: A Social History*. New Haven: Yale University Press, 1988.

Anderson, Margo J., and Stephen E. Fienberg. *Who Counts? The Politics of Census-Taking in Contemporary America*. New York: Russell Sage Foundation, 1999.

Arena, Richard. "Joseph Garnier, libéral orthodoxe et théoricien éclectique." *L'économie politique en France au XIXe siècle*, ed. Y. Breton and M. Lutfalla. Paris: Economica, 1991.

Armatte, Michel. "Une discipline dans tous ses états: La statistique à travers ses traités (1800–1914)." *Revue de synthèse*, 4th ser., 2 (April–June 1991): 161–205.

Barnes, Barry, and Steven Shapin. *Natural Order: Historical Studies of Scientific Culture*. Beverly Hills, Calif.: Sage, 1979.

Behar, Cem L. "Malthus and the Development of Demographic Analysis." *Population Studies* 41 (1987): 269–81.

Ben-David, Joseph, and Randall Collins. "Social Factors in the Origins of a New Science: The Case of Psychology." *American Sociological Review* 31, no. 4 (1966): 451–65.

Biagoli, Mario, ed. *The Science Studies Reader*. New York: Routledge, 1999.

Biersack, Aletta, and Lynn Avery Hunt. *The New Cultural History*. Berkeley: University of California Press, 1989.

Bourguet, Marie-Noëlle. *Déchiffrer la France: La statistique départementale à l'époque napoléonienne, ordres sociaux*. Paris: Archives contemporaines, 1988.

Brais, Bernard. "Désirée Magloire Bourneville and French Anticlericalism during the Third Republic." *Doctors, Politics and Society: Historical Essays*, ed. D. Porter and R. Porter. Amsterdam: Clio Medica, 1993.

Brand, Jeanne L. *Doctors and the State: The British Medical Profession and Government Action in Public Health, 1870–1912*. Baltimore: Johns Hopkins University Press, 1965.

Breton, Yves. "La place de la statistique et de l'arithmétique politique dans la méthodologie économique de Jean-Baptiste Say." *Revue économique* 37, no. 6 (1986): 1033–58.

———. "L'économie politique et les mathématiques en France, 1800–1940." *Histoire et mesure* 7, nos. 1–2 (1992): 25–52.

Breton, Yves, and Michel Lutfalla. *L'économie politique en France au XIXᵉ siècle*. Paris: Economica, 1991.

Brian, Eric. *La mesure de l'état: Recherches sur la division sociale du travail statistique au XVIIIᵉ et XIXᵉ siècles*. Paris: Albin Michel, 1990.

———. "Bibliographie des comptes rendus officiels du congrès international de statistique (1853–1878)." *Annales de démographie historique: Études, chronique, bibliographie, documents*, 1990, 469–79.

———. "Des courbes qui parlent dans un brouhaha de chiffres." *Mémoire vive* 5 (1991): 3–20.

———. "Le prix Montyon de statistique à l'académie royale des sciences pendant la restauration." *Revue de synthèse*, 4th ser., 2 (1991): 207–36.

Brown, Lucy. *The Board of Trade and the Free Trade Movement*. Oxford: Clarendon, 1958.

Bryant, Christopher G. A. *Positivism in Social Theory and Research*. New York: St. Martin's, 1985.

Bulmer, Martin, Kevin Bales, and Kathryn Kish Sklar, eds. *The Social Survey in Historical Perspective, 1880–1940*. Cambridge: Cambridge University Press, 1991.

Cahan, David, ed. *From Natural Philosophy to the Sciences: Writing the History of Nineteenth-Century Science*. Chicago: University of Chicago Press, 2003.

Cambrosio, Alberto, and Peter Keating. "The Disciplinary Stake: The Case of Chronobiology." *Social Studies of Science* 13 (1983): 323–53.

Cardwell, Donald S. L. *The Organisation of Science in England: A Retrospect*. Melbourne: Heinemann, 1957.

Castel, Robert. "From Dangerousness to Risk." *The Foucault Effect*, ed. G. G. Burchell, Colin Gordon, and Peter Miller. Chicago: University of Chicago Press, 1991.

——. *From Manual Workers to Wage Laborers: Transformation of the Social Question*. New Brunswick, N.J.: Transaction, 2003.

Charbit, Yves. *Du malthusianisme au populationnisme: Les économistes français et la population, 1840–1870*. Paris: Presses universitaires de France, 1981.

Chartier, Roger. *Cultural History: Between Practices and Representations*. Cornell: Cornell University Press, 1993.

Clark, Elizabeth A. *History, Theory, Text: Historians and the Linguistic Turn*. Cambridge: Harvard University Press, 2004.

Clarke, Adele. *Disciplining Reproduction*. Berkeley: University of California Press, 1996.

Cohn, Bernard S. "The Census, Social Structure and Objectification in South Asia." *An Anthropologist among the Historians and Other Essays*. Delhi: Oxford University Press, 1988.

——. *Colonialism and Its Forms of Knowledge: The British in India*. Princeton: Princeton University Press, 1996.

Cole, Joshua. *The Power of Large Numbers: Population and Politics in Nineteenth-Century France*. Ithaca: Cornell University Press, 2000.

Coleman, William. *Death Is a Social Disease: Public Health and Political Economy in Early Industrial France*. Madison: University of Wisconsin Press, 1982.

——. "The Cognitive Basis of the Discipline: Claude Bernard on Physiology." *Isis* 76 (1985): 49–70.

Collini, Stefan. *Liberalism and Sociology: L. T. Hobhouse and Political Argument in England, 1880–1914*. Cambridge: Cambridge University Press, 1983.

Collins, Randall. 1998. "The Transformation of Philosophy." *The Rise of the Social Sciences and the Formation of Modernity: Conceptual Change in Context, 1750–1850*, ed. J. Heilbron, L. Magnusson, and B. Wittrock. Boston: Kluwer Academic, 1998.

Converse, Jean M. *Survey Research in the United States: Roots and Emergence, 1890–1960*. Berkeley: University of California Press, 1987.

Corrigan, Philip Richard D., and Derek Sayer. *The Great Arch: English State Formation as Cultural Revolution*. Oxford: Basil Blackwell, 1985.

Crawford, Elisabeth. "The Prize System of the Academy of Sciences, 1850–1914." *The Organization of Science and Technology in France, 1808–1914*, ed. R. Fox and G. Weisz. Cambridge: Cambridge University Press, 1980.

Crombie, A. C. *Styles of Scientific Thinking in the European Tradition: The History of Argument and Explanation Especially in the Mathematical and Biomedical Sciences and Arts*. London: Duckworth, 1994.

Cullen, M. J. "The Making of the Civil Registration Act of 1836." *Journal of Ecclesiastical History* 25, no. 1 (1974): 39–59.

——. *The Statistical Movement in Early Victorian Britain: The Foundations of Empirical Social Research*. Hassocks: Harvester, 1975.

Curtis, Bruce. "Social Investment in Medical Forms: The 1866 Cholera Scare and Beyond." *Canadian Historical Review* 81, no. 4 (2000).

——. *The Politics of Population.* Toronto: University of Toronto Press, 2001.

Daston, Lorraine. *Classical Probability in the Enlightenment.* Princeton: Princeton University Press, 1988.

——. "Objectivity and the Escape from Perspective." *Social Studies of Science* 22, no. 4 (1992): 597–618.

——. "Reply to James Chandler's Commentary on 'Marvelous Facts and Miraculous Evidence.'" Unpublished MS, Chicago Evidence Conference, 21–24 May 1992.

Daston, Lorraine, and Michael Otte, eds. "Styles in Science." *Science in Context* 4 (1991) [special issue].

Davidson, Arnold I. *The Emergence of Sexuality: Historical Epistemology and the Formation of Concepts.* Cambridge: Harvard University Press, 2001.

Dean, Mitchell. *The Constitution of Poverty: Toward a Genealogy of Liberal Governance.* London: Routledge, 1991.

Desrosières, Alain. "How to Make Things Which Hold Together: Social Science, Statistics and the State." *Discourses on Society: The Shaping of the Social Science Disciplines,* ed. P. Wagner, B. Wittrock, and R. Whitley. Dordrecht: Kluwer Academic, 1991.

——. "L'ingénieur d'état et le père de famille: Émile Cheysson et la statistique." *Annales des mines* 2 (1986): 66–80.

——. "Official Statistics and Medicine in Nineteenth-Century France: The SGF as a Case Study." *Social History of Medicine* 6, no. 3 (1991): 515–37.

——. "L'opposition entre deux formes d'enquête: Monographie et statistique." *Justesse et justice dans le travail,* ed. É. Statistique. Paris: Presses universitaires de France, 1989.

——. "The Part in Relation to the Whole: How to Generalize? The Prehistory of Representative Sampling." *The Social Survey in Historical Perspective, 1880–1940,* ed. M. Bulmer, K. Bales, and K. K. Sklar. Cambridge: Cambridge University Press, 1991.

——. *The Politics of Large Numbers: A History of Statistical Reasoning.* Cambridge: Harvard University Press, 1998.

Donzelot, Jacques. *L'invention du social: Essai sur le déclin des passions politiques.* Paris: Fayard, 1984.

Duff, E. Grant. "Address of the President of Section F . . . of the British Association at the Fifty-first Meeting Held at York, in August 1881." *Journal of the Statistical Society of London* 41 (1881): 647–59.

Dumont, Louis. *Essays on Individualism: Modern Ideology in Anthropological Perspective.* Chicago: University of Chicago, 1986.

Dupâquier, Jacques, and Michel Dupâquier. *Histoire de la démographie: La statistique de la population des origines à 1914.* Paris: Librairie academique Perrin, 1985.

Dupâquier, Michel. "La famille Bertillon et la naissance d'une nouvelle science sociale: La démographie." *Annales de démographie historique: Études, chronique, bibliographie, documents*, 1983, 293–311.

Edge, David O. *Astronomy Transformed: The Emergence of Radio Astronomy in Britain*. New York: John Wiley and Sons, 1976.

Elesh, David. "The Manchester Statistical Society: A Case Study of Discontinuity in the History of Empirical Social Research." *The Establishment of Empirical Sociology: Studies in Continuity, Discontinuity, and Institutionalization*, ed. A. Oberschall. New York: Harper and Row, 1972.

Elwitt, Sanford. "Social Reform and Social Order in Late Nineteenth-Century France: The Musée Social and Its Friends." *French Historical Studies* 2 (1980): 431–51.

Etzkowitz, Harry. "The Entrepreneurial University and the Emergence of Democratic Corporatism." *Universities and the Global Knowledge Economy*, ed. H. Etzkowitz and L. A. Leydesdorff. London: Pinter, 1997.

Ewald, François. *L'état providence*. Paris: B. Grasset, 1986.

Eyler, John M. *Victorian Social Medicine: The Ideas and Methods of William Farr*. Baltimore: Johns Hopkins University Press, 1979.

——. *Sir Arthur Newsholme and State Medicine, 1885–1935*. Cambridge: Cambridge University Press, 1997.

Faure, Oliver. "The Social History of Health in France: A Survey of Recent Developments." *Social History of Medicine: The Journal of the Society for the Social History of Medicine* 3, no. 3 (1990): 437–51.

Finer, S. E. *The Life and Times of Sir Edwin Chadwick*. London: Methuen, 1952.

Foucault, Michel. *The History of Sexuality*. Vol. 1. New York: Vintage, 1980.

——. "Les Mailles de pouvoir." *Dits et écrits*, ed. M. Foucault, D. Defert, and F. Ewald. Paris: Gallimard, 1994.

Fourcade-Gourinchas, Marion. "Politics, Institutional Structures and the Rise of Economics: A Comparative Study." *Theory and Society* 30, no. 3 (2001): 397–447.

Fournier, Marcel. "La démographie comme discipline." *Sociologie et sociétés* 19, no. 1 (1987): 163–65.

Fox, Robert, and George Weisz, eds. *The Organization of Science and Technology in France, 1808–1914*. Cambridge: Cambridge University Press, 1980.

Fuller, Steve. "Disciplinary Boundaries and the Rhetoric of the Social Sciences." *Knowledges: Historical and Critical Studies in Disciplinarity*, ed. E. Messer-Davidow, D. R. Shumway, and D. Sylvan. Charlottesville: University Press of Virginia, 1993.

——. *Science*. Minneapolis: University of Minnesota Press, 1997.

Funtowicz, S. O., and J. R. Ravetz. "The Emergence of Post-Normal Science." *Science, Politics and Morality: Scientific Uncertainty and Decision Making*, ed. R. v. Schomberg. Dordrecht: Kluwer Academic, 1993.

Furner, Mary O. *Advocacy and Objectivity: A Crisis in the Professionalization of American Social Science, 1865–1905*. Lexington: University Press of Kentucky, 1975.

Gaziano, Emanuel. "Ecological Metaphors as Scientific Boundary Work: Innovations and Authority in Interwar Sociology and Biology." *American Journal of Sociology* 102 (1996): 974–97.

Gibbons, Michael, Camille Limoges, Helga Nowotny, Simon Schwartzman, Peter Scott, and Martin Trow. *The New Production of Knowledge: the Dynamics of Science and Research in Contemporary Societies*. London: Sage, 1994.

Gieryn, Thomas F. "Boundaries of Science." *Handbook of Science and Technology Studies*, ed. S. Jasanoff, G. E. Markle, J. C. Petersen, and T. Pinch. Thousand Oaks, Calif.: Sage, 1995.

Gigerenzer, Gerd, et. al. *The Empire of Chance: How Probability Changed Science and Everyday Life*. Cambridge: Cambridge University Press, 1989.

Gille, Bertrand. *Les sources statistiques de l'histoire de France*. Paris: Minard, 1964.

Glass, David V. "Some Aspects of the Development of Demography." *Journal of the Royal Society of Arts* 104 (1956): 854–68.

——. *Numbering the People: the Eighteenth-Century Population Controversy and the Development of Census and Vital Statistics in Britain*. Farnborough, Hants: Saxon House, 1973.

Godin, Benoit, and Yves Gingras. "The Place of Universities in the System of Knowledge Production." *Research Policy* 29 (2000): 273–78.

Goldman, Lawrence. "The Social Science Association, 1857–1886: A Context for Mid-Victorian England." *English Historical Review*, 1986, 95–134.

——. "Statistics and the Science of Society in Early Victorian Britain: An Intellectual Context for the General Register Office." *Social History of Medicine: The Journal of the Society for the Social History of Medicine* 4 (1991): 415–34.

——. *Science, Reform and Politics in Victorian Britain: The Social Science Association, 1857–1886*. Cambridge: Cambridge University Press, 2002.

Gordon, Colin. "Governmental Rationality: An Introduction." *The Foucault Effect*, ed. G. G. Burchell, Colin Gordon, and Peter Miller. Chicago: University of Chicago Press, 1991.

Graham, Loren, Wolf Lepenies, and Peter Weingart, eds. *Functions and Uses of Disciplinary Histories*. Dordrecht: D. Reidel, 1983.

Grebenik, E. "Demography, Democracy, and Demonology." *Population and Development Review* 15, no. 1 (1989): 1–22.

Greenhalgh, Susan. "The Social Construction of Population Science: An Intellectual, Institutional, and Political History of Twentieth-Century Demography." *Comparative Studies in Society and History* 38, no. 1 (1996): 26–66.

Griffin, Larry J. "Narrative, Event-Structure Analysis, and Causal Interpretation in Historical Sociology." *American Journal of Sociology* 98, no. 5 (1996):1094–1133.

Hacking, Ian. *The Emergence of Probability*. Cambridge: Cambridge University Press, 1975.

——. "Biopower and the Avalanche of Printed Numbers." *Humanities in Society* 5 (1982): 279–95.

———. "Nineteenth Century Cracks in the Concept of Determinism." *Journal of the History of Ideas* 44 (1983): 455–75.

———. *Representing and Intervening*. Cambridge: Cambridge University Press, 1983.

———. "Prussian Numbers, 1860–1882." *The Probabilistic Revolution*, vol. 1, ed. L. Krüger, L. Daston, and M. Heidelberger. Cambridge: MIT Press, 1987.

———. *The Taming of Chance*. Cambridge: Cambridge University Press, 1990.

———. "Statistical Language, Statistical Truth and Statistical Reason: The Self-authentification of a Style of Scientific Reasoning." *The Social Dimensions of Science*, ed. E. McMullin. Notre Dame: University of Notre Dame Press, 1992.

———. "'Style' for Historians and Philosophers." *Studies in History and Philosophy of Science* 23, no. 1 (1992): 1–20.

Hallyn, Fernand. *Metaphor and Analogy in the Sciences*. Boston: Kluwer Academic, 2000.

Hamlin, Christopher. *Public Health and Social Justice in the Age of Chadwick*. New York: Cambridge University Press, 1998.

Hammond, Michael. "Anthropology as a Weapon of Social Combat in Late-Nineteenth-Century France." *Journal of the History of the Behavioral Sciences* 16 (1980): 118–32.

Hanley, James. "Edwin Chadwick and the Poverty of Statistics." *Medical History* 46 (2002): 21–40.

Hardy, Anne. "Public Health and the Expert: The London Medical Officers of Health, 1856–1900." *Government and Expertise: Specialists, Administrators, and Professionals, 1860–1919*, ed. R. M. MacLeod. Cambridge: Cambridge University Press, 1988.

Harvey, Joy. "Evolutionism Transformed: Positivists and Materialists in the Société d'Anthropologie de Paris from Second Empire to Third Republic." *The Wider Domain of Evolutionary Thought*, ed. D. R. Oldroyd and I. Langham. Dordrecht: D. Reidel, 1983.

———. *Almost a Man of Genius: Clemence Royer, Feminism and Nineteenth-Century Science*. New Brunswick, N.J.: Rutgers University Press, 1997.

Hauser, Philip Morris, and Otis Dudley Duncan. *The Study of Population: An Inventory and Appraisal*. Chicago: University of Chicago Press, 1964.

Hennock, E. P. "Central/Local Government Relations in England: An Outline, 1800–1950." *Urban History Yearbook*, 1982, 38–49.

Hess, David J. *Science Studies: An Advanced Introduction*. New York: New York University Press, 1997.

Higgs, Edward. *A Clearer Sense of the Census: The Victorian Censuses and Historical Research*. London: HMSO, 1996.

———. "A Cuckoo in the Nest? The Origins of Civil Registration and State Medical Statistics in England and Wales." *Continuity and Change* 11, no. 1 (1996): 115–34.

Hilts, Victor L. "Aliis Exterendum, or, the Origins of the Statistical Society of London." *Isis* 69 (1978): 21–43.

———. *Statist and Statistician: The Development of Science*. New York: Arno, 1981.

Hodgson, Dennis. "Demography as Social Science and Policy Science." *Population and Development Review* 9, no. 1 (1983): 1–33.

———. "Orthodoxy and Revisionism in American Demography." *Population and Development Review* 14, no. 4 (1988): 541–69.

Holmes, Frederic L. "The Intake-Output Method of Quantification in Physiology." *Historical Studies in the Physical and Biological Sciences* 17 (1987): 236–70.

Hooper, Wynnard. "The Method of Statistical Analysis." *Journal of the Statistical Society of London*, 1881, 44.

Horne, Janet R. *A Social Laboratory for Modern France: The Musée Social and the Rise of the Welfare State*. Durham: Duke University Press, 2003.

Horvarth, Robert A. "De Christophe Bernoulli à Achille Guillard: Les tentatives de création d'une discipline démographique autonome au milieu du XIXᵉ siècle." *Population* 35, nos. 4–5 (1980): 893–909.

Huch, Ronald K. "The National Association for the Promotion of Social Science: Its Contribution to Victorian Health Reform, 1857–1886." *Albion* 17, no. 3 (1985): 279–300.

Jasanoff, Sheila, Gerald E. Markle, James C. Petersen, and Trevor Pinch, eds. *Handbook of Science and Technology Studies*. Thousand Oaks, Calif.: Sage, 1995.

Jepperson, Ronald L. "Political Modernities: Disentangling Two Underlying Dimensions of Institutional Differentiation." *Sociological Theory* 20, no. 1 (2002): 61–85.

Kadish, Alon. *The Oxford Economists in the Late Nineteenth Century*. Oxford: Clarendon, 1982.

Kang, Zheng. "La société de statistique de Paris au XIXᵉ siècle: Un lieu de savoir social." *Cahiers du centre de recherches historiques*, 1989.

———. "Lieu de savoir social: La société de statistique de Paris au XIXᵉ siècle (1860–1910)." Diss., École des hautes études en sciences sociales, 1989.

Keller, Evelyn Fox. "Gender and Science: Origin, History, and Politics." *Osiris* 10 (1995): 27–38.

Kevles, Daniel J. *In the Name of Eugenics: Genetics and the Uses of Human Heredity*. Berkeley: University of California Press, 1985.

Kinchy, A. J., and D. L. Kleinman. "Organizing Credibility: Discursive and Organizational Orthodoxy on the Borders of Ecology and Politics." *Social Studies of Science* 33, no. 6 (2003): 869–96.

Klein, Julie-Thompson. *Crossing Boundaries: Knowledge, Disciplinarities and Interdisciplinarities*. Charlottesville: University Press of Virginia, 1996.

Kohler, Robert E. *From Medical Chemistry to Biochemistry: The Making of a Biomedical Discipline*. Cambridge: Cambridge University Press, 1982.

Kohn, Hans. *The Age of Nationalism: The First Era of Global History*. New York: Harper, 1962.

Krüger, Lorenz, Lorraine Daston, and Michael Heidelberger, eds. *The Probabilistic Revolution*. Vol. 1. Cambridge: MIT Press, 1987.

Krüger, Lorenz, Gerd Gigerenzer, and Mary S. Morgan, eds. *The Probabilistic Revolution*. Vol. 2. Cambridge: MIT Press, 1987.

Kudlick, Catherine J. "The Culture of Statistics and the Crisis of Cholera in Paris, 1830–1850." *Re-creating Authority in Revolutionary France*, ed. B. T. Ragan and E. A. Williams. New Brunswick, N.J.: Rutgers University Press, 1992.

Kuisel, Richard F. *Capitalism and the State in Modern France: Renovation and Economic Management in the Twentieth Century*. Cambridge: Cambridge University Press, 1983.

Kuklick, Henrika. "Boundary Maintenance in American Sociology: Limitations to Academic 'Professionalism.'" *Journal of the History of the Behavioral Sciences* 16, no. 3 (1980): 201–19.

La Berge, Ann F. "Edwin Chadwick and the French Connection." *Bulletin of the History of Medicine* 62 (1988): 23–41.

Latour, Bruno. *Science in Action: How to Follow Scientists and Engineers through Society*. Milton Keynes: Open University Press, 1987.

Lécuyer, Bernard-Pierre. "Probability in Vital and Social Statistics: Quetelet, Farr, and the Bertillons." *The Probabilistic Revolution*, vol. 1, ed. L. Krüger, L. Daston, and M. Heidelberger. Cambridge: MIT Press, 1987.

Le Mée, R. "La statistique démographique officielle de 1815 à 1870 en France." *Annales de démographie historique: Études, chronique, bibliographie, documents*, 1979, 251–79.

Lenoir, Timothy. "Disciplinary Boundaries and the Rhetoric of the Social Sciences." *Knowledges: Historical and Critical Studies in Disciplinarity*, E. Messer-Davidow, D. R. Shumway, and D. Sylvan. Charlottesville: University Press of Virginia, 1993.

Léonard, Jacques. *La médecine entre les savoirs et les pouvoirs: Histoire intellectuelle et politique de la médecine française au XIXᵉ siècle*. Paris: Aubier Montaigne, 1981.

Lesch, John E. "The Paris Academy of Medicine and Experimental Science, 1820–1848." *The Investigative Enterprise: Experimental Physiology in Nineteenth-Century Medicine*, ed. W. Coleman and F. L. Holmes. Berkeley: University of California Press, 1988.

Le Van-Lemesle, Lucette. "La promotion de l'économie politique en France au XIXᵉ siècle jusqu'a son introduction dans les facultés (1815–1881)." *Revue d'histoire moderne et contemporaine* 27 (1980): 270–94.

Levine, Donald Nathan. *Visions of the Sociological Tradition*. Chicago: University of Chicago Press, 1995.

Lewis, Richard Albert. *Edwin Chadwick and the Public Health Movement, 1832–1854*. London: Longmans, Green, 1952.

Leydesdorff, Loet, and Henry Etzkowitz. "Emergence of a Triple Helix of University-Industry-Government Relations." *Science and Public Policy* 23 (1996): 279–86.

———. "The Endless Transition: A Triple-Helix of University-Industry-Government Relations." *Minerva* 36 (1998): 203–18.

Lilienfeld, Abraham M. "Times, Places, and Persons: Aspects of the History of

Epidemiology." *Henry E. Sigerist Supplements to the Bulletin of the History of Medicine*, new ser., 4 (1980). Baltimore: Johns Hopkins University Press.

Lutfalla, Michel. "Le 'journal des économistes.'" *Revue d'histoire économique et sociale* 50, no. 4 (1972): 494–517.

MacKenzie, Donald A. *Statistics in Britain, 1865–1930: The Social Construction of Scientific Knowledge*. Edinburgh: Edinburgh University Press, 1981.

MacLaughlin, Neil G. "Why Do Schools of Thought Fail? Neo-Freudianism as a Case Study in the Sociology of Knowledge." *Journal of the History of the Behavioral Sciences* 34, no. 2 (1998): 113–34.

MacLeod, Roy M. "The Anatomy of State Medicine: Concept and Application." *Medicine and Science in the 1860s: Proceedings of the Sixth British Congress on the History of Medicine, University of Sussex, 6–9 September 1967*, ed. F. N. L. Poynter (1968).

———, ed. *Government and Expertise: Specialists, Administrators, and Professionals, 1860–1919*. Cambridge: Cambridge University Press, 1988.

Maloney, John. *Marshall, Orthodoxy and the Professionalisation of Economics*. Cambridge: Cambridge University Press, 1985.

Martin, Emily. "The Egg and the Sperm: How Science Has Constructed a Romance Based on Sterotypical Male-Female Roles." *Journal of Women in Culture and Society* 16, no. 3 (1991): 485–501.

McCormmach, Russell. Editor's Foreword. *Historical Studies in the Physical Sciences* 3 (1971): ix–xxiv.

Ménard, Claude. "Trois formes de résistance aux statistiques: Say, Cournot, Walras." *Pour une histoire de la statistique*. Paris: Institut national de la statistique et des études économiques, 1977.

Messer-Davidow, Ellen, David R. Shumway, and David Sylvan, eds. *Knowledges: Historical and Critical Studies in Disciplinarity*. Charlottesville: University Press of Virginia, 1993.

Miller, Peter, and Nikolas Rose. "Governing Economic Life." *Economy and Society* 19, no. 1 (1990): 1–31.

Mirowski, Philip. *More Heat than Light: Economics and Social Physics*. Cambridge: Cambridge University Press, 1989.

Mirowski, Philip, and Esther-Mirjam Sent. Introduction. *Science Bought and Sold*, ed. P. Mirowski and E.-M. Sent. Chicago: University of Chicago Press, 2002.

Morrell, Jack, and Arnold Thackray. *Gentlemen of Science: Early Years of the British Association for the Advancement of Science*. Oxford: Clarendon, 1981.

Murard, Lion, and Patrick Zylberman. *L'hygiène dans la République: La santé publique en France, ou, l'utopie contrariée (1870–1918)*. Paris: Fayard, 1996.

Nicolet, Claude. *L'idée républicaine en France, 1789–1924: Essai d'histoire critique*. Paris: Gallimard, 1982.

Nicolson, Malcolm. "National Styles, Divergent Classifications: A Comparative Case Study from the History of French and American Plant Ecology." *Knowledge and Society: Studies in the Sociology of Culture Past and Present* 8 (1989): 139–86.

Nobles, Melissa. *Shades of Citizenship: Race and the Census in Modern Politics*. Stanford: Stanford University Press, 2000.

Nord, Philip G. *The Republican Moment: The Struggle for Democracy in Nineteenth-Century France*. Cambridge: Harvard University Press, 1995.

Notestein, Frank W. "Demography in the United States: A Partial Account of the Development of the Field." *Population and Development Review* 8, no. 4 (1982): 651–87.

Nowotny, Helga, Peter Scott, and Michael Gibbons. *Re-thinking Science: Knowledge and the Public in an Age of Uncertainty*. Oxford: Polity, 2001.

Nye, Mary Jo. "National Styles? French and English Chemistry in the 19th and Early 20th Centuries." *Osiris* 8 (1993): 30–49.

Oberschall, Anthony, ed. *The Establishment of Empirical Sociology: Studies in Continuity, Discontinuity, and Institutionalization*. New York: Harper and Row, 1972.

Otte, Michael. "Style as a Historical Category." *Science in Context* 4, no. 2 (1991): 233–64.

Palsky, Gilles. *Des chiffres et des cartes: Naissance et développement de la cartographie quantitative au XIXᵉ siècle*. Paris: Ministère de l'enseignment supérieur et de la recherche, Comité des travaux historiques et scientifiques, 1996.

Parkes, E. A. *A Manual of Practical Hygiene: Prepared Especially for Use in the Medical Service of the Army*. London: John Churchill and Sons, 1864.

Patriarca, Silvana. *Numbers and Nationhood: Writing Statistics in Nineteenth-Century Italy*. Cambridge: Cambridge University Press, 1996.

Paul, Harry W. *From Knowledge to Power: The Rise of the Science Empire in France, 1860–1939*. Cambridge: Cambridge University Press, 1985.

Perrot, Jean-Claude, and Stuart J. Woolf. *State and Statistics in France, 1789–1815*. London: Harwood Academic, 1984.

Pestre, Dominique. *The Evolution of Knowledge Domains: Interdisciplinarity and Core Knowledge*. Report written for the Scientific Council of the CNRS, Paris, 2002, reproduced on www.interdisciplines.org/interdisciplinarity/papers/8.

——. "Regimes of Knowledge Production in Society: Towards a More Social and Political Reading." *Minerva* 41, no. 3 (2003): 245–61.

Pick, Daniel. *Faces of Degeneration: A European Disorder, c.1848–c.1918*. Cambridge: Cambridge University Press, 1989.

Pickstone, John. "How Might We Map the Cultural Fields of Science? Politics and Organisms in Restoration France." *History of Science* 37 (1999): 347–64.

Platt, Jennifer. *A History of Sociological Research Methods in America, 1920–1960*. Cambridge: Cambridge University Press, 1996.

Plessis, Alain. *The Rise and Fall of the Second Empire, 1852–1871*. Cambridge: Cambridge University Press, 1985.

Poovey, Mary. *Making a Social Body: British Cultural Formation, 1830–1864*. Chicago: University of Chicago Press, 1995.

——. *A History of the Modern Fact: Problems of Knowledge in the Sciences of Wealth and Society*. Chicago: University of Chicago Press, 1998.

Porter, Dorothy, and Roy Porter. "The Politics of Prevention: Anti-Vaccinationism and Public Health in Nineteenth-Century England." *Medical History* 32 (1988): 231–52.

Porter, Roy. "Gentlemen and Geology: The Emergence of a Scientific Career, 1660–1920." *Historical Journal* 21, no. 4 (1978): 809–36.

Porter, Theodore M. *The Rise of Statistical Thinking, 1820–1900*. Princeton: Princeton University Press, 1986.

——. "Lawless Society: Social Science and the Reinterpretation of Statistics in Germany, 1850–1880." *The Probabilistic Revolution*, vol. 1, ed. L. Krüger, L. Daston, and M. Heidelberger. Cambridge: MIT Press, 1987.

——. *Trust in Numbers: The Pursuit of Objectivity in Science and Public Life*. Princeton: Princeton University Press, 1995.

——. "Statistics and Statistical Methods." *The Modern Social Sciences*. Cambridge: Cambridge University Press, 2003.

Ramsden, Edmund. "Carving up Population Science: Eugenics, Demography and the Controversy over the 'Biological Law' of Population Growth." *Social Studies of Science* 32, nos. 5–6 (2002): 857–99.

——. "Mapping Populations and Population Science: Demography, Eugenics and the Logistic Curve Controversy." Unpublished MS, 2002.

Rasmussen, Anne. "Les congrès internationaux liés aux expositions universelles de Paris (1867–1900)." *Mil Neuf Cent* 7 (1989): 23–44.

Renneville, Marc. "Politiques de l'hygiène à l'AFAS." *Les hygiénistes*, ed. P. Bourdelais. Paris: Belin, 2001.

Richards, Joan L. "Rigor and Clarity: Foundations of Mathematics in France and England, 1800–1840." *Science in Context* 4, no. 2 (1991): 297–319.

Riley, James C. *Population Thought in the Age of the Demographic Revolution*. Durham: Carolina Academic, 1985.

Rodgers, Brian. "The Social Science Association, 1857–1886." *Manchester School of Economic and Social Studies* 20, no. 3 (1952): 283–310.

Rollet-Echalier, Catherine. "La politique à l'égard de la petite enfance sous la IIIᵉ république." *Population* 2 (1991): 349–58.

Rosanvallon, Pierre. *Le peuple introuvable: Histoire de la représentation démocratique en France*. Paris: Gallimard, 2002.

Rosen, George. *A History of Public Health*. Baltimore: Johns Hopkins University Press, 1993.

Rosenberg, Charles. "Toward an Ecology of Knowledge: On Discipline, Context, and History." *The Organization of Knowledge in Modern America, 1860–1920*, ed. J. Voss and A. Oleson. Baltimore: Johns Hopkins University Press, 1979.

Rosental, Paul André. *L'intelligence démographique*. Paris: Odile Jacob, 2003.

Russell, Colin A. *Science and Social Change, 1700–1900*. Hong Kong: Macmillan, 1983.

Ryder, N. B. "Notes on the Concept of a Population." *American Journal of Sociology* 69, no. 5 (1964): 447–63.

Savoye, Antoine. *Les débuts de la sociologie empirique: Études socio-historiques, 1830–1930*. Paris: Méridiens Klincksieck, 1994.

Schabas, Margaret. "Alfred Marshall, W. Stanley Jevons, and the Mathematization of Economics." *Isis* 80 (1989): 60–73.

———. "Mathematics and the Economics Profession in Late Victorian England." *The Estate of Social Knowledge*, ed. J. Brown and D. K. Van Keuren. Baltimore: Johns Hopkins University Press, 1991.

Schiller, Francis. *Paul Broca, Founder of French Anthropology, Explorer of the Brain*. Berkeley: University of California Press, 1979.

Schofer, Evan, and Marion Fourcade-Gourinchas. "The Structural Contexts of Civic Engagement: Voluntary Association Membership in Comparative Perspective." *American Sociological Review* 66 (2001): 806–28.

Schweber, Libby. "Controverses et styles de raisonnement: Débats sur la statistique de population au XIXᵉ siècle en France et en Angleterre." *Enquête* 5 (1997): 83–108.

Scott, James C. *Seeing like a State: How Certain Schemes to Improve the Human Condition Have Failed*. New Haven: Yale University Press, 1998.

Scott, Joan Wallach. *Gender and the Politics of History*. New York: Columbia University Press, 1988.

Sewell, William H. "A Theory of Structure: Duality, Agency, and Transformation." *American Journal of Sociology* 98, no. 1 (1992): 1–29.

———. "Historical Events as Transformation of Structures: Inventing Revolution at the Bastille." *Theory and Society* 25 (1996): 841–81.

Shapin, Steven. "Here and Everywhere: Sociology of Scientific Knowledge." *Annual Review of Sociology* 21 (1995): 289–321.

Shapin, Steven, and Simon Schaffer. *Leviathan and the Air-Pump: Hobbes, Boyle, and the Experimental Life*. Princeton: Princeton University Press, 1989.

Shapin, Steven, and Arnold Thackray. "Prosopography as a Research Tool in History of Science: The British Scientific Community, 1700–1900." *History of Science* 12 (1974): 1–28.

Shinn, Terry. "Change or Mutation? Reflections on the Foundations of Contemporary Sciences." *Social Science Information* 38, no. 1 (1999): 149–76.

Simon, John. *English Sanitary Institutions, Reviewed in Their Course of Development, and in Some of Their Political and Social Relations*. London, 1890.

Skerry, Peter. *Counting on the Census? Race, Group Identity and the Evasion of Politics*. Washington: Brookings Institution Press, 2000.

Soffer, Reba N. "Why Do Disciplines Fail? The Strange Case of British Sociology." *English Historical Review* 97 (1982): 767–802.

Somers, Margaret R. "Where Is Sociology after the Historic Turn? Knowledge Cultures, Narrativity, and Historical Epistemologies." *The Historic Turn in the Human Sciences*, ed. T. J. McDonald. Ann Arbor: University of Michigan Press, 1996.

Spengler, Joseph J. "French Population Theory since 1800." *Journal of Political Economy* 44, no. 5 (1936): 577–611, 743–66.

——. *France Faces Depopulation*. Durham: Duke University Press, 1938.

Steimetz, George. *Regulating the Social: The Welfare State and Local Politics in Imperial Germany*. Princeton: Princeton University Press, 1993.

Stigler, Stephen M. *The History of Statistics: The Measurement of Uncertainty before 1900*. Cambridge: Belknap Press of Harvard University Press, 1986.

Sussman, George D. *Selling Mothers' Milk: The Wet-Nursing Business in France, 1715–1914*. Urbana: University of Illinois Press, 1982.

Szreter, Simon. "The GRO and the Public Health Movement in Britain, 1837–1914." *Social History of Medicine* 4 (1991): 435–63.

——. "Introduction: The GRO and the Historians." *Social History of Medicine* 4 (1991): 401–14.

——. *Fertility, Class and Gender in Britain, 1860–1940*. Cambridge: Cambridge University Press, 1996.

——. "Demography, History of." *International Encyclopedia of the Social and Behavioral Sciences*, ed. N. J. Smelser and P. B. Baltes. New York: Macmillan, 2001.

Talmy, Robert. *Histoire du mouvement familial en France*. Paris: Union nationale des caisses d'allocation, 1962.

Thévenot, Laurent. "Rules and Implements: Investment in Forms." *Social Science Information* 23, no. 1 (1984): 1–45.

Tiles, Mary. "The Normal and Pathological: The Concept of a Scientific Medicine." *British Journal for the Philosophy of Science* 44 (1993): 729–42.

Tribe, Keith. "Political Economy to Economics via Commerce: The Evolution of British Academic Economics, 1860–1920." *Discourses on Society: The Shaping of the Social Science Disciplines*, ed. P. Wagner, B. Wittrock, and R. Whitley. Dordrecht: Kluwer Academic, 1991.

Turner, Stephen P., and Jonathan H. Turner. *The Impossible Science: An Institutional Analysis of American Sociology*. Newbury Park, Calif.: Sage, 1990.

Vilquin, Eric. "La naissance de la démographie." *Population et famille* 39, no. 3 (1976): 145–64.

Walter, Richard D. "What Became of the Degenerate? A Brief History of a Concept." *Journal of the History of Medicine and Allied Sciences* 9, no. 4 (1956): 422–29.

Warwick, Andrew. *Masters of Theory: Cambridge and the Rise of Mathematical Physics*. Chicago: University of Chicago Press, 2003.

Weingart, Peter. "From 'Finalization' to 'Mode 2': Old Wine in New Bottles." *Social Science Information* 36, no. 4 (1997): 591–613.

Weisz, George. "Reform and Conflict in French Medical Education, 1870–1914." *The Organization of Science and Technology in France, 1808–1914*, ed. R. Fox and G. Weisz. Cambridge: Cambridge University Press, 1980.

——. *The Emergence of Modern Universities in France, 1863–1914*. Princeton: Princeton University Press, 1983.

Wessely, Anna. "Transporting 'Style' from the History of Art to the History of Science." *Science in Context* 4, no. 2 (1991): 265–78.

Westergaard, Harold. *Contributions to the History of Statistics*. London, 1932.

Whitley, Richard. "Umbrella and Polytheistic Scientific Disciplines and Their Elites." *Social Studies of Science* 6 (1976): 471–97.

Williams, Elizabeth A. "Anthropological Institutions in Nineteenth-Century France." *Isis* 76 (1985): 331–48.

Williams, Raymond. *Politics and Letters*. London: Schocken, 1979.

Woolf, Stuart. "Statistics and the Modern State." *Comparative Studies in Society and History* 31 (1989): 588–604.

Wrigley, E.A., ed. *Nineteenth-Century Society: Essays in the Use of Quantitative Methods for the Study of Social Data*. Cambridge: Cambridge University Press, 1972.

Yeo, Eileen. *The Contest for Social Science: Relations and Representations of Gender and Class*. London: Rivers Oram, 1996.

INDEX

Académie des sciences morales et politiques, 37–38, 47, 78–79, 87

Académie des sciences, 168, 191, 217; Prix Montyon, 82–84, 138, 241 n. 11

Académie impériale de medicine, 53, 68; on causes of death, 161, 164; on infant mortality, 70–71; numerical method and, 65

Académie royale de médecine, 22

Acclimatisation, 72

Administrative statistics: British, 106–7, 128, 171; French, 51–52, 59, 171; inadequacy for science of, 38, 40, 157; international congresses and, 31–32, 151; medical statistics and, 161, 163–64; municipal bureaus and, 64, 147, 158–64, 209; scientific uses of, 36, 44, 84–86, 106, 119, 122–24, 145, 150–51, 159–64; state centralization and, 30, 219; writings on, 25–27

Anthropology, 145–48, 137, 155, 165; polygenism and, 62–63

Averages, 38, 43, 55–56, 62, 195–96, 204

Bernard, Claude, 56

Bertillon, Jacques, 146, 164–66, 172

Bertillon, Louis Adolphe: Académie de médecine and, 57–60, 80–82, 86–88; Académie des sciences and, 85–88; anthropology and, 60–64; on averages, 55–56; *La démographie figurée*, 77–80, 82–86; on depopulation, 57, 68, 74, 76, 145; disciplinary activity and, 74, 89–90, 137, 153–54; on measurement of mortality, 57–59; Municipal Bureau of Statistics and, 160–64; "new" medicine and, 53, 56; on population movement, 75–77, 143–50; positivist societies and, 42; public hygiene and, 54; Quetelet and, 62–63, 128; "scientific" approach and, 143–45; Statistical Society of Paris and, 58–60, 157, 166; vaccine and, 57–58

Bienaymé, Jules, 83–84, 86

Birth rates, 42, 76, 87, 172, 186–87; decline in, 38, 68, 71, 77 161

Block, Maurice, 169

Board of Trade, 101

British Medical Association, 117–18, 163–64, 193

Broca, Paul, 242 n. 35; Société d'Anthropologie and, 61, 137; on statistics, 70–73, 80–81

Brochard, André-Théodore, 71

Burdett, Henry C., 206–7

Bureau de statistique de la République, 82, 241 n. 30

Cameralism, 22–23

Censuses: British (1841), 31; conduct of, 171; forms for, 151; French (1856, 1866), 68, 70; use of data from, 58, 110, 196–97; writings on, 25

population, 37–38, 41–42, 45; on
political economy, 37, 39, 45; positivist social science and, 41–42; on "scientific" approach, 108, 122; Statistical
Society of Paris and, 50–53; statistique humaine and, 36, 42–45
Guy, William: "scientific" approach
and, 129–30, 201–3; Social Science
Association and, 125–26; Statistical
Society of London and, 121

Hacking, Ian, 20, 22–23, 26, 218
Haussmann, Georges Eugène, 58
Historical epistemology, 8, 17

Infant mortality, 55, 70–71, 80–81, 84,
87, 147, 161; wet-nursing and, 57, 71,
73
International Conference of Statistics,
152–54
International Congress of Demography: First, 147–48, 160–61; Second,
164–65
International Congress of Hygiene, 164
International Congress of Statistics,
32, 121, 141, 207–8; Theory and
Methods section of, 122–23, 207–8
International Institute of Statistics,
209–11

Lavergne, Léonce de, 68
Legoyt, Alfred, 51, 123, 166, 239 n. 5;
on depopulation, 69; descriptive
approach and, 59–60
Levasseur, Émile: Commission on
Municipal Statistics and, 160; International Congress of Demography
and, 137, 143, 148–49; report on *La
démographie figurée*, 79; Statistical
Society of Paris and, 166–68, 172,
203–4
"Liberal administrative sector," 139–41,
153, 166, 174

Liberal states: public health and, 39; science and, 3, 12–13; statistical styles
and, 1, 23, 218; statistics and, 3, 5–6,
23, 29–30; types of, 5, 218–19
Local Government Board, 192
Loua, Toussaint, 152–54, 160, 166–67

Malthus, Thomas Robert, 37, 45, 68, 101
Manchester Statistical Society, 98, 100–
101
Marshall, Alfred D.: disciplinary strategy and, 206, 210–11; mathematical
statistics and, 203, 205, 234 n. 61
Mathematical statistics, 183, 188–89,
191, 201–2, 205–6, 210–11, 216;
writings on, 20–24
Measurement of error, 195–96, 204–5
Medical Congress of France, 74
Medical Department of the Privy Council, 6, 112, 116, 130, 192
"Medical-municipal sector," 139–41,
145–46, 153–54, 165–66, 174
Medical officers of health, 116, 192–94,
197–98, 200, 211, 217, 224; teaching
manuals for, 195
Medicine: "new" (France), 53, 56, 60–
61, 137; numerical method and, 61,
65, 80–81, 95–96
Migration, 59, 69–70, 73, 76
Moreau de Jonnès, Alexandre, 51, 55,
78, 80, 84, 99, 128, 162, 167
Morel, Bénédict Augustin, 69
Mortality, 63, 66, 77, 87, 115, 150, 186–
88; healthy district rate and, 109, 127,
180, 186, 244 n. 8; interpretation of,
55–56, 63, 69, 97, 107–12, 196; measurement of, 37, 54–57, 59, 84, 95,
108–9, 112–15, 197; tables, 55, 58,
95, 97, 109–14, 123, 128
Mouat, Frederic J., 201–2
Municipal Bureau of Statistics for the
City of Paris, 158–63
Museum of Natural History, 62

Libby Schweber is a reader in the Department of
Sociology, University of Reading.

Library of Congress Cataloging-in-Publication Data
Schweber, Libby.
Disciplining statistics : demography and vital
statistics in France and England 1830–1885 /
Libby Schweber.
p. cm. — (Politics, history, and culture)
Includes bibliographical references and index.
ISBN-13: 978-0-8223-3825-3 (cloth : alk. paper)
ISBN-10: 0-8223-3825-4 (cloth : alk. paper)
ISBN-13: 978-0-8223-3814-7 (pbk. : alk. paper)
ISBN-10: 0-8223-3814-9 (pbk. : alk. paper)
1. Demography — France — History — 19th century.
2. France — Statistics, Vital — History — 19th century.
3. Demography — England — History — 19th century.
4. England — Statistics, Vital — History — 19th
century. I. Title. II. Series.
HB853.F8S38 2006
304.60944'09034 — dc22   2006010426